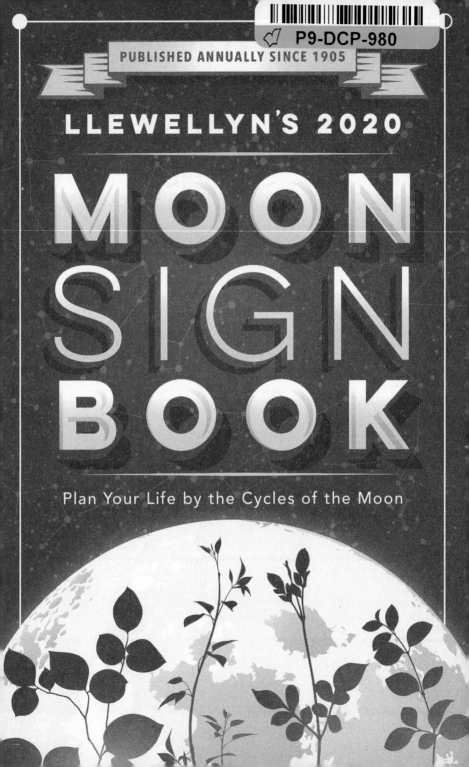

LLEWELLYN'S 2020

MOON SIGN BOOK

Plan Your Life by the Cycles of the Moon

Llewellyn's 2020 Moon Sign Book®

ISBN 978-0-7387-4946-4

Cover design by Kevin R. Brown
Editing by Annie Burdick
Stock photography models used for illustrative purposes only and may not endorse or represent the book's subject.
Interior photographs: Getty Images
Copyright 2019 Llewellyn Worldwide Ltd. All rights reserved.
Typography owned by Llewellyn Worldwide Ltd.

Weekly tips by Penny Kelly, Mireille Blacke, and Charlie Rainbow Wolf.

Any Internet references contained in this work are current at publication time, but the publisher cannot guarantee that a specific location will continue to be maintained.

Astrological data compiled and programmed by Rique Pottenger. Based on the earlier work of Neil F. Michelsen.

You can order Llewellyn annuals and books from *New Worlds*, Llewellyn's catalog. To request a free copy of the catalog, call toll-free 1-877-NEW-WRLD, or visit our website at www.llewellyn.com.

Llewellyn Publications is a registered trademark of Llewellyn Worldwide Ltd.
2143 Wooddale Drive, Woodbury, MN 55125-2989 USA
Moon Sign Book® is registered in U.S. Patent and Trademark Office.
Moon Sign Book is a trademark of Llewellyn Worldwide Ltd. (Canada).

Llewellyn Publications
A Division of Llewellyn Worldwide Ltd.
2143 Wooddale Drive
Woodbury, MN 55125-3989
www.llewellyn.com

Printed in the United States of America

Table of Contents

The Methods of the *Moon Sign Book*

Whether we live in simple, primitive times or a time of high technology and mass communication, we need our connection to Mother Nature and an understanding of how all of her systems work together—soil, sun, wind, water, plants, animals, people, and planets.

The connections among elements of nature become especially relevant when we recognize that many energies—both subtle and obvious—flow through our world and affect all things. Ancient civilizations knew about these changing energies and were much more attuned to the subtle effects that they had on us.

In the world of unseen energies, it has long been accepted in many quarters that the position of the planets makes a difference in the energy flowing around planet Earth. Those who question these energy flows are often sadly divorced from nature.

Imagine placing a large rock in the waters of a flowing stream or creek. Immediately you would notice numerous changes in the flow of the water moving over, around, and past the rock.

It is no different with our solar system. We live on a planet that floats in a solar sea of energies and frequency waves. As the planets move around the sun, the currents of energy flowing through the solar sea change in the same way that flowing water changes around the rock placed in a creek or stream…and we are affected by those changes at every level—physically, mentally, emotionally, and spiritually.

The ability to detect these changes and their effect on us has long been organized into knowledge systems, and the *Moon Sign Book* has always been a stable anchor in maintaining this knowledge and recognizing its importance. We call these organized methods of gaining knowledge *astrology*, and ancient cultures around the globe used this as their science. It was how they found and maintained a sense of prediction, control, and security, something we are still striving for even today as we try to anticipate the cycles and events of our daily lives.

Although there are several ways of organizing and assessing these energy flows based on planetary positions, the *Moon Sign Book* uses the tropical system, which says that spring officially begins when the Sun is directly over the equator at noon, something that occurs around March 20 to 21 every year. Once that moment has been determined, the rest of the zodiac calendar is laid out at thirty-degree intervals. This allows us to be precise, but also flex with the changing nature of all things, including our solar system. We support a knowledge base that upholds the ancient wisdom and teaches it to all who are interested. We invite you to read what we have written here and to celebrate the interactions of these energies with the plants, animals, earth, and stars that share this time and space with us.

Weekly Almanac

Your Guide to
Lunar Gardening
& Good Timing for Activities

♑ January

December 29–January 4

Determine that the thing can and shall be done, and then we shall find the way. ~ABRAHAM LINCOLN

Date	Qtr.	Sign	Activity
Jan. 4, 11:15 am– Jan. 6, 9:11 pm	2nd	Taurus	Plant annuals for hardiness. Trim to increase growth.

Rubbing alcohol is a wonderful companion for frosty mornings. Make your own de-icer by mixing half water and half rubbing alcohol in a spray bottle. Mist down your windows when you are expecting frost. If you get caught short, use the same mixture to dissolve ice from your windshield and external mirrors.

_____

_____

_____

_____

◗

January 2
11:45 pm EST

		JANUARY				
S	M	T	W	T	F	S
			1	2	3	4
5	6	7	8	9	10	11
12	13	14	15	16	17	18
19	20	21	22	23	24	25
26	27	28	29	30	31	

January 5–11 ♑

Think only of the past as its remembrance gives you pleasure.

~JANE AUSTEN

Date	Qtr.	Sign	Activity
Jan. 4, 11:15 am–Jan. 6, 9:11 pm	2nd	Taurus	Plant annuals for hardiness. Trim to increase growth.
Jan. 9, 3:43 am–Jan. 10, 2:21 pm	2nd	Cancer	Plant grains, leafy annuals. Fertilize (chemical). Graft or bud plants. Irrigate. Trim to increase growth.
Jan. 10, 2:21 pm–Jan. 11, 7:16 am	3rd	Cancer	Plant biennials, perennials, bulbs and roots. Prune. Irrigate. Fertilize (organic).
Jan. 11, 7:16 am–Jan. 13, 9:06 am	3rd	Leo	Cultivate. Destroy weeds and pests. Harvest fruits and root crops for food. Trim to retard growth.

A powerful way to expand your perception is to take a drawing or painting class. Sign up for a class at your local art institute, community college, or adult education program. You will become aware of light and shadow, texture, line, positive and negative space, and details you never noticed before—all of which make you more aware!

○
January 10
2:21 pm EST

JANUARY

S	M	T	W	T	F	S
			1	2	3	4
5	6	7	8	9	10	11
12	13	14	15	16	17	18
19	20	21	22	23	24	25
26	27	28	29	30	31	

♑ January 12–18

Things change, people change, but that doesn't mean you should forget the past.   ~GAIL CARSON LEVINE

Date	Qtr.	Sign	Activity
Jan. 11, 7:16 am– Jan. 13, 9:06 am	3rd	Leo	Cultivate. Destroy weeds and pests. Harvest fruits and root crops for food. Trim to retard growth.
Jan. 13, 9:06 am– Jan. 15, 10:43 am	3rd	Virgo	Cultivate, especially medicinal plants. Destroy weeds and pests. Trim to retard growth.
Jan. 17, 1:20 pm– Jan. 19, 5:41 pm	4th	Scorpio	Plant biennials, perennials, bulbs and roots. Prune. Irrigate. Fertilize (organic).

Interested in shedding a few pounds? Consider adopting one of the following behavior changes that people who have successfully kept off excess weight practice daily. Chew food twenty times per bite. Put your fork down between bites. Drink sixty-four ounces of no-calorie fluids each day. Before eating, ask yourself if you're physically hungry or eating due to boredom, anger, sadness, etc. Sleep at least seven hours each night. Move your body every day.

January 17
7:58 am EST

JANUARY

S	M	T	W	T	F	S
			1	2	3	4
5	6	7	8	9	10	11
12	13	14	15	16	17	18
19	20	21	22	23	24	25
26	27	28	29	30	31	

January 19–25 ~~~

The ornament of a house is the friends who frequent it.
~RALPH WALDO EMERSON

Date	Qtr.	Sign	Activity
Jan. 19, 5:41 pm– Jan. 22, 12:00 am	4th	Sagittarius	Cultivate. Destroy weeds and pests. Harvest fruits and root crops for food. Trim to retard growth.
Jan. 22, 12:00 am– Jan. 24, 8:20 am	4th	Capricorn	Plant potatoes and tubers. Trim to retard growth.
Jan. 24, 8:20 am– Jan. 24, 4:42 pm	4th	Aquarius	Cultivate. Destroy weeds and pests. Harvest fruits and root crops for food. Trim to retard growth.

Coffee filters do far more than just strain coffee. Put them between plates to help avoid cracking and chipping in storage. They're great under fried food to absorb the extra fat. In the bottom of a plant pot, a filter prevents the soil from escaping when you water. They make good dusters for your TV or computer monitor, and will clean your mirrors without leaving lint behind.

●

January 24
4:24 pm EST

JANUARY

S	M	T	W	T	F	S
			1	2	3	4
5	6	7	8	9	10	11
12	13	14	15	16	17	18
19	20	21	22	23	24	25
26	27	28	29	30	31	

≈ February

January 26–February 1

When you've finished getting yourself ready in the morning, you must go get the planet ready.

~ANTOINE DE SAINT-EXUPÉRY, *THE LITTLE PRINCE*

Date	Qtr.	Sign	Activity
Jan. 26, 6:44 pm– Jan. 29, 6:51 am	1st	Pisces	Plant grains, leafy annuals. Fertilize (chemical). Graft or bud plants. Irrigate. Trim to increase growth.
Jan. 31, 7:28 pm– Feb. 1, 8:42 pm	1st	Taurus	Plant annuals for hardiness. Trim to increase growth.
Feb. 1, 8:42 pm– Feb. 3, 6:29 am	2nd	Taurus	Plant annuals for hardiness. Trim to increase growth.
Jan 31, 7:47 pm– Feb 3, 8:03 am	4th	Capricorn	Plant potatoes and tubers. Trim to retard growth.

Buy a cookbook that interests you and experiment with new kinds of ingredients and food preparation techniques. Keep high-density nutrition in mind as you treat yourself to a new kitchen tool necessary for making excellent meals.

☽

February 1
8:42 pm EST

FEBRUARY

S	M	T	W	T	F	S
						1
2	3	4	5	6	7	8
9	10	11	12	13	14	15
16	17	18	19	20	21	22
23	24	25	26	27	28	29

February 2–8 ～～～

The meaning of life is to find your gift. The purpose of life is
to give it away.   ~PABLO PICASSO

Date	Qtr.	Sign	Activity
Feb. 1, 8:42 pm– Feb. 3, 6:29 am	2nd	Taurus	Plant annuals for hardiness. Trim to increase growth.
Feb. 5, 2:03 pm– Feb. 7, 5:45 pm	2nd	Cancer	Plant grains, leafy annuals. Fertilize (chemical). Graft or bud plants. Irrigate. Trim to increase growth.

Lack of sunshine during winter months is associated with
higher risk for mood swings, irritability, fatigue, anxiety, and
depression. Dark winter skies have been linked to lower levels
of serotonin and dopamine, leading to many of these symptoms.
Eating more protein-rich foods like extra-lean meat, chicken, and
fish, and low-fat dairy has been shown to boost energy and mood.
If symptoms of depression persist, seek attention from your
health care provider.

FEBRUARY

S	M	T	W	T	F	S
						1
2	3	4	5	6	7	8
9	10	11	12	13	14	15
16	17	18	19	20	21	22
23	24	25	26	27	28	29

≈≈ February 9–15

Change will not come if we wait for some other person or some other time. We are the ones we've been waiting for. We are the change that we seek.   ∼Barack Obama

Date	Qtr.	Sign	Activity
Feb. 9, 2:33 am– Feb. 9, 6:39 pm	3rd	Leo	Cultivate. Destroy weeds and pests. Harvest fruits and root crops for food. Trim to retard growth.
Feb. 9, 6:39 pm– Feb. 11, 6:37 pm	3rd	Virgo	Cultivate, especially medicinal plants. Destroy weeds and pests. Trim to retard growth.
Feb. 13, 7:37 pm– Feb. 15, 5:17 pm	3rd	Scorpio	Plant biennials, perennials, bulbs and roots. Prune. Irrigate. Fertilize (organic).
Feb. 15, 5:17 pm– Feb. 15, 11:07 pm	4th	Scorpio	Plant biennials, perennials, bulbs and roots. Prune. Irrigate. Fertilize (organic).

Colorful seed packets can be turned into paper beads! You'll need scissors, glue, some Mod Podge, and a skewer. Open the packet flat and cut long triangular strips. Wrap the paper around the skewer, thick end first, and seal with a dab of glue on the point. Seal with Mod Podge, remove from the skewer, and string them together for an ornamental delight.

February 9
2:33 am EST

February 15
5:17 pm EST

FEBRUARY

S	M	T	W	T	F	S
						1
2	3	4	5	6	7	8
9	10	11	12	13	14	15
16	17	18	19	20	21	22
23	24	25	26	27	28	29

February 16–22 〜〜〜

There is no cosmetic for beauty like happiness.

~MARGUERITE GARDINER

Date	Qtr.	Sign	Activity
Feb. 15, 11:07 pm– Feb. 18, 5:37 am	4th	Sagittarius	Cultivate. Destroy weeds and pests. Harvest fruits and root crops for food. Trim to retard growth.
Feb. 18, 5:37 am– Feb. 20, 2:42 pm	4th	Capricorn	Plant potatoes and tubers. Trim to retard growth.
Feb. 20, 2:42 pm– Feb. 23, 1:37 am	4th	Aquarius	Cultivate. Destroy weeds and pests. Harvest fruits and root crops for food. Trim to retard growth.

Many methods have been used to keep eyes from watering while slicing onions, but the best way to avoid tears is to use onion goggles. (Yes, really!) But there's no need to buy trendy or expensive onion eyewear; swim or safety goggles work just as well to stop the airborne, tear-inducing sulfur molecules from penetrating your eye membranes. Chop away!

FEBRUARY						
S	M	T	W	T	F	S
						1
2	3	4	5	6	7	8
9	10	11	12	13	14	15
16	17	18	19	20	21	22
23	24	25	26	27	28	29

♓ February
February 23–29

*Unthinking respect for authority is the greatest enemy
of truth.*   ~ALBERT EINSTEIN

Date	Qtr.	Sign	Activity
Feb. 23, 1:37 am– Feb. 23, 10:32 am	4th	Pisces	Plant biennials, perennials, bulbs and roots. Prune. Irrigate. Fertilize (organic).
Feb. 23, 10:32 am– Feb. 25, 1:47 pm	1st	Pisces	Plant grains, leafy annuals. Fertilize (chemical). Graft or bud plants. Irrigate. Trim to increase growth.
Feb. 28, 2:30 am– Mar. 1, 2:21 pm	1st	Taurus	Plant annuals for hardiness. Trim to increase growth.

If your indoor mat has become worn and inefficient, don't throw it away. Place it outside the door, and put your new mat inside. That way, the worst of the shoe soil is left outside, extending the life of your inside mat, and giving it more of a chance to keep your floors clean.

_____

_____

_____

_____

*February 23
10:32 am EST*

FEBRUARY

S	M	T	W	T	F	S
						1
2	3	4	5	6	7	8
9	10	11	12	13	14	15
16	17	18	19	20	21	22
23	24	25	26	27	28	29

March 1–7 ✂

You're afraid of making mistakes. Don't be. Mistakes can be
profited by.   ∼RAY BRADBURY, *FARENHEIT 451*

Date	Qtr.	Sign	Activity
Feb. 28, 2:30 am– Mar. 1, 2:21 pm	1st	Taurus	Plant annuals for hardiness. Trim to increase growth.
Mar. 3, 11:25 pm– Mar. 6, 4:27 am	2nd	Cancer	Plant grains, leafy annuals. Fertilize (chemical). Graft or bud plants. Irrigate. Trim to increase growth.

Fall in love with color and texture. Look at your room, home, or apartment with a discerning eye and ask yourself what it says about you. If it's blah or boring, consider taking a walk on the wild side by changing the wall color, or adding some nubby woven rugs or wall hangings.

◑

March 2
2:57 pm EST

MARCH

S	M	T	W	T	F	S
1	2	3	4	5	6	7
8	9	10	11	12	13	14
15	16	17	18	19	20	21
22	23	24	25	26	27	28
29	30	31				

March 8–14

It is a capital mistake to theorize before you have all the evidence. It biases the judgment.   ~·Sherlock Holmes

Date	Qtr.	Sign	Activity
Mar. 9, 1:48 pm– Mar. 10, 6:03 am	3rd	Virgo	Cultivate, especially medicinal plants. Destroy weeds and pests. Trim to retard growth.
Mar. 12, 5:28 am– Mar. 14, 7:09 am	3rd	Scorpio	Plant biennials, perennials, bulbs and roots. Prune. Irrigate. Fertilize (organic).
Mar. 14, 7:09 am– Mar. 16, 5:34 am	3rd	Sagittarius	Cultivate. Destroy weeds and pests. Harvest fruits and root crops for food. Trim to retard growth.

When tomato planting starts, wait for the soil to warm up before you transplant them into the ground. Just be patient. They really don't like "cold toes" and will significantly slow down growth if you hurry to get them in the ground. In addition, if you can place your tomatoes near a big boulder or southern-facing wall, do so. They'll love the heat source throughout the season.

_____

_____

_____

_____

Daylight Saving Time begins
March 8, 2:00 am

O

March 9
1:48 pm EDT

MARCH

S	M	T	W	T	F	S
1	2	3	4	5	6	7
8	9	10	11	12	13	14
15	16	17	18	19	20	21
22	23	24	25	26	27	28
29	30	31				

March 15–21   🐟

In my experience, there's no such thing as luck.

~GEORGE LUCAS

Date	Qtr.	Sign	Activity
Mar. 14, 7:09 am–Mar. 16, 5:34 am	3rd	Sagittarius	Cultivate. Destroy weeds and pests. Harvest fruits and root crops for food. Trim to retard growth.
Mar. 16, 5:34 am–Mar. 16, 12:25 pm	4th	Sagittarius	Cultivate. Destroy weeds and pests. Harvest fruits and root crops for food. Trim to retard growth.
Mar. 16, 12:25 pm–Mar. 18, 9:16 pm	4th	Capricorn	Plant potatoes and tubers. Trim to retard growth.
Mar. 18, 9:16 pm–Mar. 21, 8:33 am	4th	Aquarius	Cultivate. Destroy weeds and pests. Harvest fruits and root crops for food. Trim to retard growth.
Mar. 21, 8:33 am–Mar. 23, 8:58 pm	4th	Pisces	Plant biennials, perennials, bulbs and roots. Prune. Irrigate. Fertilize (organic).

When spring rolls around, spend a day washing the windows in your house or apartment. Make this a symbolic task in which you imagine you are washing the inside of your consciousness in order to see the truth of your own life. You'll be amazed at what you become aware of.

◑

March 16
5:34 am EDT

MARCH

S	M	T	W	T	F	S
1	2	3	4	5	6	7
8	9	10	11	12	13	14
15	16	17	18	19	20	21
22	23	24	25	26	27	28
29	30	31				

♈ March 22–28

*Life moves pretty fast. If you don't stop and look around once
in a while, you could miss it.*   ⁓FERRIS BUELLER

Date	Qtr.	Sign	Activity
Mar. 21, 8:33 am– Mar. 23, 8:58 pm	4th	Pisces	Plant biennials, perennials, bulbs and roots. Prune. Irrigate. Fertilize (organic).
Mar. 23, 8:58 pm– Mar. 24, 5:28 am	4th	Aries	Cultivate. Destroy weeds and pests. Harvest fruits and root crops for food. Trim to retard growth.
Mar. 26, 9:37 am– Mar. 28, 9:38 pm	1st	Taurus	Plant annuals for hardiness. Trim to increase growth.

Spice up your seedlings. Add strong smelling spices like cinnamon, cloves, or garlic to your potting soil. Many herbs and spices are powerful antioxidants, and they will help protect your seedlings from the pathogens that could attack and weaken—or even destroy—them. Dust the top of the soil with the spices when you sow the seeds, and top off occasionally after watering.

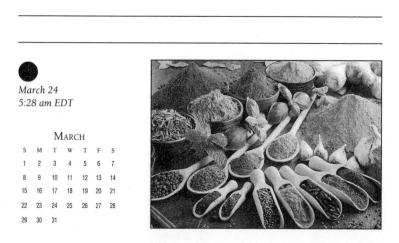

March 24
5:28 am EDT

MARCH

S	M	T	W	T	F	S
1	2	3	4	5	6	7
8	9	10	11	12	13	14
15	16	17	18	19	20	21
22	23	24	25	26	27	28
29	30	31				

April ♈

March 29–April 4

We celebrate the past to awaken the future.

~John F. Kennedy

Date	Qtr.	Sign	Activity
Mar. 31, 7:43 am– Apr. 1, 6:21 am	1st	Cancer	Plant grains, leafy annuals. Fertilize (chemical). Graft or bud plants. Irrigate. Trim to increase growth.
Apr. 1, 6:21 am– Apr. 2, 2:26 pm	2nd	Cancer	Plant grains, leafy annuals. Fertilize (chemical). Graft or bud plants. Irrigate. Trim to increase growth.

Many garden plants—including roses and ferns—appreciate the nutrients in used tea bags. Remove the staple (if there is one), tear the bag open, and sprinkle the contents onto the soil. Tea will also help your compost decompose, as well as deter any unwanted garden pests from becoming too much of a nuisance.

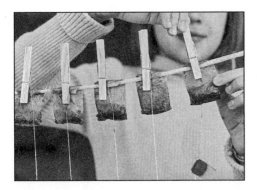

◐

April 1
6:21 am EDT

April

S	M	T	W	T	F	S
			1	2	3	4
5	6	7	8	9	10	11
12	13	14	15	16	17	18
19	20	21	22	23	24	25
26	27	28	29	30		

♈ April 5–11

Relaxed, playful, harmonious moments are the birth ground
of creativity.   .~AMIT RAY

Date	Qtr.	Sign	Activity
Apr. 6, 5:16 pm– Apr. 7, 10:35 pm	2nd	Libra	Plant annuals for fragrance and beauty. Trim to increase growth.
Apr. 8, 4:17 pm– Apr. 10, 4:35 pm	3rd	Scorpio	Plant biennials, perennials, bulbs and roots. Prune. Irrigate. Fertilize (organic).
Apr. 10, 4:35 pm– Apr. 12, 8:05 pm	3rd	Sagittarius	Cultivate. Destroy weeds and pests. Harvest fruits and root crops for food. Trim to retard growth.

Research has shown that spending time in nature has been associated with reduced symptoms of depression and anxiety, in addition to increased self-esteem. Green walks can actually help boost short-term memory by up to 20 percent. Even a small dose (as little as five minutes) of exposure to natural settings each day can benefit a person's well-being. Consider short outdoor walks or hikes during lunch breaks or after dinner.

_____

_____

_____

_____

○
April 7
10:35 pm EDT

APRIL

S	M	T	W	T	F	S
			1	2	3	4
5	6	7	8	9	10	11
12	13	14	15	16	17	18
19	20	21	22	23	24	25
26	27	28	29	30		

April 12–18 ♈

Even goats may have starlight in their eyes.

~Robert Service

Date	Qtr.	Sign	Activity
Apr. 12, 8:05 pm– Apr. 14, 6:56 pm	3rd	Capricorn	Plant potatoes and tubers. Trim to retard growth.
Apr. 14, 6:56 pm– Apr. 15, 3:37 am	4th	Capricorn	Plant potatoes and tubers. Trim to retard growth.
Apr. 15, 3:37 am– Apr. 17, 2:29 pm	4th	Aquarius	Cultivate. Destroy weeds and pests. Harvest fruits and root crops for food. Trim to retard growth.
Apr. 17, 2:29 pm– Apr. 20, 3:00 am	4th	Pisces	Plant biennials, perennials, bulbs and roots. Prune. Irrigate. Fertilize (organic).

Goldenrod is considered a weed in many areas, while others cultivate it as a herbaceous border in the garden! The flowers have a myriad of uses. Soap makers use them for color and texture. In herbal medicine they're used for tinctures, salves, and teas. Dyers use the goldenrod flowers mixed with a mordant to color their fabric and wool. In the kitchen, goldenrod honey and goldenrod cordial are sweet treats indeed.

◐

April 14
6:56 pm EDT

APRIL

S	M	T	W	T	F	S
			1	2	3	4
5	6	7	8	9	10	11
12	13	14	15	16	17	18
19	20	21	22	23	24	25
26	27	28	29	30		

♈ April 19–25

Live and let live.   ～Proverb

Date	Qtr.	Sign	Activity
Apr. 17, 2:29 pm– Apr. 20, 3:00 am	4th	Pisces	Plant biennials, perennials, bulbs and roots. Prune. Irrigate. Fertilize (organic).
Apr. 20, 3:00 am– Apr. 22, 3:36 pm	4th	Aries	Cultivate. Destroy weeds and pests. Harvest fruits and root crops for food. Trim to retard growth.
Apr. 22, 3:36 pm– Apr. 22, 10:26 pm	4th	Taurus	Plant potatoes and tubers. Trim to retard growth.
Apr. 22, 10:26 pm– Apr. 25, 3:20 am	1st	Taurus	Plant annuals for hardiness. Trim to increase growth.

Mercury Retrograde is a time for stepping back, surveying your entire situation, and assessing where you're at and what needs to be changed, refined, or rethought. Look up the next period of Mercury Retrograde (on page 160) and use this three-week period as quiet time in your life.

_____

_____

_____

_____

April 22
10:26 pm EDT

APRIL

S	M	T	W	T	F	S
			1	2	3	4
5	6	7	8	9	10	11
12	13	14	15	16	17	18
19	20	21	22	23	24	25
26	27	28	29	30		

May ♉

April 26–May 2

People in their right minds never take pride in their talents.
~HARPER LEE, *TO KILL A MOCKINGBIRD*

Date	Qtr.	Sign	Activity
Apr. 27, 1:28 pm– Apr. 29, 9:06 pm	1st	Cancer	Plant grains, leafy annuals. Fertilize (chemical). Graft or bud plants. Irrigate. Trim to increase growth.

Save your citrus! Lemon and orange peels make great deodorizers. Throw one down the garbage disposal for a fresh-scented drain. If you've got a kitchen container that has a stale smell lingering, store a slice of lemon in it for a few days. Lemon also helps to remove stains from cutting boards and countertops, and lemon juice will loosen stuck-on food from dishes.

◗
April 30
4:38 pm EDT

		MAY				
S	M	T	W	T	F	S
					1	2
3	4	5	6	7	8	9
10	11	12	13	14	15	16
17	18	19	20	21	22	23
24	25	26	27	28	29	30
31						

May 3–9

If all Printers were determin'd not to print anything till they were sure it would offend nobody, there would be very little printed.   ~BENJAMIN FRANKLIN

Date	Qtr.	Sign	Activity
May 4, 3:09 am–May 6, 3:05 am	2nd	Libra	Plant annuals for fragrance and beauty. Trim to increase growth.
May 6, 3:05 am–May 7, 6:45 am	2nd	Scorpio	Plant grains, leafy annuals. Fertilize (chemical). Graft or bud plants. Irrigate. Trim to increase growth.
May 7, 6:45 am–May 8, 3:15 am	3rd	Scorpio	Plant biennials, perennials, bulbs and roots. Prune. Irrigate. Fertilize (organic).
May 8, 3:15 am–May 10, 5:39 am	3rd	Sagittarius	Cultivate. Destroy weeds and pests. Harvest fruits and root crops for food. Trim to retard growth.

Low levels of vitamin D could raise your risk of developing chronic headaches, osteoporosis, and seasonal affective disorder (SAD). Most people should consume at least 600 international units (IU) daily, but if foods like fish, fortified milk, and cereals aren't doing the trick, ask your doctor about supplementation or spend at least fifteen minutes in the sun each day.

O
May 7
6:45 am EDT

MAY

S	M	T	W	T	F	S
					1	2
3	4	5	6	7	8	9
10	11	12	13	14	15	16
17	18	19	20	21	22	23
24	25	26	27	28	29	30
31						

May 24–May 30   ♊

Big things are often just little things that people notice.
~MARKUS ZUSAK, *I AM THE MESSENGER*

Date	Qtr.	Sign	Activity
May 24, 7:09 pm– May 27, 2:33 am	1st	Cancer	Plant grains, leafy annuals. Fertilize (chemical). Graft or bud plants. Irrigate. Trim to increase growth.

Create a landscape for birds and four-footed wildlife or a nectar garden for native bees, butterflies, and other pollinators in your own backyard. Utilize native plants to benefit more species of birds and insects. Select plants and flowers that help birds transition from the grass up to the tallest trees, moving from low plants like violets to knee-highs like cone flowers to plants that are waist-high and provide cover and foraging areas for birds.

_____

_____

_____

_____

◐
May 29
11:30 pm EDT

MAY

S	M	T	W	T	F	S
					1	2
3	4	5	6	7	8	9
10	11	12	13	14	15	16
17	18	19	20	21	22	23
24	25	26	27	28	29	30
31						

♊ June
May 31–June 6

It's hard to leave when you can't find the door.

~JOE WALSH

Date	Qtr.	Sign	Activity
May 31, 10:38 am–Jun. 2, 12:06 pm	2nd	Libra	Plant annuals for fragrance and beauty. Trim to increase growth.
Jun. 2, 12:06 pm–Jun. 4, 1:17 pm	2nd	Scorpio	Plant grains, leafy annuals. Fertilize (chemical). Graft or bud plants. Irrigate. Trim to increase growth.
Jun. 5, 3:12 pm–Jun. 6, 3:44 pm	3rd	Sagittarius	Cultivate. Destroy weeds and pests. Harvest fruits and root crops for food. Trim to retard growth.
Jun. 6, 3:44 pm–Jun. 8, 8:54 pm	3rd	Capricorn	Plant potatoes and tubers. Trim to retard growth.

Slugs are damaging, and because of their two-year life cycle, they're hard to eradicate once they take hold. Don't delay: as soon as you see a slug, break out the beer. Slugs love it, and if you put some beer in a shallow dish, they'll climb in and drown. Pick them out and feed them to the local ducks; although if ducks are roaming in your veggies, they may munch on your seedlings!

○
June 5
3:12 pm EDT

JUNE

S	M	T	W	T	F	S
	1	2	3	4	5	6
7	8	9	10	11	12	13
14	15	16	17	18	19	20
21	22	23	24	25	26	27
28	29	30				

June 7–13 ♊

A person who has not done one-half his day's work by ten
o'clock, runs a chance of leaving the other half undone.
                    ~EMILY BRONTË, *WUTHERING HEIGHTS*

Date	Qtr.	Sign	Activity
Jun. 6, 3:44 pm– Jun. 8, 8:54 pm	3rd	Capricorn	Plant potatoes and tubers. Trim to retard growth.
Jun. 8, 8:54 pm– Jun. 11, 5:32 am	3rd	Aquarius	Cultivate. Destroy weeds and pests. Harvest fruits and root crops for food. Trim to retard growth.
Jun. 11, 5:32 am– Jun. 13, 2:24 am	3rd	Pisces	Plant biennials, perennials, bulbs and roots. Prune. Irrigate. Fertilize (organic).
Jun. 13, 2:24 am– Jun. 13, 5:03 pm	4th	Pisces	Plant biennials, perennials, bulbs and roots. Prune. Irrigate. Fertilize (organic).

Make this your year to reconnect with Mother Nature. Make a commitment to spend at least one hour outside every week when you can be completely devoted to the trees, the weather, the soil, and the local plants. Notice how your awareness changes!

◐
June 13
2:24 am EDT

		JUNE				
S	M	T	W	T	F	S
	1	2	3	4	5	6
7	8	9	10	11	12	13
14	15	16	17	18	19	20
21	22	23	24	25	26	27
28	29	30				

♊ June 14–20

Is there a movie I think I should have won the Oscar for?
Yeah. All of them.   ∼MORGAN FREEMAN

Date	Qtr.	Sign	Activity
Jun. 13, 5:03 pm– Jun. 16, 5:35 am	4th	Aries	Cultivate. Destroy weeds and pests. Harvest fruits and root crops for food. Trim to retard growth.
Jun. 16, 5:35 am– Jun. 18, 5:00 pm	4th	Taurus	Plant potatoes and tubers. Trim to retard growth.
Jun. 18, 5:00 pm– Jun. 21, 2:02 am	4th	Gemini	Cultivate. Destroy weeds and pests. Harvest fruits and root crops for food. Trim to retard growth.

Cleaning out that closet? Consider each item and ask: Have I used it in the past year? Does it have either sentimental or monetary value to me? If yes in either case, keep it another year. If no, discard. Then ask, might it come in handy someday? If yes, but no specifics come to mind, you're probably holding on to clutter. Put the item in a donate or discard box and keep going!

JUNE

S	M	T	W	T	F	S
	1	2	3	4	5	6
7	8	9	10	11	12	13
14	15	16	17	18	19	20
21	22	23	24	25	26	27
28	29	30				

June 21–27 ♋

If you have a garden and a library, you have everything
you need.   ~Cicero

Date	Qtr.	Sign	Activity
Jun. 18, 5:00 pm– Jun. 21, 2:02 am	4th	Gemini	Cultivate. Destroy weeds and pests. Harvest fruits and root crops for food. Trim to retard growth.
Jun. 21, 2:02 am– Jun. 21, 2:41 am	4th	Cancer	Plant biennials, perennials, bulbs and roots. Prune. Irrigate. Fertilize (organic).
Jun. 21, 2:41 am– Jun. 23, 8:33 am	1st	Cancer	Plant grains, leafy annuals. Fertilize (chemical). Graft or bud plants. Irrigate. Trim to increase growth.
Jun. 27, 4:16 pm– Jun. 28, 4:16 am	1st	Libra	Plant annuals for fragrance and beauty. Trim to increase growth.

Pretend you are in a school of lifelong learning…except you are both teacher and student. Select a subject of study that you're interested in, create a list of books you must read on your subject, assign yourself a project in which you must do something with what you learn, and set a deadline to accomplish this. You'll be surprised at how powerful self-education is!

●

June 21
2:41 am EDT

			June			
S	M	T	W	T	F	S
	1	2	3	4	5	6
7	8	9	10	11	12	13
14	15	16	17	18	19	20
21	22	23	24	25	26	27
28	29	30				

♋ July

June 28–July 4

Hope is a good thing, maybe the best of things. And no good thing ever dies.

~ANDY DUFRESNE, *THE SHAWSHANK REDEMPTION*

Date	Qtr.	Sign	Activity
Jun. 28, 4:16 am– Jun. 29, 6:48 pm	2nd	Libra	Plant annuals for fragrance and beauty. Trim to increase growth.
Jun. 29, 6:48 pm– Jul. 1, 9:21 pm	2nd	Scorpio	Plant grains, leafy annuals. Fertilize (chemical). Graft or bud plants. Irrigate. Trim to increase growth.
Jul. 4, 12:48 am– Jul. 5, 12:44 am	2nd	Capricorn	Graft or bud plants. Trim to increase growth.

If you've got an oil or grease stain on your clothing, bring some chalk to the rescue! Simply use white chalk (available from most craft or value stores) to pretreat your clothing or linens before laundering. This method also works for dirty shirt collars, and should you have a pair of suede shoes that need brightening, use chalk on them too, followed by a soft bristled brush.

◗

June 28
4:16 am EDT

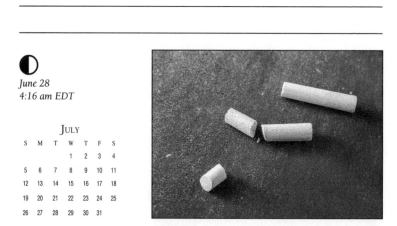

JULY

S	M	T	W	T	F	S
			1	2	3	4
5	6	7	8	9	10	11
12	13	14	15	16	17	18
19	20	21	22	23	24	25
26	27	28	29	30	31	

July 5–11

You can never get a cup of tea large enough or a book long enough to suit me.
    ~C.S. LEWIS

Date	Qtr.	Sign	Activity
Jul. 5, 12:44 am–Jul. 6, 6:08 am	3rd	Capricorn	Plant potatoes and tubers. Trim to retard growth.
Jul. 6, 6:08 am–Jul. 8, 2:13 pm	3rd	Aquarius	Cultivate. Destroy weeds and pests. Harvest fruits and root crops for food. Trim to retard growth.
Jul. 8, 2:13 pm–Jul. 11, 1:06 am	3rd	Pisces	Plant biennials, perennials, bulbs and roots. Prune. Irrigate. Fertilize (organic).
Jul. 11, 1:06 am–Jul. 12, 7:29 pm	3rd	Aries	Cultivate. Destroy weeds and pests. Harvest fruits and root crops for food. Trim to retard growth.

Are you owned by a finicky feline? Save wasted cat food, money, and lots of frustration and do not serve cold cat food. When feeding wet food, make sure it's at room or body temperature. Cold food straight from the refrigerator may cause stomach upset and also isn't as appealing. Take up the dish after twenty or thirty minutes to prevent hardening or spoiling. Your picky cat will appreciate it!

○
July 5
12:44 am EDT

JULY

S	M	T	W	T	F	S
			1	2	3	4
5	6	7	8	9	10	11
12	13	14	15	16	17	18
19	20	21	22	23	24	25
26	27	28	29	30	31	

July 12–18

It isn't enough to talk about peace. One must believe in it.
And it isn't enough to believe in it. One must work at it.

~ELEANOR ROOSEVELT

Date	Qtr.	Sign	Activity
Jul. 12, 7:29 pm– Jul. 13, 1:34 pm	4th	Aries	Cultivate. Destroy weeds and pests. Harvest fruits and root crops for food. Trim to retard growth.
Jul. 13, 1:34 pm– Jul. 16, 1:19 am	4th	Taurus	Plant potatoes and tubers. Trim to retard growth.
Jul. 16, 1:19 am– Jul. 18, 10:24 am	4th	Gemini	Cultivate. Destroy weeds and pests. Harvest fruits and root crops for food. Trim to retard growth.
Jul. 18, 10:24 am– Jul. 20, 1:33 pm	4th	Cancer	Plant biennials, perennials, bulbs and roots. Prune. Irrigate. Fertilize (organic).

Keep your coffee grounds! They're so useful in so many ways. Not only are they a great non-toxic fertilizer, but they also help to deter garden pests. If you're into nature crafts, they make a wonderful dye for cotton fabric, as well as an interesting inclusion for handmade paper.

July 12
7:29 pm EDT

JULY

S	M	T	W	T	F	S
			1	2	3	4
5	6	7	8	9	10	11
12	13	14	15	16	17	18
19	20	21	22	23	24	25
26	27	28	29	30	31	

July 19–25 ♋

There's nothing we can't do if we work hard, never sleep, and
shirk all other responsibilities in our lives.

~LESLIE KNOPE, *PARKS AND RECREATION*

Date	Qtr.	Sign	Activity
Jul. 18, 10:24 am–Jul. 20, 1:33 pm	4th	Cancer	Plant biennials, perennials, bulbs and roots. Prune. Irrigate. Fertilize (organic).
Jul. 20, 1:33 pm–Jul. 20, 4:16 pm	1st	Cancer	Plant grains, leafy annuals. Fertilize (chemical). Graft or bud plants. Irrigate. Trim to increase growth.
Jul. 24, 9:54 pm–Jul. 27, 12:12 am	1st	Libra	Plant annuals for fragrance and beauty. Trim to increase growth.

Pick a weekend to drive as far as you can go in one direction and still make it back home by the end of the weekend. While driving, alternate between listening to audiobooks or YouTube videos, and periods of just looking at the countryside while thinking about what you've just listened to. Consider this your private "windshield university think-tank time."

●
July 20
1:33 pm EDT

JULY

S	M	T	W	T	F	S
		1	2	3	4
5	6	7	8	9	10	11
12	13	14	15	16	17	18
19	20	21	22	23	24	25
26	27	28	29	30	31

♌ **August**

July 26–August 1

Kindness is language the deaf can hear and the blind can see.
~MARK TWAIN

Date	Qtr.	Sign	Activity
Jul. 24, 9:54 pm– Jul. 27, 12:12 am	1st	Libra	Plant annuals for fragrance and beauty. Trim to increase growth.
Jul. 27, 12:12 am– Jul. 27, 8:33 am	1st	Scorpio	Plant grains, leafy annuals. Fertilize (chemical). Graft or bud plants. Irrigate. Trim to increase growth.
Jul. 27, 8:33 am– Jul. 29, 3:25 am	2nd	Scorpio	Plant grains, leafy annuals. Fertilize (chemical). Graft or bud plants. Irrigate. Trim to increase growth.
Jul. 31, 7:58 am– Aug. 2, 2:11 pm	2nd	Capricorn	Graft or bud plants. Trim to increase growth.

When building meals, make sure your plate is ablaze with color. Missing a splash of yellow? Add ½ cup of whole kernel corn to your dish. Need to jazz up your morning oatmeal? Add a pop of violet with blueberries. Mixed into smoothies or tossed into your favorite soup, it's easy to add color, nutrition, flavor, and texture to meals.

July 27
8:33 am EDT

AUGUST

S	M	T	W	T	F	S
						1
2	3	4	5	6	7	8
9	10	11	12	13	14	15
16	17	18	19	20	21	22
23	24	25	26	27	28	29
30	31					

August 2–8 ♌

The final forming of a person's character lies in their
own hands.   ~ANNE FRANK

Date	Qtr.	Sign	Activity
Jul. 31, 7:58 am– Aug. 2, 2:11 pm	2nd	Capricorn	Graft or bud plants. Trim to increase growth.
Aug. 3, 11:59 am– Aug. 4, 10:28 pm	3rd	Aquarius	Cultivate. Destroy weeds and pests. Harvest fruits and root crops for food. Trim to retard growth.
Aug. 4, 10:28 pm– Aug. 7, 9:05 am	3rd	Pisces	Plant biennials, perennials, bulbs and roots. Prune. Irrigate. Fertilize (organic).
Aug. 7, 9:05 am– Aug. 9, 9:28 pm	3rd	Aries	Cultivate. Destroy weeds and pests. Harvest fruits and root crops for food. Trim to retard growth.

Removing sweat stains can be tricky and frustrating. Many solutions are touted, with the key ingredient ranging from Borax to vodka. One non-alcoholic option is to mix up a baking soda and water paste and apply with a clean toothbrush to dissolve perspiration. Soak in ¼ cup of oxygen bleach alternative and warm water in the washing machine or a small bucket for a couple of hours or overnight. (Vodka shot optional.)

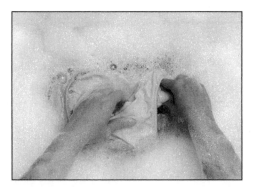

○
August 3
11:59 am EDT

AUGUST

S	M	T	W	T	F	S
						1
2	3	4	5	6	7	8
9	10	11	12	13	14	15
16	17	18	19	20	21	22
23	24	25	26	27	28	29
30	31					

August 9–15

We do not conceive of sudden, radical, irrational change as built into the very fabric of existence. Yet it is.
~MICHAEL CRICHTON, JURASSIC PARK

Date	Qtr.	Sign	Activity
Aug. 9, 9:28 pm– Aug. 11, 12:45 pm	3rd	Taurus	Plant potatoes and tubers. Trim to retard growth.
Aug. 11, 12:45 pm– Aug. 12, 9:46 am	4th	Taurus	Plant potatoes and tubers. Trim to retard growth.
Aug. 12, 9:46 am– Aug. 14, 7:35 pm	4th	Gemini	Cultivate. Destroy weeds and pests. Harvest fruits and root crops for food. Trim to retard growth.
Aug. 14, 7:35 pm– Aug. 17, 1:38 am	4th	Cancer	Plant biennials, perennials, bulbs and roots. Prune. Irrigate. Fertilize (organic).

You don't need expensive garden netting to protect your young plants from unwanted invaders. Hit the thrift stores and pick up old lace curtains. They're lightweight and let in the sun and rain, but won't inhibit the growth of the plant. Anchor them at the edges with staples or stones. Not only are they much less expensive than garden cloth, but you're also upcycling!

◐
August 11
12:45 pm EDT

AUGUST

S	M	T	W	T	F	S
						1
2	3	4	5	6	7	8
9	10	11	12	13	14	15
16	17	18	19	20	21	22
23	24	25	26	27	28	29
30	31					

August 16–22

If you have good thoughts they will shine out of your face like
sunbeams and you will always look lovely.

~ROALD DAHL

Date	Qtr.	Sign	Activity
Aug. 14, 7:35 pm–Aug. 17, 1:38 am	4th	Cancer	Plant biennials, perennials, bulbs and roots. Prune. Irrigate. Fertilize (organic).
Aug. 17, 1:38 am–Aug. 18, 10:42 pm	4th	Leo	Cultivate. Destroy weeds and pests. Harvest fruits and root crops for food. Trim to retard growth.
Aug. 21, 5:16 am–Aug. 23, 6:16 am	1st	Libra	Plant annuals for fragrance and beauty. Trim to increase growth.

After a summer of gardening, your hands can look pretty rough. Soak them in a bowl of warm water to which you've added two heaping tablespoons of baking soda, two heaping tablespoons of salt, and four to five drops of lavender or another favorite essential oil. You and your hands will be greatly renewed.

August 18
10:42 pm EDT

AUGUST

S	M	T	W	T	F	S
						1
2	3	4	5	6	7	8
9	10	11	12	13	14	15
16	17	18	19	20	21	22
23	24	25	26	27	28	29
30	31					

♍ August 23–29

If you are eating well and your condition is pure and clean,
life itself becomes like the dreams or visions that you have
when sleeping.   ~Michio Kushi

Date	Qtr.	Sign	Activity
Aug. 21, 5:16 am– Aug. 23, 6:16 am	1st	Libra	Plant annuals for fragrance and beauty. Trim to increase growth.
Aug. 23, 6:16 am– Aug. 25, 8:49 am	1st	Scorpio	Plant grains, leafy annuals. Fertilize (chemical). Graft or bud plants. Irrigate. Trim to increase growth.
Aug. 27, 1:37 pm– Aug. 29, 8:37 pm	2nd	Capricorn	Graft or bud plants. Trim to increase growth.

When choosing an avocado at the grocery store, you want it to feel like a tennis ball. It should have a slight "give," but should not feel mushy. If all your grocery store has are under-ripe avocadoes (green and really hard), that's fine! Take them home and leave them on the counter until they have that tennis ball feel. Once that happens, place them in your fridge and you'll be all set!

_____

_____

_____

_____

August 25
1:58 pm EDT

AUGUST

S	M	T	W	T	F	S
						1
2	3	4	5	6	7	8
9	10	11	12	13	14	15
16	17	18	19	20	21	22
23	24	25	26	27	28	29
30	31					

September ♍

August 30–September 5

There are two great days in a person's life—the day we are born and the day we discover why.   ～ANONYMOUS

Date	Qtr.	Sign	Activity
Sep. 1, 5:34 am– Sep. 2, 1:22 am	2nd	Pisces	Plant grains, leafy annuals. Fertilize (chemical). Graft or bud plants. Irrigate. Trim to increase growth.
Sep. 2, 1:22 am– Sep. 3, 4:22 pm	3rd	Pisces	Plant biennials, perennials, bulbs and roots. Prune. Irrigate. Fertilize (organic).
Sep. 3, 4:22 pm– Sep. 6, 4:43 am	3rd	Aries	Cultivate. Destroy weeds and pests. Harvest fruits and root crops for food. Trim to retard growth.

Eggplant is high in fiber, low in calories, and full of nutrients. Even better, it's available year-round with peak season in August and September in the US. Store fresh eggplant at room temperature to maintain better texture and flavor, and use within a few days to avoid softening and wrinkling. Do not consume eggplant leaves, as they are toxic. But do add this diverse plant to your recipe arsenal for better health!

○
September 2
1:22 am EDT

SEPTEMBER

S	M	T	W	T	F	S
		1	2	3	4	5
6	7	8	9	10	11	12
13	14	15	16	17	18	19
20	21	22	23	24	25	26
27	28	29	30			

♍ September 6–12

Even darkness must pass. A new day will come, and when the sun shines, it'll shine out the clearer.

~SAMWISE GAMGEE, *THE TWO TOWERS*

Date	Qtr.	Sign	Activity
Sep. 6, 4:43 am– Sep. 8, 5:28 pm	3rd	Taurus	Plant potatoes and tubers. Trim to retard growth.
Sep. 8, 5:28 pm– Sep. 10, 5:26 am	3rd	Gemini	Cultivate. Destroy weeds and pests. Harvest fruits and root crops for food. Trim to retard growth.
Sep. 10, 5:26 am– Sep. 11, 4:23 am	4th	Gemini	Cultivate. Destroy weeds and pests. Harvest fruits and root crops for food. Trim to retard growth.
Sep. 11, 4:23 am– Sep. 13, 11:32 am	4th	Cancer	Plant biennials, perennials, bulbs and roots. Prune. Irrigate. Fertilize (organic).

Protein is an important nutrient for creating a sense of satiety, or fullness. Additionally, it helps buffer intense spikes and valleys in blood sugar caused by meals rich in carbohydrates. Balance the carbs from grains, fruit, and vegetables with high-quality lean protein sources (chicken, eggs, soy products). You'll feel fuller throughout the day and less likely to grab unhealthy snacks!

◖
September 10
5:26 am EDT

SEPTEMBER

S	M	T	W	T	F	S
		1	2	3	4	5
6	7	8	9	10	11	12
13	14	15	16	17	18	19
20	21	22	23	24	25	26
27	28	29	30			

September 13–19 ♍

Expect nothing. Live frugally on surprise.   ∼ALICE WALKER

Date	Qtr.	Sign	Activity
Sep. 13, 11:32 am– Sep. 15, 2:37 pm	4th	Leo	Cultivate. Destroy weeds and pests. Harvest fruits and root crops for food. Trim to retard growth.
Sep. 15, 2:37 pm– Sep. 17, 7:00 am	4th	Virgo	Cultivate, especially medicinal plants. Destroy weeds and pests. Trim to retard growth.
Sep. 17, 2:56 pm– Sep. 19, 2:33 pm	1st	Libra	Plant annuals for fragrance and beauty. Trim to increase growth.
Sep. 19, 2:33 pm– Sep. 21, 3:32 pm	1st	Scorpio	Plant grains, leafy annuals. Fertilize (chemical). Graft or bud plants. Irrigate. Trim to increase growth.

Clean with vinegar! A spray bottle filled with white vinegar works both as a degreaser and a disinfectant. To trap annoying fruit flies in the house, put ¼ cup of cider vinegar and ½ teaspoon of dishwashing liquid into a dish and put plastic wrap over the top. Poke some holes in the plastic and watch it catch the flies. You can also soak smelly cleaning cloths in vinegar before washing them to get rid of the odor.

● September 17
7:00 am EDT

SEPTEMBER

S	M	T	W	T	F	S
		1	2	3	4	5
6	7	8	9	10	11	12
13	14	15	16	17	18	19
20	21	22	23	24	25	26
27	28	29	30			

♎ September 20–26

Of course, when they bring the maple syrup after the pancakes, it will definitely be too late.

~RAYMOND BABBITT, *RAIN MAN*

Date	Qtr.	Sign	Activity
Sep. 19, 2:33 pm– Sep. 21, 3:32 pm	1st	Scorpio	Plant grains, leafy annuals. Fertilize (chemical). Graft or bud plants. Irrigate. Trim to increase growth.
Sep. 23, 7:16 pm– Sep. 23, 9:55 pm	1st	Capricorn	Graft or bud plants. Trim to increase growth.
Sep. 23, 9:55 pm– Sep. 26, 2:08 am	2nd	Capricorn	Graft or bud plants. Trim to increase growth.

Fight "pack rat syndrome" by periodically eliminating items you no longer want in your house. One possible criterion: when you no longer notice a decorative object (such as a picture or figurine), it's time to get rid of it. Consider a trade-off system. When adding something new to the household, discard an old item. Be ruthless with your own possessions. Discard all unused junk. But don't throw out someone else's things unless they ask!

◑
September 23
9:55 pm EDT

SEPTEMBER

S	M	T	W	T	F	S
		1	2	3	4	5
6	7	8	9	10	11	12
13	14	15	16	17	18	19
20	21	22	23	24	25	26
27	28	29	30			

October ♎

September 27–October 3

We cannot sit back and hope that everything works out for
the best.   ⁓MICHELLE OBAMA

Date	Qtr.	Sign	Activity
Sep. 23, 9:55 pm– Sep. 26, 2:08 am	2nd	Capricorn	Graft or bud plants. Trim to increase growth.
Sep. 28, 11:34 am– Sep. 30, 10:47 pm	2nd	Pisces	Plant grains, leafy annuals. Fertilize (chemical). Graft or bud plants. Irrigate. Trim to increase growth.
Oct. 1, 5:05 pm– Oct. 3, 11:12 am	3rd	Aries	Cultivate. Destroy weeds and pests. Harvest fruits and root crops for food. Trim to retard growth.
Oct. 3, 11:12 am– Oct. 6, 12:03 am	3rd	Taurus	Plant potatoes and tubers. Trim to retard growth.

Roses are pretty, but did you know that most of them are edible too? We grow *Rosa rugosa* just for this purpose! It comes in many different colors, and is commonly known as a beach rose. The hips—the fruit of the rose—have culinary and medicinal uses, and we make sorbet, jelly, and wine from the petals.

○
October 1
5:05 pm EDT

OCTOBER

S	M	T	W	T	F	S
				1	2	3
4	5	6	7	8	9	10
11	12	13	14	15	16	17
18	19	20	21	22	23	24
25	26	27	28	29	30	31

♎ October 4–10

If you obey all the rules, you miss all the fun.

~Katharine Hepburn

Date	Qtr.	Sign	Activity
Oct. 3, 11:12 am– Oct. 6, 12:03 am	3rd	Taurus	Plant potatoes and tubers. Trim to retard growth.
Oct. 6, 12:03 am– Oct. 8, 11:45 am	3rd	Gemini	Cultivate. Destroy weeds and pests. Harvest fruits and root crops for food. Trim to retard growth.
Oct. 8, 11:45 am– Oct. 9, 8:40 pm	3rd	Cancer	Plant biennials, perennials, bulbs and roots. Prune. Irrigate. Fertilize (organic).
Oct. 9, 8:40 pm– Oct. 10, 8:24 pm	4th	Cancer	Plant biennials, perennials, bulbs and roots. Prune. Irrigate. Fertilize (organic).
Oct. 10, 8:24 pm– Oct. 13, 12:56 am	4th	Leo	Cultivate. Destroy weeds and pests. Harvest fruits and root crops for food. Trim to retard growth.

Need some activities to boost your mood? Put up a bird-feeder and see how many birds you can recognize. Make a list called "Things I'm Thankful For." Try a new type of food or experiment with recipes from a culture other than your own. Turn off the TV or at least stop watching depressing programs. Fly a kite. Take a walk, dance (even by yourself), and move more.

◑
October 9
8:40 pm EDT

October

S	M	T	W	T	F	S
				1	2	3
4	5	6	7	8	9	10
11	12	13	14	15	16	17
18	19	20	21	22	23	24
25	26	27	28	29	30	31

October 11–17 ♎

So often in life things that you regard as an impediment turn out to be great, good fortune. ~RUTH BADER GINSBURG

Date	Qtr.	Sign	Activity
Oct. 10, 8:24 pm– Oct. 13, 12:56 am	4th	Leo	Cultivate. Destroy weeds and pests. Harvest fruits and root crops for food. Trim to retard growth.
Oct. 13, 12:56 am– Oct. 15, 1:54 am	4th	Virgo	Cultivate, especially medicinal plants. Destroy weeds and pests. Trim to retard growth.
Oct. 16, 3:31 pm– Oct. 17, 1:05 am	1st	Libra	Plant annuals for fragrance and beauty. Trim to increase growth.
Oct. 17, 1:05 am– Oct. 19, 12:43 am	1st	Scorpio	Plant grains, leafy annuals. Fertilize (chemical). Graft or bud plants. Irrigate. Trim to increase growth.

Things grow better in well-fed soil, but you don't have to spend a fortune on treatments. Try trench composting, by burying your kitchen veggie scraps, coffee grounds, and tea leaves in a foot deep trench in your garden. Cover with more organic matter, such as autumn leaves or a few lawnmower clippings, and leave to decompose. Plant in the trenches next year, and start new trenches where you have been growing.

● *October 16*
3:31 pm EDT

OCTOBER

S	M	T	W	T	F	S
				1	2	3
4	5	6	7	8	9	10
11	12	13	14	15	16	17
18	19	20	21	22	23	24
25	26	27	28	29	30	31

♎︎ October 18–24

*The consequences of our actions are always so complicated,
so diverse, that predicting the future is a very difficult
business indeed.*   ~ALBUS DUMBLEDORE

Date	Qtr.	Sign	Activity
Oct. 17, 1:05 am– Oct. 19, 12:43 am	1st	Scorpio	Plant grains, leafy annuals. Fertilize (chemical). Graft or bud plants. Irrigate. Trim to increase growth.
Oct. 21, 2:44 am– Oct. 23, 8:17 am	1st	Capricorn	Graft or bud plants. Trim to increase growth.

Poor sleep can have a host of negative consequences on our health, safety, and well-being. It can cause impaired memory and productivity, increase risk of car accidents, and negatively impact relationships. Insomnia has been linked to magnesium and thiamine (vitamin B1) deficiencies. Limit your insomnia by eating more spinach, avocado, almonds, barley, quinoa, and oysters to boost magnesium, and asparagus, salmon, pork, and whole wheat bread or pasta to raise levels of vitamin B1.

◗
October 23
9:23 am EDT

OCTOBER

S	M	T	W	T	F	S
				1	2	3
4	5	6	7	8	9	10
11	12	13	14	15	16	17
18	19	20	21	22	23	24
25	26	27	28	29	30	31

October 25–31 ♏

*Vulnerability is the birthplace of love, belonging, joy, courage,
empathy, and creativity. It is the source of hope, empathy,
accountability, and authenticity.*   ~BRENÉ BROWN

Date	Qtr.	Sign	Activity
Oct. 25, 5:18 pm– Oct. 28, 4:45 am	2nd	Pisces	Plant grains, leafy annuals. Fertilize (chemical). Graft or bud plants. Irrigate. Trim to increase growth.
Oct. 30, 5:19 pm– Oct. 31, 10:49 am	2nd	Taurus	Plant annuals for hardiness. Trim to increase growth.
Oct. 31, 10:49 am– Nov. 2, 5:00 am	3rd	Taurus	Plant potatoes and tubers. Trim to retard growth.

We call mullein "nature's toilet paper" around here, because of its soft, silky leaves, but there's much more to this garden great than just a bit of fluff! We never mow over it because it heals the soil, feeds pollinators, and makes a great compost. As an herbal medicine, it's an expectorant, a mucilient, an analgesic, and a demulcent. It's also statuesque and pretty to grow!

○
October 31
10:49 am EDT

OCTOBER

S	M	T	W	T	F	S
				1	2	3
4	5	6	7	8	9	10
11	12	13	14	15	16	17
18	19	20	21	22	23	24
25	26	27	28	29	30	31

♏ November

November 1–7

The Cosmos is all that is or ever was or ever will be.

~CARL SAGAN

Date	Qtr.	Sign	Activity
Oct. 31, 10:49 am– Nov. 2, 5:00 am	3rd	Taurus	Plant potatoes and tubers. Trim to retard growth.
Nov. 2, 5:00 am– Nov. 4, 4:45 pm	3rd	Gemini	Cultivate. Destroy weeds and pests. Harvest fruits and root crops for food. Trim to retard growth.
Nov. 4, 4:45 pm– Nov. 7, 2:18 am	3rd	Cancer	Plant biennials, perennials, bulbs and roots. Prune. Irrigate. Fertilize (organic).
Nov. 7, 2:18 am– Nov. 8, 8:46 am	3rd	Leo	Cultivate. Destroy weeds and pests. Harvest fruits and root crops for food. Trim to retard growth.

Clean your windows with yesterday's news. The newspapers don't leave streaky marks or residue behind like some paper towels do. If you've got some grime to remove, don't use window cleaning preparations, just add vinegar! Brown packing paper works too, should you have it leftover from a parcel delivery. Do this on a dull news day and you'll avoid even more messy marks.

*Daylight Saving Time
ends November 1, 2:00 a.m.*

NOVEMBER

S	M	T	W	T	F	S
1	2	3	4	5	6	7
8	9	10	11	12	13	14
15	16	17	18	19	20	21
22	23	24	25	26	27	28
29	30					

November 8–14 ♏

It's hard for many people to believe that there are
extraordinary things inside themselves, as well as others.

    ~Elijah Price, *Unbreakable*

Date	Qtr.	Sign	Activity
Nov. 7, 2:18 am– Nov. 8, 8:46 am	3rd	Leo	Cultivate. Destroy weeds and pests. Harvest fruits and root crops for food. Trim to retard growth.
Nov. 8, 8:46 am– Nov. 9, 8:30 am	4th	Leo	Cultivate. Destroy weeds and pests. Harvest fruits and root crops for food. Trim to retard growth.
Nov. 9, 8:30 am– Nov. 11, 11:09 am	4th	Virgo	Cultivate, especially medicinal plants. Destroy weeds and pests. Trim to retard growth.
Nov. 13, 11:19 am– Nov. 15, 12:07 am	4th	Scorpio	Plant biennials, perennials, bulbs and roots. Prune. Irrigate. Fertilize (organic).

Bake a cake and decorate it for no particular reason. Then invite a friend, family member, or neighbor to share and celebrate the ordinary side of life with you.

◖

November 8
8:46 am EST

NOVEMBER

S	M	T	W	T	F	S
1	2	3	4	5	6	7
8	9	10	11	12	13	14
15	16	17	18	19	20	21
22	23	24	25	26	27	28
29	30					

♏ November 15–21

Don't raise your voice, improve your argument.

~Desmond Tutu

Date	Qtr.	Sign	Activity
Nov. 15, 12:07 am– Nov. 15, 10:47 am	1st	Scorpio	Plant grains, leafy annuals. Fertilize (chemical). Graft or bud plants. Irrigate. Trim to increase growth.
Nov. 17, 11:35 am– Nov. 19, 3:25 pm	1st	Capricorn	Graft or bud plants. Trim to increase growth.
Nov. 21, 11:06 pm– Nov. 21, 11:45 pm	1st	Pisces	Plant grains, leafy annuals. Fertilize (chemical). Graft or bud plants. Irrigate. Trim to increase growth.
Nov. 21, 11:45 pm– Nov. 24, 10:05 am	2nd	Pisces	Plant grains, leafy annuals. Fertilize (chemical). Graft or bud plants. Irrigate. Trim to increase growth.

Rubbing alcohol is an asset in the garden when it comes to cleaning your tools and storing them away. Not only does the alcohol make removing stuck dirt and grime easier, but it also prevents fungus and other pathogens from living and perhaps breeding on your items when you're not using them. Use a mist of half alcohol and half water once they're cleaned, and store them in your usual place.

◗ ●

November 15   November 21
12:07 am EST   11:45 pm EST

NOVEMBER

S	M	T	W	T	F	S
1	2	3	4	5	6	7
8	9	10	11	12	13	14
15	16	17	18	19	20	21
22	23	24	25	26	27	28
29	30					

November 22–28

*Here and there an individual or group dares to love, and rises
to the majestic heights of moral maturity. So in a real sense
this is a great time to be alive.* ~MARTIN LUTHER KING JR.

Date	Qtr.	Sign	Activity
Nov. 21, 11:45 pm– Nov. 24, 10:05 am	2nd	Pisces	Plant grains, leafy annuals. Fertilize (chemical). Graft or bud plants. Irrigate. Trim to increase growth.
Nov. 26, 10:43 pm– Nov. 29, 11:16 am	2nd	Taurus	Plant annuals for hardiness. Trim to increase growth.

Perennial "miracle diets" waste time and money, and potentially risk your health. To spot one, ask if: 1) Unrealistic promises are made. 2) No solid research supports claims. 3) Major food groups are restricted. 4) Less than three meals are eaten per day. 5) A celebrity or someone without credentials endorses it. 6) Something exotic or unusual is consumed, or required for purchase. 7) It sounds too good to be true. (It is.)

		NOVEMBER				
S	M	T	W	T	F	S
1	2	3	4	5	6	7
8	9	10	11	12	13	14
15	16	17	18	19	20	21
22	23	24	25	26	27	28
29	30					

↗ **December**

November 29–December 5

There are many ways of going forward, but only one way of standing still.   ~FRANKLIN D. ROOSEVELT

Date	Qtr.	Sign	Activity
Nov. 26, 10:43 pm– Nov. 29, 11:16 am	2nd	Taurus	Plant annuals for hardiness. Trim to increase growth.
Nov. 30, 4:30 am– Dec. 1, 10:33 pm	3rd	Gemini	Cultivate. Destroy weeds and pests. Harvest fruits and root crops for food. Trim to retard growth.
Dec. 1, 10:33 pm– Dec. 4, 7:53 am	3rd	Cancer	Plant biennials, perennials, bulbs and roots. Prune. Irrigate. Fertilize (organic).
Dec. 4, 7:53 am– Dec. 6, 2:46 pm	3rd	Leo	Cultivate. Destroy weeds and pests. Harvest fruits and root crops for food. Trim to retard growth.

Dandelions have many culinary uses. They were introduced to North America in the 1600s by settlers who cultivated them for food and medicine. Dandelion greens are delicious in a salad, and the flowers make a very pretty jelly. The roasted root makes a coffee type drink. If you're lucky, perhaps you know someone who makes dandelion wine!

O
November 30
4:30 am EST

DECEMBER

S	M	T	W	T	F	S
		1	2	3	4	5
6	7	8	9	10	11	12
13	14	15	16	17	18	19
20	21	22	23	24	25	26
27	28	29	30	31		

December 6–12

The person, be it gentleman or lady, who has not pleasure in a good novel, must be intolerably stupid.   ~JANE AUSTEN

Date	Qtr.	Sign	Activity
Dec. 6, 2:46 pm– Dec. 7, 7:37 pm	3rd	Virgo	Cultivate, especially medicinal plants. Destroy weeds and pests. Trim to retard growth.
Dec. 7, 7:37 pm– Dec. 8, 7:01 pm	4th	Virgo	Cultivate, especially medicinal plants. Destroy weeds and pests. Trim to retard growth.
Dec. 10, 8:59 pm– Dec. 12, 9:39 pm	4th	Scorpio	Plant biennials, perennials, bulbs and roots. Prune. Irrigate. Fertilize (organic).
Dec. 12, 9:39 pm– Dec. 14, 11:17 am	4th	Sagittarius	Cultivate. Destroy weeds and pests. Harvest fruits and root crops for food. Trim to retard growth.

If you have trouble meditating, try knitting, crochet, or needle-work as a form of active meditation. It is quiet, allows you to think deeply, and keeps your hands busy while your mind is free. Choose each knitting, crochet, or sewing project as if it were an expression of what you are trying to accomplish in meditation… for example, peace of mind, insight into a situation, or a more expansive consciousness.

◑
December 7
7:37 pm EST

DECEMBER

S	M	T	W	T	F	S
		1	2	3	4	5
6	7	8	9	10	11	12
13	14	15	16	17	18	19
20	21	22	23	24	25	26
27	28	29	30	31		

December 13–19

*I don't want to repeat my innocence. I want the pleasure of
losing it again.*   ∼F. Scott Fitzgerald

Date	Qtr.	Sign	Activity
Dec. 12, 9:39 pm– Dec. 14, 11:17 am	4th	Sagittarius	Cultivate. Destroy weeds and pests. Harvest fruits and root crops for food. Trim to retard growth.
Dec. 14, 10:35 pm– Dec. 17, 1:27 am	1st	Capricorn	Graft or bud plants. Trim to increase growth.
Dec. 19, 7:39 am– Dec. 21, 5:32 pm	1st	Pisces	Plant grains, leafy annuals. Fertilize (chemical). Graft or bud plants. Irrigate. Trim to increase growth.

I f your hands are dry, cracked, and bleeding from the cold
temperatures and winter air, try this home remedy. Rub a skin-
healing ointment (like Aquaphor) on your hands, place a sock
over each, and then go to bed. Leaving the ointment to soak in
overnight (but not smear all over your sheets) will help your
hands heal much more quickly and will heal those spots that
crack and bleed throughout the day.

_____

_____

_____

_____

●

December 14
11:17 am EST

December

S	M	T	W	T	F	S
		1	2	3	4	5
6	7	8	9	10	11	12
13	14	15	16	17	18	19
20	21	22	23	24	25	26
27	28	29	30	31		

December 20–26

Don't waste your energy trying to educate or change opinions;
go over, under, through, and opinions will change organically
when you're the boss. Or they won't. Who cares? Do your
thing, and don't care if they like it.   ~TINA FEY

Date	Qtr.	Sign	Activity
Dec. 19, 7:39 am– Dec. 21, 5:32 pm	1st	Pisces	Plant grains, leafy annuals. Fertilize (chemical). Graft or bud plants. Irrigate. Trim to increase growth.
Dec. 24, 5:55 am– Dec. 26, 6:33 pm	2nd	Taurus	Plant annuals for hardiness. Trim to increase growth.

When summer comes, wallow in the heat. When autumn arrives, bask in the briskness. When winter comes, play in the snow. And when spring arrives, start your life over as if it's all new and beautiful and you are a flower about to bloom.

◐
December 21
6:41 pm EST

DECEMBER

S	M	T	W	T	F	S
		1	2	3	4	5
6	7	8	9	10	11	12
13	14	15	16	17	18	19
20	21	22	23	24	25	26
27	28	29	30	31		

♑ December 27–January 2, 2021

*Don't be too timid and squeamish about your actions. All life
is an experiment. The more experiments you make the better.*
~RALPH WALDO EMERSON

Date	Qtr.	Sign	Activity
Dec. 29, 5:28 am– Dec. 29, 10:28 pm	2nd	Cancer	Plant grains, leafy annuals. Fertilize (chemical). Graft or bud plants. Irrigate. Trim to increase growth.
Dec. 29, 10:28 pm– Dec. 31, 1:58 pm	3rd	Cancer	Plant biennials, perennials, bulbs and roots. Prune. Irrigate. Fertilize (organic).

Need something to look forward to? Start planning a trip! The trip can fit your budget—anything from a night or two of camping to a weeklong tropical adventure or a month of backpacking in Europe. Making fun future plans can be a great use of time and gives you something to get excited about! If you're not ready to travel, even planning a special date night or friend outing can be a great way to avoid feeling a new year slump.

_____

_____

_____

_____

○
December 29
10:28 pm EST

DECEMBER

S	M	T	W	T	F	S
		1	2	3	4	5
6	7	8	9	10	11	12
13	14	15	16	17	18	19
20	21	22	23	24	25	26
27	28	29	30	31		

Gardening by the Moon

Welcome to the world of gardening by the Moon! Unlike most gardening advice, this article is not about how to garden, it's about when to garden. Timing is everything; if you know how to use the Moon, you'll not only be in sync with nature but you can sit back and watch your garden grow beyond your wildest dreams.

Gardening by the Moon is nothing new. It's been around since ancient times when people used both the Sun and the Moon to predict the tides, as well as fertility and growth cycles for plants and animals.

Lunar gardening is simple and the results are immediate. It doesn't matter whether you're a beginner gardener with a single pot or an old hand with years of master gardening experience— your garden will grow bigger and better if you follow the cycles of the Moon and match up the right time with the right garden activity. When the temperature has dropped and the sun is low on the horizon you can apply what you've learned to your indoor plants as well.

The sky is a celestial clock, with the Sun and the Moon as the "hands" that tell the time. The Sun tells the season, and the light and location of the Moon tell the best times for birth, growth, and death in the garden. The Moon doesn't generate any light by itself, but as it circles the Earth it reflects the light of the Sun, which makes the Moon look like it's getting bigger and smaller. The cyclical increases and decreases in the light of the Moon are phases and tell times of growth.

Moon Phases

The theory behind gardening by the Moon is "as the Moon goes, so goes the garden." The Earth circles around the Sun once a year but the Moon has a much shorter "life span" of twenty-eight to thirty days. Every month, as the light of the Moon increases and decreases, it mirrors the cycle of birth, growth, and death in the garden. After adjusting your garden activities to the light of the Moon you'll be amazed to see how well your garden grows.

The **waxing phase** is the growth cycle in the garden. It begins with the New Moon and lasts for two weeks. Each month the Moon is "born" at the New Moon (day one) and grows bigger and brighter until it reaches maturity at the Full Moon (day fourteen). When the light of the Moon is increasing it's the best time of the month to sow seeds, plant leafy annuals, and cut back or prune plants to encourage bigger growth.

The **waning phase** is the declining cycle in the garden. It begins with the Full Moon (day fourteen) and lasts for two weeks. The Moon grows older after the Full Moon as the light begins to decrease, until it disappears or "dies" at day twenty-eight. The decreasing light of the Moon is the time to plant bulbs, root vegetables, and perennials that store their energy underground. The waning Moon phase is also a good time for garden maintenance, including weeding, raking, deadheading, mowing, working the soil, destroying insects, and burning brush.

How can you tell if the Moon is waxing or waning?

Cup your right hand into a C shape and look up into the sky. If the crescent Moon fits into the closed part of your right hand, it's a waxing Moon.

Cup your left hand into a C shape and look up into the sky. If the crescent Moon fits into the closed part of your left hand, it's a waning Moon.

New Moon and Full Moon

Every month, the Moon takes one day off. This time-out between waning and waxing is called the New Moon. The time-out between waxing and waning is called the Full Moon. When the Moon reaches either of these stopping points, it's time for you to follow its example and take a one-day break from the garden.

Moon Signs

Once you know the Moon phases, the next step is to locate where the Moon is in the zodiac. The Moon hangs out in each of the zodiac signs for two to three days per month.

There's no such thing as a "bad" time in the garden, but there are Moon signs that are better for growth and others that are better for digging and weeding. Growth times alternate every two to three days with maintenance times. The trick is knowing which one is which.

The grow signs are Taurus, Cancer, Libra, Scorpio, Capricorn, and Pisces. When the Moon is in these signs it's time to seed and plant.

The no-grow/maintenance signs are Aries, Gemini, Leo, Virgo, Sagittarius, and Aquarius. When the Moon is in these signs it's time for digging, weeding, mowing, and pruning.

Remember: It's always a good time to garden something!

Putting It All Together

In order to get started, you'll need three tools: a calendar with New and Full Moons, the Moon tables (pg. 136), and the Moon phases and signs below.

Then follow these simple steps:

1. Mark your calendar with your time frame for gardening.

2. Figure out when the Moon is waxing (1st and 2nd quarters) and waning (3rd and 4th quarters). Use the tables in the Weekly Almanac section.

3. Locate the Moon by zodiac sign.

4. Check out the gardening advice below, which takes into account the Moon's phase and sign.

Moon Phases and Signs

Note: Can be applied to any calendar year.

Waxing Aries Moon (October–April)

Aries is one of the three fire signs that is hot and barren. Seeds planted under a waxing Aries Moon tend to be bitter or bolt quickly, but if you're feeling lucky you could try your hand at hot and spicy peppers or herbs that thrive in dry heat.

Waning Aries Moon (April–October)

The decreasing light of the waning Aries Moon makes these two to three days a good time to focus on harvesting, cutting back, mowing the lawn, and getting rid of pests.

Waxing Taurus Moon (November–May)

Taurus is one of the three semi-fruitful earth signs. These days are perfect ones to establish your garden by planting or fertilizing annuals. Annuals with outside seeds like lettuces, cabbage, corn, and broccoli grow faster when planted under a waxing Taurus Moon that is one to seven days old. Vegetables with inside seeds like cucumbers, melons, squash, tomatoes, and beans should be planted when the Moon is seven to twelve days old. Annual flowers can be planted any time during this two-week phase.

Waning Taurus Moon (May–November)

The decreasing light of this semi-fruitful waning Taurus Moon gives you a perfect two- or three-day window for planting perennials or digging in root vegetables and flower bulbs.

Waxing Gemini Moon (December–June)

Gemini is one of the three dry and barren signs. But with the light of the Moon increasing you can use these two to three days to prune or cut back plants you want to flourish and grow bigger.

Waning Gemini Moon (June–December)

Gemini can be all over the place, so use these couple of dry and barren days when the light is decreasing to weed invasive plants that are out of control.

Waxing Cancer Moon (January–July)

Cancer is one of the three wet and fruitful signs, so when the Moon is waxing in Cancer it's the perfect time to plant seeds or set out seedlings and annual flowers that live for only one season. Annuals with outside seeds grow faster when planted under a Moon that is one to seven days old. Vegetables with inside seeds should be planted when the Moon is seven to twelve days old. Annual flowers can be planted any time during these two weeks.

Waning Cancer Moon (July–January)

Plant perennials, root vegetables, and bulbs to your heart's content under the decreasing light of this fruitful Moon.

Waxing Leo Moon (February–August)

The light of the Moon is increasing but Leo is one of the three hot and barren fire signs. Use the two or three days of this waxing Leo Moon to cut and prune the plants and shrubs you want to be the king or queen of your garden.

Waning Leo Moon (August–February)

With the light of the Moon decreasing, this Leo Moon is a good period to dig the soil, destroy pests and insects, and burn brush.

Waxing Virgo Moon (March–September)

Virgo is a semi-barren sign, which is good for fertilizing (Virgo is a "greenie" type that loves organics) and for planting woody vines and hardy herbs.

Waning Virgo Moon (September–March)

With the light of this semi-barren Moon decreasing for a couple of days, plan to hoe those rows and get rid of your weeds. Harvest Moon in September.

Waxing Libra Moon (October–April)

Libra is a semi-fruitful sign focused on beauty. Because the Moon is growing brighter in Libra, these two to three days are a great time to give your flower garden some heavy-duty TLC.

Waning Libra Moon (April–October)

If you want to encourage re-blooming, try deadheading your vegetables and flowers under the light of this decreasing Libra Moon. Harvest your flowers.

Waxing Scorpio Moon (November–May)

Scorpio is one of the three wet and fruitful signs. When the Moon is waxing in Scorpio it's the perfect time for planting annuals that have a bite, like arugula and hot peppers. Annuals with outside seeds grow faster when planted under a Moon that is one to seven days old. Vegetables with inside seeds should be planted when the Moon is seven to twelve days old. Annual flowers can be planted anytime during this two-week phase.

Waning Scorpio Moon (May–November)

With the light of the Moon decreasing in Scorpio, a sign that likes strong and intense flavors, this is the perfect period to plant hardy perennials, garlic bulbs, and onion sets.

Waxing Sagittarius Moon (June–December)

Sagittarius is one of the three hot and barren signs. Because Sagittarius prefers roaming to staying still, this waxing Moon is not good time for planting. But you can encourage growth during the two or three days when the light is increasing by cutting back, mowing, and pruning.

Waning Sagittarius Moon (December–June)

It's time to discourage growth during the days when the light of the Moon is decreasing in Sagittarius. Cut back, mow the lawn, prune, and destroy pests and insects you never want to darken your garden again.

Waxing Capricorn Moon (July–January)

Capricorn is a semi-fruitful earth sign. The couple of days when the light of the Moon is increasing in Capricorn are good for getting the garden into shape, setting out plants and transplants, and fertilizing.

Waning Capricorn Moon (January–July)

The decreasing light of this fruitful Capricorn Moon is the perfect window for digging and dividing bulbs and pinching back suckers to encourage bigger blooms on your flowers and vegetables.

Waxing Aquarius Moon (August–February)

Aquarius is a dry and barren sign. However, the increasing light of the Aquarian Moon makes this a good opportunity to experiment by pruning or cutting back plants you want to flourish.

Waning Aquarius Moon (February–August)

The light of the Moon is decreasing. Use this time to harvest or to weed, cut back, and prune the shrubs and plants that you want to banish forever from your garden. Harvest vegetables.

Waxing Pisces Moon (September–March)

When the Moon is increasing in fruitful Pisces, it's a perfect period for planting seeds and annuals. Annuals with outside seeds grow faster when planted under a Moon that is one to seven days old. Vegetables with inside seeds should be planted when the Moon is seven to twelve days old. Annual flowers can be planted any time during these two weeks.

Waning Pisces Moon (March–September)

With the light of the Moon decreasing it's time to plant all perennials, bulbs, and root vegetables except potatoes. Garden lore has it that potatoes planted under a Pisces Moon tend to grow bumps or "toes," because Pisces is associated with the feet.

Here's hoping that this has inspired you to give gardening by the Moon a try. Not only is it the secret ingredient that will make your garden more abundant, but you can use it as long as the Sun is in the sky and the Moon circles the Earth!

A Guide to Planting

Plant	Quarter	Sign
Annuals	1st or 2nd	
Apple tree	2nd or 3rd	Cancer, Pisces, Virgo
Artichoke	1st	Cancer, Pisces
Asparagus	1st	Cancer, Scorpio, Pisces
Aster	1st or 2nd	Virgo, Libra
Barley	1st or 2nd	Cancer, Pisces, Libra, Capricorn, Virgo
Beans (bush & pole)	2nd	Cancer, Taurus, Pisces, Libra
Beans (kidney, white & navy)	1st or 2nd	Cancer, Pisces
Beech tree	2nd or 3rd	Virgo, Taurus
Beets	3rd	Cancer, Capricorn, Pisces, Libra
Biennials	3rd or 4th	
Broccoli	1st	Cancer, Scorpio, Pisces, Libra
Brussels sprouts	1st	Cancer, Scorpio, Pisces, Libra
Buckwheat	1st or 2nd	Capricorn
Bulbs	3rd	Cancer, Scorpio, Pisces
Bulbs for seed	2nd or 3rd	
Cabbage	1st	Cancer, Scorpio, Pisces, Taurus, Libra
Canes (raspberry, blackberry & gooseberry)	2nd	Cancer, Scorpio, Pisces
Cantaloupe	1st or 2nd	Cancer, Scorpio, Pisces, Taurus, Libra
Carrots	3rd	Cancer, Scorpio, Pisces, Taurus, Libra
Cauliflower	1st	Cancer, Scorpio, Pisces, Libra
Celeriac	3rd	Cancer, Scorpio, Pisces
Celery	1st	Cancer, Scorpio, Pisces
Cereals	1st or 2nd	Cancer, Scorpio, Pisces, Libra
Chard	1st or 2nd	Cancer, Scorpio, Pisces
Chicory	2nd or 3rd	Cancer, Scorpio, Pisces
Chrysanthemum	1st or 2nd	Virgo

Plant	Quarter	Sign
Coreopsis	2nd or 3rd	Libra
Corn	1st	Cancer, Scorpio, Pisces
Corn for fodder	1st or 2nd	Libra
Cosmos	2nd or 3rd	Libra
Cress	1st	Cancer, Scorpio, Pisces
Crocus	1st or 2nd	Virgo
Cucumber	1st	Cancer, Scorpio, Pisces
Daffodil	1st or 2nd	Libra, Virgo
Dahlia	1st or 2nd	Libra, Virgo
Deciduous trees	2nd or 3rd	Cancer, Scorpio, Pisces, Virgo, Libra
Eggplant	2nd	Cancer, Scorpio, Pisces, Libra
Endive	1st	Cancer, Scorpio, Pisces, Libra
Flowers	1st	Cancer, Scorpio, Pisces, Libra, Taurus, Virgo
Garlic	3rd	Libra, Taurus, Pisces
Gladiola	1st or 2nd	Libra, Virgo
Gourds	1st or 2nd	Cancer, Scorpio, Pisces, Libra
Grapes	2nd or 3rd	Cancer, Scorpio, Pisces, Virgo
Hay	1st or 2nd	Cancer, Scorpio, Pisces, Libra, Taurus
Herbs	1st or 2nd	Cancer, Scorpio, Pisces
Honeysuckle	1st or 2nd	Scorpio, Virgo
Hops	1st or 2nd	Scorpio, Libra
Horseradish	1st or 2nd	Cancer, Scorpio, Pisces
Houseplants	1st	Cancer, Scorpio, Pisces, Libra
Hyacinth	3rd	Cancer, Scorpio, Pisces
Iris	1st or 2nd	Cancer, Virgo
Kohlrabi	1st or 2nd	Cancer, Scorpio, Pisces, Libra
Leek	2nd or 3rd	Sagittarius
Lettuce	1st	Cancer, Scorpio, Pisces, Libra, Taurus
Lily	1st or 2nd	Cancer, Scorpio, Pisces
Maple tree	2nd or 3rd	Taurus, Virgo, Cancer, Pisces
Melon	2nd	Cancer, Scorpio, Pisces

Plant	Quarter	Sign
Morning glory	1st or 2nd	Cancer, Scorpio, Pisces, Virgo
Oak tree	2nd or 3rd	Taurus, Virgo, Cancer, Pisces
Oats	1st or 2nd	Cancer, Scorpio, Pisces, Libra
Okra	1st or 2nd	Cancer, Scorpio, Pisces, Libra
Onion seed	2nd	Cancer, Scorpio, Sagittarius
Onion set	3rd or 4th	Cancer, Pisces, Taurus, Libra
Pansies	1st or 2nd	Cancer, Scorpio, Pisces
Parsley	1st	Cancer, Scorpio, Pisces, Libra
Parsnip	3rd	Cancer, Scorpio, Taurus, Capricorn
Peach tree	2nd or 3rd	Cancer, Taurus, Virgo, Libra
Peanuts	3rd	Cancer, Scorpio, Pisces
Pear tree	2nd or 3rd	Cancer, Scorpio, Pisces, Libra
Peas	2nd	Cancer, Scorpio, Pisces, Libra
Peony	1st or 2nd	Virgo
Peppers	2nd	Cancer, Scorpio, Pisces
Perennials	3rd	
Petunia	1st or 2nd	Libra, Virgo
Plum tree	2nd or 3rd	Cancer, Pisces, Taurus, Virgo
Poppies	1st or 2nd	Virgo
Portulaca	1st or 2nd	Virgo
Potatoes	3rd	Cancer, Scorpio, Libra, Taurus, Capricorn
Privet	1st or 2nd	Taurus, Libra
Pumpkin	2nd	Cancer, Scorpio, Pisces, Libra
Quince	1st or 2nd	Capricorn
Radishes	3rd	Cancer, Scorpio, Pisces, Libra, Capricorn
Rhubarb	3rd	Cancer, Pisces
Rice	1st or 2nd	Scorpio
Roses	1st or 2nd	Cancer, Virgo
Rutabaga	3rd	Cancer, Scorpio, Pisces, Taurus
Saffron	1st or 2nd	Cancer, Scorpio, Pisces

Plant	Quarter	Sign
Salsify	1st	Cancer, Scorpio, Pisces
Shallot	2nd	Scorpio
Spinach	1st	Cancer, Scorpio, Pisces
Squash	2nd	Cancer, Scorpio, Pisces, Libra
Strawberries	3rd	Cancer, Scorpio, Pisces
String beans	1st or 2nd	Taurus
Sunflowers	1st or 2nd	Libra, Cancer
Sweet peas	1st or 2nd	Any
Tomatoes	2nd	Cancer, Scorpio, Pisces, Capricorn
Trees, shade	3rd	Taurus, Capricorn
Trees, ornamental	2nd	Libra, Taurus
Trumpet vine	1st or 2nd	Cancer, Scorpio, Pisces
Tubers for seed	3rd	Cancer, Scorpio, Pisces, Libra
Tulips	1st or 2nd	Libra, Virgo
Turnips	3rd	Cancer, Scorpio, Pisces, Taurus, Capricorn, Libra
Valerian	1st or 2nd	Virgo, Gemini
Watermelon	1st or 2nd	Cancer, Scorpio, Pisces, Libra

Companion Planting Guide

Plant	Companions	Hindered by
Asparagus	Tomatoes, parsley, basil	None known
Beans	Tomatoes, carrots, cucumbers, garlic, cabbage, beets, corn	Onions, gladiolas
Beets	Onions, cabbage, lettuce, mint, catnip	Pole beans
Broccoli	Beans, celery, potatoes, onions	Tomatoes
Cabbage	Peppermint, sage, thyme, tomatoes	Strawberries, grapes
Carrots	Peas, lettuce, chives, radishes, leeks, onions, sage	Dill, anise
Citrus trees	Guava, live oak, rubber trees, peppers	None known
Corn	Potatoes, beans, peas, melon, squash, pumpkin, sunflowers, soybeans	Quack grass, wheat, straw, mulch
Cucumbers	Beans, cabbage, radishes, sunflowers, lettuce, broccoli, squash	Aromatic herbs
Eggplant	Green beans, lettuce, kale	None known
Grapes	Peas, beans, blackberries	Cabbage, radishes
Melons	Corn, peas	Potatoes, gourds
Onions, leeks	Beets, chamomile, carrots, lettuce	Peas, beans, sage
Parsnip	Peas	None known
Peas	Radishes, carrots, corn, cucumbers, beans, tomatoes, spinach, turnips	Onion, garlic
Potatoes	Beans, corn, peas, cabbage, hemp, cucumbers, eggplant, catnip	Raspberries, pumpkins, tomatoes, sunflowers
Radishes	Peas, lettuce, nasturtiums, cucumbers	Hyssop
Spinach	Strawberries	None known
Squash/Pumpkin	Nasturtiums, corn, mint, catnip	Potatoes
Tomatoes	Asparagus, parsley, chives, onions, carrots, marigolds, nasturtiums, dill	Black walnut roots, fennel, potatoes
Turnips	Peas, beans, brussels sprouts	Potatoes

Plant	Companions	Uses
Anise	Coriander	Flavor candy, pastry, cheeses, cookies
Basil	Tomatoes	Dislikes rue; repels flies and mosquitoes
Borage	Tomatoes, squash	Use in teas
Buttercup	Clover	Hinders delphinium, peonies, monkshood, columbine
Catnip		Repels flea beetles
Chamomile	Peppermint, wheat, onions, cabbage	Roman chamomile may control damping-off disease; use in herbal sprays
Chervil	Radishes	Good in soups and other dishes
Chives	Carrots	Use in spray to deter black spot on roses
Coriander	Plant anywhere	Hinders seed formation in fennel
Cosmos		Repels corn earworms
Dill	Cabbage	Hinders carrots and tomatoes
Fennel	Plant in borders	Disliked by all garden plants
Horseradish		Repels potato bugs
Horsetail		Makes fungicide spray
Hyssop		Attracts cabbage flies; harmful to radishes
Lavender	Plant anywhere	Use in spray to control insects on cotton, repels clothes moths
Lovage		Lures horn worms away from tomatoes
Marigolds		Pest repellent; use against Mexican bean beetles and nematodes
Mint	Cabbage, tomatoes	Repels ants, flea beetles, cabbage worm butterflies
Morning glory	Corn	Helps melon germination
Nasturtium	Cabbage, cucumbers	Deters aphids, squash bugs, pumpkin beetles
Okra	Eggplant	Attracts leafhopper (lure insects from other plants)
Parsley	Tomatoes, asparagus	Freeze chopped-up leaves to flavor foods
Purslane		Good ground cover
Rosemary		Repels cabbage moths, bean beetles, carrot flies
Savory		Plant with onions for added sweetness
Tansy		Deters Japanese beetles, striped cucumber beetles, squash bugs
Thyme		Repels cabbage worms

Moon Void-of-Course

By Kim Rogers-Gallagher

The Moon circles the Earth in about twenty-eight days, moving through each zodiac sign in two-and-a-half days. As she passes through the thirty degrees of each sign, she "visits" with the planets in numerical order, forming aspects with them. Because she moves one degree in just two to two and a half hours, her influence on each planet lasts only a few hours. She eventually reaches the planet that's in the highest degree of any sign and forms what will be her final aspect before leaving the sign. From this point until she enters the next sign, she is referred to as void-of-course.

Think of it this way: the Moon is the emotional "tone" of the day, carrying feelings with her particular to the sign she's "wearing" at the moment. After she has contacted each of the planets, she symbolically "rests" before changing her costume, so her instinct is temporarily on hold. It's during this time that many people feel "fuzzy" or "vague." Plans or decisions made now often do not pan out. Without the instinctual "knowing" the Moon provides as she touches each planet, we tend to be unrealistic or exercise poor judgment. The traditional definition of the void Moon is that "nothing will come of this." Actions initiated under a void Moon are often wasted, irrelevant, or incorrect—usually because information is hidden, missing, or has been overlooked.

Although it's not a good time to initiate plans, routine tasks seem to go along just fine. This period is ideal for reflection. On the lighter side, remember there are good uses for the void Moon. It is the period when the universe seems to be most open to loopholes. It's a great time to make plans you don't want to fulfill or schedule things you don't want to do. See the tables on pages 76–81 for a schedule of the Moon's void-of-course times.

Last Aspect   Moon Enters New Sign

			January		
1	9:14 pm	1	Aries	11:00 pm
3	8:18 pm	4	Taurus	11:15 am
6	7:08 am	6	Gemini	9:11 pm
8	5:16 pm	9	Cancer	3:43 am
10	6:58 pm	11	Leo	7:16 am
13	8:42 am	13	Virgo	9:06 am
15	7:12 am	15	Libra	10:43 am
17	7:58 am	17	Scorpio	1:20 pm
19	4:22 pm	19	Sagittarius	5:41 pm
20	11:46 pm	22	Capricorn	12:00 am
23	9:08 pm	24	Aquarius	8:20 am
25	2:06 pm	26	Pisces	6:44 pm
28	8:08 pm	29	Aries	6:51 am
31	10:10 am	31	Taurus	7:28 pm
			February		
3	6:28 am	3	Gemini	6:29 am
5	9:20 am	5	Cancer	2:03 pm
7	10:43 am	7	Leo	5:45 pm
9	11:08 am	9	Virgo	6:39 pm
11	1:26 pm	11	Libra	6:37 pm
13	4:40 pm	13	Scorpio	7:37 pm
15	5:20 pm	15	Sagittarius	11:07 pm
18	4:03 am	18	Capricorn	5:37 am
20	9:18 am	20	Aquarius	2:42 pm
21	11:08 pm	23	Pisces	1:37 am
25	9:12 am	25	Aries	1:47 pm
27	10:25 pm	28	Taurus	2:30 am

Last Aspect   Moon Enters New Sign

		March			
1	10:52 am	1	Gemini	2:21 pm
3	9:20 pm	3	Cancer	11:25 pm
6	2:11 am	6	Leo	4:27 am
8	4:12 am	8	Virgo	6:47 am
10	4:32 am	10	Libra	6:03 am
12	4:12 am	12	Scorpio	5:28 am
14	6:06 am	14	Sagittarius	7:09 am
16	5:34 am	16	Capricorn	12:25 pm
18	8:48 pm	18	Aquarius	9:16 pm
20	5:00 am	21	Pisces	8:33 am
23	10:51 am	23	Aries	8:58 pm
26	3:16 am	26	Taurus	9:37 am
28	7:05 pm	28	Gemini	9:38 pm
30	11:10 am	31	Cancer	7:43 am
		April			
2	12:49 pm	2	Leo	2:26 pm
3	3:29 pm	4	Virgo	5:18 pm
6	9:29 am	6	Libra	5:16 pm
8	8:50 am	8	Scorpio	4:17 pm
10	3:35 pm	10	Sagittarius	4:35 pm
12	7:46 am	12	Capricorn	8:05 pm
14	7:47 pm	15	Aquarius	3:37 am
17	10:34 am	17	Pisces	2:29 pm
19	7:31 pm	20	Aries	3:00 am
22	8:32 am	22	Taurus	3:36 pm
24	8:43 pm	25	Gemini	3:20 am
27	1:00 pm	27	Cancer	1:28 pm
29	3:29 pm	29	Leo	9:06 pm

Last Aspect   Moon Enters New Sign

		May		
1	12:04 pm	2	Virgo	1:35 am
3	10:25 pm	4	Libra	3:09 am
5	10:31 pm	6	Scorpio	3:05 am
7	10:39 pm	8	Sagittarius	3:15 am
10	2:11 am	10	Capricorn	5:39 am
12	6:30 am	12	Aquarius	11:39 am
14	10:03 am	14	Pisces	9:24 pm
17	3:59 am	17	Aries	9:36 am
19	4:33 pm	19	Taurus	10:10 pm
22	4:01 am	22	Gemini	9:36 am
24	7:09 am	24	Cancer	7:09 pm
26	9:06 pm	27	Leo	2:33 am
28	9:30 am	29	Virgo	7:40 am
31	5:17 am	31	Libra	10:38 am
		June		
2	6:40 am	2	Scorpio	12:06 pm
4	7:36 am	4	Sagittarius	1:17 pm
6	12:10 am	6	Capricorn	3:44 pm
8	2:06 pm	8	Aquarius	8:54 pm
10	10:35 am	11	Pisces	5:32 am
13	8:45 am	13	Aries	5:03 pm
15	8:49 pm	16	Taurus	5:35 am
18	8:02 am	18	Gemini	5:00 pm
20	5:48 pm	21	Cancer	2:02 am
23	3:20 am	23	Leo	8:33 am
24	1:34 am	25	Virgo	1:05 pm
27	4:02 pm	27	Libra	4:16 pm
29	9:02 am	29	Scorpio	6:48 pm

Last Aspect   Moon Enters New Sign

		July		
1	9:20 pm	1	Sagittarius	9:21 pm
3	9:06 am	4	Capricorn	12:48 am
6	5:35 am	6	Aquarius	6:08 am
7	12:37 am	8	Pisces	2:13 pm
10	11:49 pm	11	Aries	1:06 am
13	11:54 am	13	Taurus	1:34 pm
15	11:21 pm	16	Gemini	1:19 am
17	5:14 pm	18	Cancer	10:24 am
20	1:55 pm	20	Leo	4:16 pm
21	8:27 pm	22	Virgo	7:40 pm
24	7:08 pm	24	Libra	9:54 pm
26	9:09 pm	27	Scorpio	12:12 am
29	12:01 am	29	Sagittarius	3:25 am
30	8:08 pm	31	Capricorn	7:58 am
		August		
2	9:59 am	2	Aquarius	2:11 pm
4	5:45 pm	4	Pisces	10:28 pm
7	8:53 am	7	Aries	9:05 am
9	3:50 pm	9	Taurus	9:28 pm
12	3:55 am	12	Gemini	9:46 am
14	7:19 am	14	Cancer	7:35 pm
16	7:59 pm	17	Leo	1:38 am
19	1:38 am	19	Virgo	4:20 am
20	11:37 pm	21	Libra	5:16 am
23	12:20 am	23	Scorpio	6:16 am
25	2:27 am	25	Sagittarius	8:49 am
27	8:00 am	27	Capricorn	1:37 pm
29	3:31 pm	29	Aquarius	8:37 pm

Last Aspect   Moon Enters New Sign

		September		
1	12:56 am	1	Pisces	5:34 am
3	10:34 am	3	Aries	4:22 pm
6	12:45 am	6	Taurus	4:43 am
8	8:47 am	8	Gemini	5:28 pm
11	12:48 am	11	Cancer	4:23 am
13	8:05 am	13	Leo	11:32 am
15	11:09 am	15	Virgo	2:37 pm
17	7:42 am	17	Libra	2:56 pm
19	10:29 am	19	Scorpio	2:33 pm
21	2:13 pm	21	Sagittarius	3:32 pm
23	1:31 pm	23	Capricorn	7:16 pm
25	11:36 pm	26	Aquarius	2:08 am
28	3:18 am	28	Pisces	11:34 am
30	1:30 pm	30	Aries	10:47 pm
		October		
3	1:47 am	3	Taurus	11:12 am
5	2:41 pm	6	Gemini	12:03 am
7	9:57 pm	8	Cancer	11:45 am
10	12:04 pm	10	Leo	8:24 pm
12	10:29 am	13	Virgo	12:56 am
14	6:47 pm	15	Libra	1:54 am
16	6:11 pm	17	Scorpio	1:05 am
18	5:43 pm	19	Sagittarius	12:43 am
20	11:38 pm	21	Capricorn	2:44 am
23	12:35 am	23	Aquarius	8:17 am
24	5:54 pm	25	Pisces	5:18 pm
27	8:46 pm	28	Aries	4:45 am
30	12:12 pm	30	Taurus	5:19 pm

Last Aspect   Moon Enters New Sign

		November			
1	9:29 pm	2		Gemini	5:00 am
4	8:49 am	4		Cancer	4:45 pm
6	8:27 pm	7		Leo	2:18 am
9	6:05 am	9		Virgo	8:30 am
11	5:58 am	11		Libra	11:09 am
13	6:32 am	13		Scorpio	11:19 am
15	6:13 am	15		Sagittarius	10:47 am
17	2:55 am	17		Capricorn	11:35 am
19	11:30 am	19		Aquarius	3:25 pm
20	7:49 pm	21		Pisces	11:06 pm
24	5:44 am	24		Aries	10:05 am
26	6:46 pm	26		Taurus	10:43 pm
29	7:48 am	29		Gemini	11:16 am
30	11:22 pm	12/1		Cancer	10:33 pm
		December			
4	5:29 am	4		Leo	7:53 am
5	5:28 pm	6		Virgo	2:46 pm
8	5:35 pm	8		Libra	7:01 pm
10	7:56 pm	10		Scorpio	8:59 pm
12	8:58 pm	12		Sagittarius	9:39 pm
14	11:17 am	14		Capricorn	10:35 pm
17	12:34 am	17		Aquarius	1:27 am
19	3:45 am	19		Pisces	7:39 am
21	5:25 am	21		Aries	5:32 pm
23	5:51 pm	24		Taurus	5:55 am
26	6:32 am	26		Gemini	6:33 pm
28	10:01 pm	29		Cancer	5:28 am
31	8:45 am	31		Leo	1:58 pm

The Moon's Rhythm

The Moon journeys around Earth in an elliptical orbit that takes about 27.33 days, which is known as a sidereal month (period of revolution of one body about another). She can move up to 15 degrees or as few as 11 degrees in a day, with the fastest motion occurring when the Moon is at perigee (closest approach to Earth). The Moon is never retrograde, but when her motion is slow, the effect is similar to a retrograde period.

Astrologers have observed that people born on a day when the Moon is fast will process information differently from those who are born when the Moon is slow in motion. People born when the Moon is fast process information quickly and tend to react quickly, while those born during a slow Moon will be more deliberate.

The time from New Moon to New Moon is called the synodic month (involving a conjunction), and the average time span between this Sun-Moon alignment is 29.53 days. Since 29.53 won't divide into 365 evenly, we can have a month with two Full Moons or two New Moons.

Moon Aspects

The aspects the Moon will make during the times you are considering are also important. A trine or sextile, and sometimes a conjunction, are considered favorable aspects. A trine or sextile between the Sun and Moon is an excellent foundation for success. Whether or not a conjunction is considered favorable depends upon the planet the Moon is making a conjunction to. If it's joining the Sun, Venus, Mercury, Jupiter, or even Saturn, the aspect is favorable. If the Moon joins Pluto or Mars, however, that would not be considered favorable. There may be exceptions, but it would depend on what you are electing to do. For example, a trine to Pluto might hasten the end of a relationship you want to be free of.

It is important to avoid times when the Moon makes an aspect to or is conjoining any retrograde planet, unless, of course, you want the thing started to end in failure.

After the Moon has completed an aspect to a planet, that planetary energy has passed. For example, if the Moon squares Saturn at 10:00 am, you can disregard Saturn's influence on your activity if it will occur after that time. You should always look ahead at aspects the Moon will make on the day in question, though, because if the Moon opposes Mars at 11:30 pm on that day, you can expect events that stretch into the evening to be affected by the Moon-Mars aspect. A testy conversation might lead to an argument, or more.

Moon Signs

Much agricultural work is ruled by earth signs—Virgo, Capricorn, and Taurus. The air signs—Gemini, Aquarius, and Libra—rule flying and intellectual pursuits.

Each planet has one or two signs in which its characteristics are enhanced or "dignified," and the planet is said to "rule" that sign. The Sun rules Leo and the Moon rules Cancer, for example. The ruling planet for each sign is listed below. These should not be considered complete lists. We recommend that you purchase a book of planetary rulerships for more complete information.

Aries Moon

The energy of an Aries Moon is masculine, dry, barren, and fiery. Aries provides great start-up energy, but things started at this time may be the result of impulsive action that lacks research or necessary support. Aries lacks staying power.

Use this assertive, outgoing Moon sign to initiate change, but have a plan in place for someone to pick up the reins when you're impatient to move on to the next thing. Work that requires skillful but not necessarily patient use of tools—cutting down trees, hammering, etc.—is appropriate in Aries. Expect things to occur rapidly but to also quickly pass. If you are prone to injury or accidents, exercise caution and good judgment in Aries-related activities.

RULER: Mars

IMPULSE: Action

RULES: Head and face

Taurus Moon

A Taurus Moon's energy is feminine, semi-fruitful, and earthy. The Moon is exalted—very strong—in Taurus. Taurus is known as the farmer's sign because of its associations with farmland and precipitation that is the typical day-long "soaker" variety. Taurus energy is good to incorporate into your plans when patience, practicality, and perseverance are needed. Be aware, though, that you may also experience stubbornness in this sign.

Things started in Taurus tend to be long lasting and to increase in value. This can be very supportive energy in a marriage election. On the downside, the fixed energy of this sign resists change or the letting go of even the most difficult situations. A divorce following a marriage that occurred during a Taurus Moon may be difficult and costly to end. Things begun now tend to become habitual and hard to alter. If you want to make changes in something you started, it would be better to wait for Gemini. This is a good time to get a loan, but expect the people in charge of money to be cautious and slow to make decisions.

RULER: Venus

IMPULSE: Stability

RULES: Neck, throat, and voice

Gemini Moon

A Gemini Moon's energy is masculine, dry, barren, and airy. People are more changeable than usual and may prefer to follow intellectual pursuits and play mental games rather than apply themselves to practical concerns.

This sign is not favored for agricultural matters, but it is an excellent time to prepare for activities, to run errands, and write letters. Plan to use a Gemini Moon to exchange ideas, meet people, go on vacations that include walking or biking, or be in situations that require versatility and quick thinking on your feet.

RULER: Mercury

IMPULSE: Versatility

RULES: Shoulders, hands, arms, lungs, and nervous system

Cancer Moon

A Cancer Moon's energy is feminine, fruitful, moist, and very strong. Use this sign when you want to grow things—flowers, fruits, vegetables, commodities, stocks, or collections—for example. This sensitive sign stimulates rapport between people. Considered the most fertile of the signs, it is often associated with mothering. You can use this moontime to build personal friendships that support mutual growth.

Cancer is associated with emotions and feelings. Prominent

Cancer energy promotes growth, but it can also turn people pouty and prone to withdrawing into their shells.

Ruler: The Moon

Impulse: Tenacity

Rules: Chest area, breasts, and stomach

Leo Moon

A Leo Moon's energy is masculine, hot, dry, fiery, and barren. Use it whenever you need to put on a show, make a presentation, or entertain colleagues or guests. This is a proud yet playful energy that exudes self-confidence and is often associated with romance.

This is an excellent time for fundraisers and ceremonies or to be straightforward, frank, and honest about something. It is advisable not to put yourself in a position of needing public approval or where you might have to cope with underhandedness, as trouble in these areas can bring out the worst Leo traits. There is a tendency in this sign to become arrogant or self-centered.

Ruler: The Sun

Impulse: I am

Rules: Heart and upper back

Virgo Moon

A Virgo Moon is feminine, dry, barren, earthy energy. It is favorable for anything that needs painstaking attention—especially those things where exactness rather than innovation is preferred.

Use this sign for activities when you must analyze information or when you must determine the value of something. Virgo is the sign of bargain hunting. It's friendly toward agricultural matters with an emphasis on animals and harvesting vegetables. It is an excellent time to care for animals, especially training them and veterinary work.

This sign is most beneficial when decisions have already been made and now need to be carried out. The inclination here is to see details rather than the bigger picture.

There is a tendency in this sign to overdo. Precautions should be taken to avoid becoming too dull from all work and no play. Build a little relaxation and pleasure into your routine from the beginning.

RULER: Mercury

IMPULSE: Discriminating

RULES: Abdomen and intestines

Libra Moon

A Libra Moon's energy is masculine, semi-fruitful, and airy. This energy will benefit any attempt to bring beauty to a place or thing. Libra is considered good energy for starting things of an intellectual nature. Libra is the sign of partnership and unions, which makes it an excellent time to form partnerships of any kind, to make agreements, and to negotiate. Even though this sign is good for initiating things, it is crucial to work with a partner who will provide incentive and encouragement, however. A Libra Moon accentuates teamwork (particularly teams of two) and artistic work (especially work that involves color). Make use of this sign when you are decorating your home or shopping for better-quality clothing.

RULER: Venus

IMPULSE: Balance

RULES: Lower back, kidneys, and buttocks

Scorpio Moon

The Scorpio Moon is feminine, fruitful, cold, and moist. It is useful when intensity (that sometimes borders on obsession) is needed. Scorpio is considered a very psychic sign. Use this Moon sign when you must back up something you strongly believe in, such as union or employer relations. There is strong group loyalty here, but a Scorpio Moon is also a good time to end connections thoroughly. This is also a good time to conduct research.

The desire nature is so strong here that there is a tendency to manipulate situations to get what one wants or to not see one's responsibility in an act.

RULER: Pluto, Mars (traditional)

IMPULSE: Transformation

RULES: Reproductive organs, genitals, groin, and pelvis

Sagittarius Moon

The Moon's energy is masculine, dry, barren, and fiery in Sagittarius, encouraging flights of imagination and confidence in the flow of life. Sagittarius is the most philosophical sign. Candor and honesty are enhanced when the Moon is here. This is an excellent time to "get things off your chest" and to deal with institutions of higher learning, publishing companies, and the law. It's also a good time for sport and adventure.

Sagittarians are the crusaders of this world. This is a good time to tackle things that need improvement, but don't try to be the diplomat while influenced by this energy. Opinions can run strong, and the tendency to proselytize is increased.

RULER: Jupiter

IMPULSE: Expansion

RULES: Thighs and hips

Capricorn Moon

In Capricorn the Moon's energy is feminine, semi-fruitful, and earthy. Because Cancer and Capricorn are polar opposites, the Moon's energy is thought to be weakened here. This energy encourages the need for structure, discipline, and organization. This is a good time to set goals and plan for the future, tend to family business, and to take care of details requiring patience or a businesslike manner. Institutional activities are favored. This sign should be avoided if you're seeking favors, as those in authority can be insensitive under this influence.

RULER: Saturn

IMPULSE: Ambitious

RULES: Bones, skin, and knees

Aquarius Moon

An Aquarius Moon's energy is masculine, barren, dry, and airy. Activities that are unique, individualistic, concerned with humanitarian issues, society as a whole, and making improvements are favored under this Moon. It is this quality of making improvements that has caused this sign to be associated with inventors and new inventions.

An Aquarius Moon promotes the gathering of social groups for friendly exchanges. People tend to react and speak from an intellectual rather than emotional viewpoint when the Moon is in this sign.

RULER: Uranus and Saturn

IMPULSE: Reformer

RULES: Calves and ankles

Pisces Moon

A Pisces Moon is feminine, fruitful, cool, and moist. This is an excellent time to retreat, meditate, sleep, pray, or make that dreamed-of escape into a fantasy vacation. However, things are not always what they seem to be with the Moon in Pisces. Personal boundaries tend to be fuzzy, and you may not be seeing things clearly. People tend to be idealistic under this sign, which can prevent them from seeing reality.

There is a live-and-let-live philosophy attached to this sign, which in the idealistic world may work well enough, but chaos is frequently the result. That's why this sign is also associated with alcohol and drug abuse, drug trafficking, and counterfeiting. On the lighter side, many musicians and artists are ruled by Pisces. It's only when they move too far away from reality that the dark side of substance abuse, suicide, or crime takes away life.

RULER: Jupiter and Neptune

IMPULSE: Empathetic

RULES: Feet

More About Zodiac Signs

Element (Triplicity)

Each of the zodiac signs is classified as belonging to an element; these are the four basic elements:

Fire Signs

Aries, Sagittarius, and Leo are action-oriented, outgoing, energetic, and spontaneous.

Earth Signs

Taurus, Capricorn, and Virgo are stable, conservative, practical, and oriented to the physical and material realm.

Air Signs

Gemini, Aquarius, and Libra are sociable and critical, and they tend to represent intellectual responses rather than feelings.

Water Signs

Cancer, Scorpio, and Pisces are emotional, receptive, intuitive, and can be very sensitive.

Quality (Quadruplicity)

Each zodiac sign is further classified as being cardinal, mutable, or fixed. There are four signs in each quadruplicity, one sign from each element.

Cardinal Signs

Aries, Cancer, Libra, and Capricorn represent beginnings and newly initiated action. They initiate each new season in the cycle of the year.

Fixed Signs

Taurus, Leo, Scorpio, and Aquarius want to maintain the status quo through stubbornness and persistence; they represent that "between" time. For example, Leo is the month when summer really feels like summer.

Mutable Signs

Pisces, Gemini, Virgo, and Sagittarius adapt to change and tolerate situations. They represent the last month of each season, when things are changing in preparation for the coming season.

Nature and Fertility

In addition to a sign's element and quality, each sign is further classified as either fruitful, semi-fruitful, or barren. This classification is the most important for readers who use the gardening information in the **Moon Sign Book** because the timing of most events depends on the fertility of the sign occupied by the Moon. The water signs of Cancer, Scorpio, and Pisces are the most fruitful. The semi-fruitful signs are the earth signs Taurus and Capricorn, and the air sign Libra. The barren signs correspond to fire-signs Aries, Leo, and Sagittarius; air-signs Gemini and Aquarius; and earth-sign Virgo.

Good Timing

By Sharon Leah

E lectional astrology is the art of electing times to begin any under-
taking. Say, for example, you want to start a business. That business will experience ups and downs, as well as reach its potential,
according to the promise held in the universe at the time the business
was started—its birth time. The horoscope (birth chart) set for the
date, time, and place that a business starts would indicate the outcome—its potential to succeed.

So, you might ask yourself the question: If the horoscope for a
business start can show success or failure, why not begin at a time
that is more favorable to the venture? Well, you can.

While no time is perfect, there are better times and better days to
undertake specific activities. There are thousands of examples that

prove electional astrology is not only practical, but that it can make a difference in our lives. There are rules for electing times to begin various activities—even shopping. You'll find detailed instructions about how to make elections beginning on page 107.

Personalizing Elections

The election rules in this almanac are based upon the planetary positions at the time for which the election is made. They do not depend on any type of birth chart. However, a birth chart based upon the time, date, and birthplace of an event has advantages. No election is effective for every person. For example, you may leave home to begin a trip at the same time as a friend, but each of you will have a different experience according to whether or not your birth chart favors the trip.

Not all elections require a birth chart, but the timing of very important events—business starts, marriages, etc.—would benefit from the additional accuracy a birth chart provides. To order a birth chart for yourself or a planned event, visit our website at www.llewellyn.com.

Some Things to Consider

You've probably experienced good timing in your life. Maybe you were at the right place at the right time to meet a friend whom you hadn't seen in years. Frequently, when something like that happens, it is the result of following an intuitive impulse—that "gut instinct." Consider for a moment that you were actually responding to planetary energies. Electional astrology is a tool that can help you to align with energies, present and future, that are available to us through planetary placements.

Significators

Decide upon the important significators (planet, sign, and house ruling the matter) for which the election is being made. The Moon is the most important significator in any election, so the Moon should always be fortified (strong by sign and making favorable aspects to other planets). The Moon's aspects to other planets are more important than the sign the Moon is in.

Other important considerations are the significators of the Ascendant and Midheaven—the house ruling the election matter and the ruler of the sign on that house cusp. Finally, any planet or sign that has a general rulership over the matter in question should be taken into consideration.

Nature and Fertility

Determine the general nature of the sign that is appropriate for your election. For example, much agricultural work is ruled by the earth signs of Virgo, Capricorn, and Taurus; while the air signs—Gemini, Aquarius, and Libra—rule intellectual pursuits.

One Final Comment

Use common sense. If you must do something, like plant your garden or take an airplane trip on a day that doesn't have the best aspects, proceed anyway, but try to minimize problems. For example, leave early for the airport to avoid being left behind due to delays in the security lanes. When you have no other choice, do the best that you can under the circumstances at the time.

If you want to personalize your elections, please turn to page 107 for more information. If you want a quick and easy answer, you can refer to Llewellyn's Astro Almanac on the following pages.

Llewellyn's Astro Almanac

The Astro Almanac tables, beginning on the next page, can help you find the dates best suited to particular activities. The dates provided are determined from the Moon's sign, phase, and aspects to other planets. Please note that the Astro Almanac does not take personal factors, such as your Sun and Moon sign, into account. The dates are general, and they will apply for everyone. Some activities will not have ideal dates during a particular month.

Activity	January
Animals (Neuter or spay)	1, 19–24, 27, 29
Animals (Sell or buy)	3, 5, 8, 27
Automobile (Buy)	13–15, 22, 23
Brewing	18, 19
Build (Start foundation)	no ideal dates
Business (Conducting for self and others)	5, 15, 19, 30
Business (Start new)	5, 6
Can Fruits and Vegetables	18, 19
Can Preserves	18, 19
Concrete (Pour)	12
Construction (Begin new)	5, 14, 15, 30
Consultants (Begin work with)	5, 14, 15, 18, 20, 22, 25, 27, 31
Contracts (Bid on)	2, 5, 25, 27, 31
Cultivate	no ideal dates
Decorating	6–8, 24, 25
Demolition	11, 12, 19–21
Electronics (Buy)	25
Entertain Guests	8
Floor Covering (Laying new)	12–17, 24
Habits (Break)	22, 23
Hair (Cut to increase growth)	4–8, 27, 28, 31
Hair (Cut to decrease growth)	11, 19–23
Harvest (Grain for storage)	11–13
Harvest (Root crops)	11, 12, 19–21
Investments (New)	5, 15
Loan (Ask for)	4–6, 31
Massage (Relaxing)	no ideal dates
Mow Lawn (Decrease growth)	11–23
Mow Lawn (Increase growth)	1–9, 25, 27–31
Mushrooms (Pick)	9–11
Negotiate (Business for the elderly)	14, 18
Prune for Better Fruit	17–20
Prune to Promote Healing	22–24
Wean Children	20–25
Wood Floors (Installing)	22–24

Activity	February
Animals (Neuter or spay)	16–20, 23–25
Animals (Sell or buy)	2, 7, 24, 29
Automobile (Buy)	9, 11, 18–20
Brewing	14, 15
Build (Start foundation)	no ideal dates
Business (Conducting for self and others)	4, 13, 18, 28
Business (Start new)	1, 2, 29
Can Fruits and Vegetables	14, 15, 23
Can Preserves	14, 15
Concrete (Pour)	9, 21
Construction (Begin new)	1, 4, 10, 13, 18, 28, 29
Consultants (Begin work with)	1, 5, 10, 14, 19, 23, 24, 28, 29
Contracts (Bid on)	1, 5, 24, 28, 29
Cultivate	21
Decorating	3–5
Demolition	16, 17
Electronics (Buy)	no ideal dates
Entertain Guests	2, 7
Floor Covering (Laying new)	9–13, 20, 21, 23
Habits (Break)	18–21
Hair (Cut to increase growth)	1–4, 7, 24, 28, 29
Hair (Cut to decrease growth)	16–19, 23
Harvest (Grain for storage)	15
Harvest (Root crops)	9, 16, 17, 20, 21
Investments (New)	4, 13
Loan (Ask for)	1–3, 7, 8, 28, 29
Massage (Relaxing)	2, 7, 21
Mow Lawn (Decrease growth)	10–22
Mow Lawn (Increase growth)	1–7, 24–29
Mushrooms (Pick)	8–10
Negotiate (Business for the elderly)	2, 11, 15, 25
Prune for Better Fruit	13–16
Prune to Promote Healing	18–20
Wean Children	16–21
Wood Floors (Installing)	18–20

Activity	March
Animals (Neuter or spay)	16–18, 21–23
Animals (Sell or buy)	3, 8, 28
Automobile (Buy)	8, 10, 16, 18, 28
Brewing	13, 22, 23
Build (Start foundation)	1, 28
Business (Conducting for self and others)	5, 13, 18, 29
Business (Start new)	1, 28
Can Fruits and Vegetables	13, 22, 23
Can Preserves	13
Concrete (Pour)	19, 20
Construction (Begin new)	5, 9, 18, 28, 29
Consultants (Begin work with)	3, 9, 12, 13, 16, 18, 21, 23, 27, 28
Contracts (Bid on)	3, 9, 27, 28
Cultivate	15, 19, 20
Decorating	1–3, 28–30
Demolition	14, 15, 23
Electronics (Buy)	12
Entertain Guests	3, 8
Floor Covering (Laying new)	10–12, 19–21
Habits (Break)	17–20, 23
Hair (Cut to increase growth)	1, 2, 6, 26–30
Hair (Cut to decrease growth)	14–17, 21, 22
Harvest (Grain for storage)	14, 15
Harvest (Root crops)	14–16, 19, 20, 23
Investments (New)	5, 13
Loan (Ask for)	1, 6–8, 26–28
Massage (Relaxing)	28
Mow Lawn (Decrease growth)	10–23
Mow Lawn (Increase growth)	1–8, 25–31
Mushrooms (Pick)	8–10
Negotiate (Business for the elderly)	1, 23, 28
Prune for Better Fruit	12–15
Prune to Promote Healing	16–18
Wean Children	14–20
Wood Floors (Installing)	16–18

Activity	April
Animals (Neuter or spay)	14, 18, 19
Animals (Sell or buy)	6
Automobile (Buy)	5, 13, 25, 27
Brewing	9, 10, 18, 19
Build (Start foundation)	25
Business (Conducting for self and others)	3, 12, 17, 28
Business (Start new)	6, 24
Can Fruits and Vegetables	9, 10, 18, 19
Can Preserves	9, 10
Concrete (Pour)	15, 16
Construction (Begin new)	3, 6, 12, 17, 24, 28
Consultants (Begin work with)	1, 6, 10, 14, 15, 19, 21, 24, 27
Contracts (Bid on)	1, 6, 7, 24, 27
Cultivate	11, 15, 16, 20, 21
Decorating	6, 7, 25–27
Demolition	10, 11, 20, 21
Electronics (Buy)	15, 27
Entertain Guests	no ideal dates
Floor Covering (Laying new)	8, 15–17
Habits (Break)	15–17, 20, 21
Hair (Cut to increase growth)	2, 23–26, 29
Hair (Cut to decrease growth)	10–14, 18, 19, 22
Harvest (Grain for storage)	10–12
Harvest (Root crops)	10–12, 15–17, 20, 21
Investments (New)	3, 12
Loan (Ask for)	2–4, 23, 24, 29, 30
Massage (Relaxing)	2, 6, 15
Mow Lawn (Decrease growth)	8–21
Mow Lawn (Increase growth)	1–6, 23–30
Mushrooms (Pick)	6–8
Negotiate (Business for the elderly)	6, 10
Prune for Better Fruit	8–10, 12
Prune to Promote Healing	13, 14
Wean Children	11–17
Wood Floors (Installing)	13, 14

Activity	July
Animals (Neuter or spay)	no ideal dates
Animals (Sell or buy)	1, 21, 24, 26, 28
Automobile (Buy)	4, 6, 23, 24
Brewing	9, 19
Build (Start foundation)	25
Business (Conducting for self and others)	10, 15, 25, 29
Business (Start new)	24
Can Fruits and Vegetables	9, 19, 20
Can Preserves	14, 19, 20
Concrete (Pour)	7, 14
Construction (Begin new)	5, 24, 25, 29
Consultants (Begin work with)	1, 5, 9, 10, 14, 15, 19, 23, 24, 28
Contracts (Bid on)	1, 5, 23, 24, 28
Cultivate	13, 17, 18
Decorating	25, 26
Demolition	11, 12
Electronics (Buy)	no ideal dates
Entertain Guests	17, 26
Floor Covering (Laying new)	6–8, 14–18
Habits (Break)	13, 16–18
Hair (Cut to increase growth)	2, 3, 29–31
Hair (Cut to decrease growth)	8–10, 13–17, 20
Harvest (Grain for storage)	6, 7, 11
Harvest (Root crops)	6, 7, 11–13, 16, 17
Investments (New)	10, 29
Loan (Ask for)	21, 22
Massage (Relaxing)	6, 21, 26
Mow Lawn (Decrease growth)	6–19
Mow Lawn (Increase growth)	1–3, 21–31
Mushrooms (Pick)	4–6
Negotiate (Business for the elderly)	1, 10, 15, 24
Prune for Better Fruit	no ideal dates
Prune to Promote Healing	5, 6
Wean Children	2–7, 29–31
Wood Floors (Installing)	5, 6

Activity	August
Animals (Neuter or spay)	25
Animals (Sell or buy)	20, 24
Automobile (Buy)	1, 2, 13, 19, 20, 28, 29
Brewing	5, 6, 15
Build (Start foundation)	no ideal dates
Business (Conducting for self and others)	8, 14, 23, 27
Business (Start new)	20
Can Fruits and Vegetables	5, 6, 15
Can Preserves	10, 11, 15
Concrete (Pour)	4, 10, 11, 17
Construction (Begin new)	8, 11, 14, 20, 27
Consultants (Begin work with)	1, 6, 7, 11, 13, 19, 20, 23, 24, 28
Contracts (Bid on)	1, 19, 20, 23, 24, 28, 29
Cultivate	13, 14, 17, 18
Decorating	3, 21–23, 30, 31
Demolition	7, 8, 17, 18
Electronics (Buy)	13
Entertain Guests	10, 15
Floor Covering (Laying new)	4, 10–14, 18
Habits (Break)	12–14, 17
Hair (Cut to increase growth)	1, 25–28
Hair (Cut to decrease growth)	5, 6, 9–13
Harvest (Grain for storage)	4, 7–9
Harvest (Root crops)	3, 4, 7–9, 12–14, 17
Investments (New)	8, 27
Loan (Ask for)	19
Massage (Relaxing)	4, 10, 15
Mow Lawn (Decrease growth)	4–17
Mow Lawn (Increase growth)	1, 2, 19–31
Mushrooms (Pick)	2–4
Negotiate (Business for the elderly)	20
Prune for Better Fruit	no ideal dates
Prune to Promote Healing	no ideal dates
Wean Children	1–4, 26–31
Wood Floors (Installing)	no ideal dates

Activity	September
Animals (Neuter or spay)	21–23
Animals (Sell or buy)	18, 20, 22, 29
Automobile (Buy)	9, 16, 17, 24, 25
Brewing	3, 12
Build (Start foundation)	21
Business (Conducting for self and others)	7, 12, 21, 26
Business (Start new)	17
Can Fruits and Vegetables	2, 3, 12
Can Preserves	7, 8, 12
Concrete (Pour)	7, 8, 14
Construction (Begin new)	7, 12, 16, 26
Consultants (Begin work with)	2, 7, 9, 14, 16, 18, 20, 23, 25, 28, 29
Contracts (Bid on)	18, 20, 23, 25, 28, 29
Cultivate	11, 14–17
Decorating	1, 17–19, 26–28
Demolition	4, 5, 13, 14
Electronics (Buy)	9, 18
Entertain Guests	8, 14, 18
Floor Covering (Laying new)	7–11, 14–17
Habits (Break)	11, 14, 15
Hair (Cut to increase growth)	21–25, 28, 29
Hair (Cut to decrease growth)	6–10, 13
Harvest (Grain for storage)	3–5, 8–10
Harvest (Root crops)	4, 5, 8–10, 13–15
Investments (New)	7, 26
Loan (Ask for)	no ideal dates
Massage (Relaxing)	14, 18
Mow Lawn (Decrease growth)	3–16
Mow Lawn (Increase growth)	18–30
Mushrooms (Pick)	1–3, 30
Negotiate (Business for the elderly)	3, 8, 30
Prune for Better Fruit	no ideal dates
Prune to Promote Healing	no ideal dates
Wean Children	1, 22–28
Wood Floors (Installing)	no ideal dates

Activity	October
Animals (Neuter or spay)	19–21, 23
Animals (Sell or buy)	18, 27
Automobile (Buy)	13, 14, 21, 23
Brewing	9, 10
Build (Start foundation)	18
Business (Conducting for self and others)	7, 12, 20, 25
Business (Start new)	no ideal dates
Can Fruits and Vegetables	9, 10
Can Preserves	4, 9, 10
Concrete (Pour)	4, 11
Construction (Begin new)	5, 7, 12, 14, 20
Consultants (Begin work with)	5, 9, 13, 14, 17, 18, 21, 22, 25, 27
Contracts (Bid on)	17, 18, 21, 22, 25, 27
Cultivate	11–14
Decorating	16, 23–25
Demolition	1, 2, 11, 12
Electronics (Buy)	no ideal dates
Entertain Guests	9, 13
Floor Covering (Laying new)	4–8, 11–16
Habits (Break)	11, 12
Hair (Cut to increase growth)	19–22, 25–27, 30
Hair (Cut to decrease growth)	3–7, 10
Harvest (Grain for storage)	2, 6, 7
Harvest (Root crops)	2, 6, 7, 11, 12
Investments (New)	7, 25
Loan (Ask for)	30, 31
Massage (Relaxing)	3, 9
Mow Lawn (Decrease growth)	2–15
Mow Lawn (Increase growth)	17–30
Mushrooms (Pick)	1, 2, 30, 31
Negotiate (Business for the elderly)	5, 14, 18, 27
Prune for Better Fruit	no ideal dates
Prune to Promote Healing	no ideal dates
Wean Children	19–25
Wood Floors (Installing)	no ideal dates

Activity	November
Animals (Neuter or spay)	15–17, 19
Animals (Sell or buy)	17, 22, 23, 29
Automobile (Buy)	4, 9, 11, 18, 19
Brewing	5
Build (Start foundation)	no ideal dates
Business (Conducting for self and others)	5, 10, 19, 24
Business (Start new)	29
Can Fruits and Vegetables	5, 14
Can Preserves	5, 14
Concrete (Pour)	7, 8
Construction (Begin new)	1, 5, 10, 19, 24, 29
Consultants (Begin work with)	1, 4, 9, 10, 13, 15, 18, 19, 23, 29
Contracts (Bid on)	18, 19, 23, 28, 29
Cultivate	9–11
Decorating	20, 29, 30
Demolition	7, 8
Electronics (Buy)	4
Entertain Guests	2, 8
Floor Covering (Laying new)	2–4, 8–13
Habits (Break)	9
Hair (Cut to increase growth)	16–18, 21–23, 26–29
Hair (Cut to decrease growth)	1–3, 15
Harvest (Grain for storage)	2–4, 7, 8
Harvest (Root crops)	2–4, 7, 8, 30
Investments (New)	5, 24
Loan (Ask for)	26–29
Massage (Relaxing)	8, 12
Mow Lawn (Decrease growth)	2–13
Mow Lawn (Increase growth)	16–29
Mushrooms (Pick)	1, 29, 30
Negotiate (Business for the elderly)	1
Prune for Better Fruit	13–15
Prune to Promote Healing	no ideal dates
Wean Children	16–20
Wood Floors (Installing)	no ideal dates

Activity	December
Animals (Neuter or spay)	13–15, 17, 19–21
Animals (Sell or buy)	17, 22, 26
Automobile (Buy)	7, 8, 15, 26
Brewing	2, 3, 11, 12, 30, 31
Build (Start foundation)	no ideal dates
Business (Conducting for self and others)	5, 10, 19, 24
Business (Start new)	24
Can Fruits and Vegetables	2, 3, 11, 12, 30
Can Preserves	2, 3, 11, 12, 30
Concrete (Pour)	5
Construction (Begin new)	5, 8, 10, 19, 21, 24, 26
Consultants (Begin work with)	4, 8, 9, 12, 14, 17, 19, 21, 24, 26
Contracts (Bid on)	17, 19, 21, 24, 26
Cultivate	8
Decorating	17–19, 26–28
Demolition	4, 5, 13, 31
Electronics (Buy)	9, 19
Entertain Guests	no ideal dates
Floor Covering (Laying new)	1, 5–10
Habits (Break)	no ideal dates
Hair (Cut to increase growth)	15–17, 19, 20, 24–28
Hair (Cut to decrease growth)	4, 13, 14, 31
Harvest (Grain for storage)	1, 4–6, 31
Harvest (Root crops)	1, 4–6, 13, 31
Investments (New)	5, 24
Loan (Ask for)	24–26
Massage (Relaxing)	3, 17
Mow Lawn (Decrease growth)	1–13, 30, 31
Mow Lawn (Increase growth)	15–28
Mushrooms (Pick)	1, 28–30
Negotiate (Business for the elderly)	8, 12, 21, 26
Prune for Better Fruit	11, 12
Prune to Promote Healing	no ideal dates
Wean Children	13–19
Wood Floors (Installing)	no ideal dates

Choose the Best Time for Your Activities

When rules for elections refer to "favorable" and "unfavorable" aspects to your Sun or other planets, please refer to the Favorable and Unfavorable Days Tables and Lunar Aspectarian for more information. You'll find instructions beginning on page 129 and the tables beginning on page 136.

The material in this section came from several sources including: *The New A to Z Horoscope Maker* and *Delineator* by Llewellyn George (Llewellyn, 1999), *Moon Sign Book* (Llewellyn, 1945), and *Electional Astrology* by Vivian Robson (Slingshot Publishing, 2000). Robson's book was originally published in 1937.

Advertise (Internet)

The Moon should be conjunct, sextile, or trine Mercury or Uranus and in the sign of Gemini, Capricorn, or Aquarius.

Advertise (Print)

Write ads on a day favorable to your Sun The Moon should be conjunct, sextile, or trine Mercury or Venus. Avoid hard aspects to Mars and Saturn. Ad campaigns produce the best results when the Moon is well aspected in Gemini (to enhance communication) or Capricorn (to build business).

Animals

Take home new pets when the day is favorable to your Sun, or when the Moon is trine, sextile, or conjunct Mercury, Jupiter or Venus, or in the sign of Virgo or Pisces. However, avoid days when the Moon is either square or opposing the Sun, Mars, Saturn, Uranus, Neptune, or Pluto. When selecting a pet, have the Moon well aspected by the planet that rules the animal. Cats are ruled by the Sun, dogs by Mercury, birds by Venus, horses by Jupiter, and fish by Neptune. Buy large animals when the Moon is in Sagittarius or Pisces and making favorable aspects to Jupiter or Mercury. Buy animals smaller than sheep when the Moon is in Virgo with favorable aspects to Mercury or Venus.

Animals (Breed)

Animals are easiest to handle when the Moon is in Taurus, Cancer, Libra, or Pisces, but try to avoid the Full Moon. To encourage healthy births, animals should be mated so births occur when the Moon is increasing in Taurus, Cancer, Pisces, or Libra. Those born during a semi-fruitful sign (Taurus and Capricorn) will produce leaner meat. Libra yields beautiful animals for showing and racing.

Animals (Declaw)

Declaw cats for medical purposes in the dark of the Moon. Avoid the week before and after the Full Moon and the sign of Pisces.

Animals (Neuter or Spay)

Have livestock and pets neutered or spayed when the Moon is in Sagittarius, Capricorn, or Pisces, after it has passed through Scorpio, the sign that rules reproductive organs. Avoid the week before and after the Full Moon.

Animals (Sell or Buy)

In either buying or selling, it is important to keep the Moon and Mercury free from any aspect to Mars. Aspects to Mars will create discord and increase the likelihood of wrangling over price and quality. The Moon should be passing from the first quarter to full and sextile or trine Venus or Jupiter. When buying racehorses, let the Moon be in an air sign. The Moon should be in air signs when you buy birds. If the birds are to be pets, let the Moon be in good aspect to Venus.

Animals (Train)

Train pets when the Moon is in Virgo or trine to Mercury.

Animals (Train Dogs to Hunt)

Let the Moon be in Aries in conjunction with Mars, which makes them courageous and quick to learn. But let Jupiter also be in aspect to preserve them from danger in hunting.

Automobiles

When buying an automobile, select a time when the Moon is conjunct, sextile, or trine to Mercury, Saturn, or Uranus and in the sign of Gemini or Capricorn. Avoid times when Mercury is in retrograde motion.

Baking Cakes

Your cakes will have a lighter texture if you see that the Moon is in Gemini, Libra, or Aquarius and in good aspect to Venus or Mercury. If you are decorating a cake or confections are being made, have the Moon placed in Libra.

Beauty Treatments (Massage, etc.)

See that the Moon is in Taurus, Cancer, Leo, Libra, or Aquarius and in favorable aspect to Venus. In the case of plastic surgery, aspects to Mars should be avoided, and the Moon should not be in the sign ruling the part to be operated on.

Borrow (Money or Goods)

See that the Moon is not placed between 15 degrees Libra and 15 degrees Scorpio. Let the Moon be waning and in Leo, Scorpio (16 to 30 degrees), Sagittarius, or Pisces. Venus should be in good aspect to the Moon, and the Moon should not be square, opposing, or conjunct either Saturn or Mars.

Brewing

Start brewing during the third or fourth quarter, when the Moon is in Cancer, Scorpio, or Pisces.

Build (Start Foundation)

Turning the first sod for the foundation marks the beginning of the building. For best results, excavate the site when the Moon is in the first quarter of a fixed sign and making favorable aspects to Saturn.

Business (Start New)

When starting a business, have the Moon be in Taurus, Virgo, or Capricorn and increasing. The Moon should be sextile or trine Jupiter or Saturn, but avoid oppositions or squares. The planet ruling the business should be well aspected, too.

Buy Goods

Buy during the third quarter, when the Moon is in Taurus for quality or in a mutable sign (Gemini, Sagittarius, Virgo, or Pisces) for savings. Good aspects to Venus or the Sun are desirable. If you are buying for yourself, it is good if the day is favorable for your Sun sign. You may also apply rules for buying specific items.

Canning
Can fruits and vegetables when the Moon is in either the third or fourth quarter and in the water sign Cancer or Pisces. Preserves and jellies use the same quarters and the signs Cancer, Pisces, or Taurus.

Clothing
Buy clothing on a day that is favorable for your Sun sign and when Venus or Mercury is well aspected. Avoid aspects to Mars and Saturn. Buy your clothing when the Moon is in Taurus if you want to remain satisfied. Do not buy clothing or jewelry when the Moon is in Scorpio or Aries. See that the Moon is sextile or trine the Sun during the first or second quarters.

Collections
Try to make collections on days when your natal Sun is well aspected. Avoid days when the Moon is opposing or square Mars or Saturn. If possible, the Moon should be in a cardinal sign (Aries, Cancer, Libra, or Capricorn). It is more difficult to collect when the Moon is in Taurus or Scorpio.

Concrete
Pour concrete when the Moon is in the third quarter of the fixed sign Taurus, Leo, or Aquarius.

Construction (Begin New)
The Moon should be sextile or trine Jupiter. According to Hermes, no building should be begun when the Moon is in Scorpio or Pisces. The best time to begin building is when the Moon is in Aquarius.

Consultants (Work with)
The Moon should be conjunct, sextile, or trine Mercury or Jupiter.

Contracts (Bid On)

The Moon should be in Gemini or Capricorn and either the Moon or Mercury should be conjunct, sextile, or trine Jupiter.

Copyrights/Patents

The Moon should be conjunct, trine, or sextile either Mercury or Jupiter.

Coronations and Installations

Let the Moon be in Leo and in favorable aspect to Venus, Jupiter, or Mercury. The Moon should be applying to these planets.

Cultivate

Cultivate when the Moon is in a barren sign and waning, ideally the fourth quarter in Aries, Gemini, Leo, Virgo, or Aquarius. The third quarter in the sign of Sagittarius will also work.

Cut Timber

Timber cut during the waning Moon does not become worm-eaten; it will season well and not warp, decay, or snap during burning. Cut when the Moon is in Taurus, Gemini, Virgo, or Capricorn—especially in August. Avoid the water signs. Look for favorable aspects to Mars.

Decorating or Home Repairs

Have the Moon waxing and in the sign of Libra, Gemini, or Aquarius. Avoid squares or oppositions to either Mars or Saturn. Venus in good aspect to Mars or Saturn is beneficial.

Demolition

Let the waning Moon be in Leo, Sagittarius, or Aries.

Dental and Dentists

Visit the dentist when the Moon is in Virgo, or pick a day marked favorable for your Sun sign. Mars should be marked sextile, conjunct, or trine; avoid squares or oppositions to Saturn, Uranus, or Jupiter.

Teeth are best removed when the Moon is in Gemini, Virgo, Sagittarius, or Pisces and during the first or second quarter. Avoid the Full Moon! The day should be favorable for your lunar cycle, and Mars and Saturn should be marked conjunct, trine, or sextile. Fillings should be done in the third or fourth quarters in the sign of Taurus, Leo, Scorpio, or Pisces. The same applies for dentures.

Dressmaking

William Lilly wrote in 1676: "Make no new clothes, or first put them on when the Moon is in Scorpio or afflicted by Mars, for they will be apt to be torn and quickly worn out." Design, repair, and sew clothes in the first and second quarters of Taurus, Leo, or Libra on a day marked favorable for your Sun sign. Venus, Jupiter, and Mercury should be favorably aspected, but avoid hard aspects to Mars or Saturn.

Egg-Setting (see p. 161)

Eggs should be set so chicks will hatch during fruitful signs. To set eggs, subtract the number of days given for incubation or

gestation from the fruitful dates. Chickens incubate in twenty-one days, turkeys and geese in twenty-eight days.

A freshly laid egg loses quality rapidly if it is not handled properly. Use plenty of clean litter in the nests to reduce the number of dirty or cracked eggs. Gather eggs daily in mild weather and at least two times daily in hot or cold weather. The eggs should be placed in a cooler immediately after gathering and stored at 50 to 55°F. Do not store eggs with foods or products that give off pungent odors since eggs may absorb the odors.

Eggs saved for hatching purposes should not be washed. Only clean and slightly soiled eggs should be saved for hatching. Dirty eggs should not be incubated. Eggs should be stored in a cool place with the large ends up. It is not advisable to store the eggs longer than one week before setting them in an incubator.

Electricity and Gas (Install)
The Moon should be in a fire sign, and there should be no squares, oppositions, or conjunctions with Uranus (ruler of electricity), Neptune (ruler of gas), Saturn, or Mars. Hard aspects to Mars can cause fires.

Electronics (Buying)
Choose a day when the Moon is in an air sign (Gemini, Libra, Aquarius) and well aspected by Mercury and/or Uranus when buying electronics.

Electronics (Repair)
The Moon should be sextile or trine Mars or Uranus and in a fixed sign (Taurus, Leo, Scorpio, Aquarius).

Entertain Friends
Let the Moon be in Leo or Libra and making good aspects to Venus. Avoid squares or oppositions to either Mars or Saturn by the Moon or Venus.

Eyes and Eyeglasses

Have your eyes tested and glasses fitted on a day marked favorable for your Sun sign, and on a day that falls during your favorable lunar cycle. Mars should not be in aspect with the Moon. The same applies for any treatment of the eyes, which should also be started during the Moon's first or second quarter.

Fence Posts

Set posts when the Moon is in the third or fourth quarter of the fixed sign Taurus or Leo.

Fertilize and Compost

Fertilize when the Moon is in a fruitful sign (Cancer, Scorpio, Pisces). Organic fertilizers are best when the Moon is waning. Use chemical fertilizers when the Moon is waxing. Start compost when the Moon is in the fourth quarter in a water sign.

Find Hidden Treasure

Let the Moon be in good aspect to Jupiter or Venus. If you erect a horoscope for this election, place the Moon in the Fourth House.

Find Lost Articles

Search for lost articles during the first quarter and when your Sun sign is marked favorable. Also check to see that the planet ruling the lost item is trine, sextile, or conjunct the Moon. The Moon rules household utensils; Mercury rules letters and books; and Venus rules clothing, jewelry, and money.

Fishing

During the summer months, the best time of the day to fish is from sunrise to three hours after and from two hours before sunset until one hour after. Fish do not bite in cooler months until the air is warm, from noon to three pm. Warm, cloudy days are good. The most favorable winds are from the south and southwest.

Easterly winds are unfavorable. The best days of the month for fishing are when the Moon changes quarters, especially if the change occurs on a day when the Moon is in a water sign (Cancer, Scorpio, Pisces). The best period in any month is the day after the Full Moon.

Friendship

The need for friendship is greater when the Moon is in Aquarius or when Uranus aspects the Moon. Friendship prospers when Venus or Uranus is trine, sextile, or conjunct the Moon. The Moon in Gemini facilitates the chance meeting of acquaintances and friends.

Grafting or Budding

Grafting is the process of introducing new varieties of fruit on less desirable trees. For this process you should use the increasing phase of the Moon in fruitful signs such as Cancer, Scorpio, or Pisces. Capricorn may be used, too. Cut your grafts while trees are dormant, from December to March. Keep them in a cool, dark place, not too dry or too damp. Do the grafting before the sap starts to flow and while the Moon is waxing, preferably while it is in Cancer, Scorpio, or Pisces. The type of plant should determine both cutting and planting times.

Habit (Breaking)

To end an undesirable habit, and this applies to ending everything from a bad relationship to smoking, start on a day when the Moon is in the fourth quarter and in the barren sign of Gemini, Leo, or Aquarius. Aries, Virgo, and Capricorn may be suitable as well, depending on the habit you want to be rid of. Make sure that your lunar cycle is favorable. Avoid lunar aspects to Mars or Jupiter. However, favorable aspects to Pluto are helpful.

Haircuts

Cut hair when the Moon is in Gemini, Sagittarius, Pisces, Taurus, or Capricorn, but not in Virgo. Look for favorable aspects to Venus.

For faster growth, cut hair when the Moon is increasing in Cancer or Pisces. To make hair grow thicker, cut when the Moon is full in the signs of Taurus, Cancer, or Leo. If you want your hair to grow more slowly, have the Moon be decreasing in Aries, Gemini, or Virgo, and have the Moon square or opposing Saturn.

Permanents, straightening, and hair coloring will take well if the Moon is in Taurus or Leo and trine or sextile Venus. Avoid hair treatments if Mars is marked as square or in opposition, especially if heat is to be used. For permanents, a trine to Jupiter is helpful. The Moon also should be in the first quarter. Check the lunar cycle for a favorable day in relation to your Sun sign.

Harvest Crops

Harvest root crops when the Moon is in a dry sign (Aries, Leo, Sagittarius, Gemini, Aquarius) and waning. Harvest grain for storage just after the Full Moon, avoiding Cancer, Scorpio, or Pisces. Harvest in the third and fourth quarters in dry signs. Dry crops in the third quarter in fire signs.

Health

A diagnosis is more likely to be successful when the Moon is in Aries, Cancer, Libra, or Capricorn and less so when in Gemini, Sagittarius, Pisces, or Virgo. Begin a recuperation program or enter a hospital when the Moon is in a cardinal or fixed sign and the day is favorable to your Sun sign. For surgery, see "Surgical Procedures." Buy medicines when the Moon is in Virgo or Scorpio.

Home (Buy New)

If you desire a permanent home, buy when the New Moon is in a fixed sign—Taurus or Leo, for example. Each sign will affect your decision in a different way. A house bought when the Moon is in Taurus is likely to be more practical and have a country look—right down to the split-rail fence. A house purchased when the Moon is in Leo will more likely be a real showplace.

If you're buying for speculation and a quick turnover, be certain that the Moon is in a cardinal sign (Aries, Cancer, Libra, Capricorn). Avoid buying when the Moon is in a fixed sign (Leo, Scorpio, Aquarius, Taurus).

Home (Make Repairs)

In all repairs, avoid squares, oppositions, or conjunctions to the planet ruling the place or thing to be repaired. For example, bathrooms are ruled by Scorpio and Cancer. You would not want to start a project in those rooms when the Moon or Pluto is receiving hard aspects. The front entrance, hall, dining room, and porch are ruled by the Sun So you would want to avoid times when Saturn or Mars are square, opposing, or conjunct the Sun Also, let the Moon be waxing.

Home (Sell)

Make a strong effort to list your property for sale when the Sun is marked favorable in your sign and in good aspect to Jupiter. Avoid adverse aspects to as many planets as possible.

Home Furnishings (Buy New)

Saturn days (Saturday) are good for buying, and Jupiter days (Thursday) are good for selling. Items bought on days when Saturn is well aspected tend to wear longer and purchases tend to be more conservative.

Job (Start New)

Jupiter and Venus should be sextile, trine, or conjunct the Moon. A day when your Sun is receiving favorable aspects is preferred.

Legal Matters

Good Moon-Jupiter aspects improve the outcome in legal decisions. To gain damages through a lawsuit, begin the process during the increasing Moon. To avoid paying damages, a court date during the decreasing Moon is desirable. Good Moon-Sun aspects strengthen your chance of success. A well-aspected Moon in Cancer or Leo, making good aspects to the Sun, brings the best results in custody cases. In divorce cases, a favorable Moon-Venus aspect is best.

Loan (Ask For)

A first and second quarter phase favors the lender, the third and fourth quarters favor the borrower. Good aspects of Jupiter and Venus to the Moon are favorable to both, as is having the Moon in Leo or Taurus.

Machinery, Appliances, or Tools (Buy)

Tools, machinery, and other implements should be bought on days when your lunar cycle is favorable and when Mars and Uranus are trine, sextile, or conjunct the Moon. Any quarter of the Moon is suitable. When buying gas or electrical appliances, the Moon should be in Aquarius.

Make a Will

Let the Moon be in a fixed sign (Taurus, Leo, Scorpio, or Aquarius) to ensure permanence. If the Moon is in a cardinal sign (Aries, Cancer, Libra, or Capricorn), the will could be altered. Let the Moon be waxing—increasing in light—and in good aspect to Saturn, Venus, or Mercury. In case the will is made in an emergency during illness and the Moon is slow in motion, void-of-course, combust, or under the Sun's beams, the testator will die and the will remain unaltered. There is some danger that it will be lost or stolen, however.

Marriage

The best time for marriage to take place is when the Moon is increasing, but not yet full. Good signs for the Moon to be in are Taurus, Cancer, Leo, or Libra.

The Moon in Taurus produces the most steadfast marriages, but if the partners later want to separate, they may have a difficult time. Make sure that the Moon is well aspected, especially to Venus or Jupiter. Avoid aspects to Mars, Uranus, or Pluto and the signs Aries, Gemini, Virgo, Scorpio, or Aquarius.

The values of the signs are as follows:

- Aries is not favored for marriage
- Taurus from 0 to 19 degrees is good, the remaining degrees are less favorable
- Cancer is unfavorable unless you are marrying a widow
- Leo is favored, but it may cause one party to deceive the other as to his or her money or possessions
- Virgo is not favored except when marrying a widow
- Libra is good for engagements but not for marriage
- Scorpio from 0 to 15 degrees is good, but the last 15 degrees are entirely unfortunate. The woman may be fickle, envious, and quarrelsome
- Sagittarius is neutral
- Capricorn, from 0 to 10 degrees, is difficult for marriage;

however, the remaining degrees are favorable, especially when marrying a widow
- Aquarius is not favored
- Pisces is favored, although marriage under this sign can incline a woman to chatter a lot

These effects are strongest when the Moon is in the sign. If the Moon and Venus are in a cardinal sign, happiness between the couple may not continue long.

On no account should the Moon apply to Saturn or Mars, even by good aspect.

Medical Treatment for the Eyes

Let the Moon be increasing in light and motion and making favorable aspects to Venus or Jupiter and be unaspected by Mars. Keep the Moon out of Taurus, Capricorn, or Virgo. If an aspect between the Moon and Mars is unavoidable, let it be separating.

Medical Treatment for the Head

If possible, have Mars and Saturn free of hard aspects. Let the Moon be in Aries or Taurus, decreasing in light, in conjunction or aspect with Venus or Jupiter and free of hard aspects. The Sun should not be in any aspect to the Moon.

Medical Treatment for the Nose

Let the Moon be in Cancer, Leo, or Virgo and not aspecting Mars or Saturn and also not in conjunction with a retrograde or weak planet.

Mining

Saturn rules mining. Begin work when Saturn is marked conjunct, trine, or sextile. Mine for gold when the Sun is marked conjunct, trine, or sextile. Mercury rules quicksilver, Venus rules copper, Jupiter rules tin, Saturn rules lead and coal, Uranus rules radioactive elements, Neptune rules oil, the Moon rules water. Mine for these items when the ruling planet is marked conjunct, trine, or sextile.

Move to New Home

If you have a choice, and sometimes you don't, make sure that Mars is not aspecting the Moon. Move on a day favorable to your Sun sign or when the Moon is conjunct, sextile, or trine the Sun

Mow Lawn

Mow in the first and second quarters (waxing phase) to increase growth and lushness, and in the third and fourth quarters (waning phase) to decrease growth.

Negotiate

When you are choosing a time to negotiate, consider what the meeting is about and what you want to have happen. If it is agreement or compromise between two parties that you desire, have the Moon be in the sign of Libra. When you are making contracts, it is best to have the Moon in the same element. For example, if your concern is communication, then elect a time when the Moon is in an air sign. If, on the other hand, your concern is about possessions, an earth sign would be more appropriate. Fixed signs are unfavorable, with the exception of Leo; so are cardinal signs, except for Capricorn. If you are negotiating the end of something, use the rules that apply to ending habits.

Occupational Training

When you begin training, see that your lunar cycle is favorable that day and that the planet ruling your occupation is marked conjunct or trine.

Paint

Paint buildings during the waning Libra or Aquarius Moon. If the weather is hot, paint when the Moon is in Taurus. If the weather is cold, paint when the Moon is in Leo. Schedule the painting to start in the fourth quarter as the wood is drier and paint will penetrate wood better. Avoid painting around the New Moon, though, as the wood is likely to be damp, making the paint subject to scalding when hot weather hits it. If the temperature is below 70°F, it is not advisable to paint while the Moon is in Cancer, Scorpio, or Pisces as the paint is apt to creep, check, or run.

Party (Host or Attend)

A party timed so the Moon is in Gemini, Leo, Libra, or Sagittarius, with good aspects to Venus and Jupiter, will be fun and well attended. There should be no aspects between the Moon and Mars or Saturn.

Pawn

Do not pawn any article when Jupiter is receiving a square or opposition from Saturn or Mars or when Jupiter is within 17 degrees of the Sun, for you will have little chance to redeem the items.

Pick Mushrooms

Mushrooms, one of the most promising traditional medicines in the world, should be gathered at the Full Moon.

Plant

Root crops, like carrots and potatoes, are best if planted in the sign Taurus or Capricorn. Beans, peas, tomatoes, peppers, and other fruit-bearing plants are best if planted in a sign that supports seed growth. Leaf plants, like lettuce, broccoli, or cauliflower, are best planted when the Moon is in a water sign.

It is recommended that you transplant during a decreasing Moon, when forces are streaming into the lower part of the plant. This helps root growth.

Promotion (Ask For)

Choose a day favorable to your Sun sign. Mercury should be marked conjunct, trine, or sextile. Avoid days when Mars or Saturn is aspected.

Prune

Prune during the third and fourth quarter of a Scorpio Moon to retard growth and to promote better fruit. Prune when the Moon is in cardinal Capricorn to promote healing.

Reconcile with People

If the reconciliation is with a woman, let Venus be strong and well aspected. If elders or superiors are involved, see that Saturn is receiving good aspects; if the reconciliation is between young people or between an older and younger person, see that Mercury is well aspected.

Romance

There is less control of when a romance starts, but romances begun under an increasing Moon are more likely to be permanent or satisfying, while those begun during the decreasing Moon tend to transform the participants. The tone of the relationship can be guessed from the sign the Moon is in. Romances begun with the Moon in Aries may be impulsive. Those begun in Capricorn will take greater effort to bring to a desirable conclusion, but they may be very rewarding. Good aspects between the Moon and Venus will have a positive influence on the relationship. Avoid unfavorable aspects to Mars, Uranus, and Pluto. A decreasing Moon, particularly the fourth quarter, facilitates ending a relationship and causes the least pain.

Roof a Building

Begin roofing a building during the third or fourth quarter, when the Moon is in Aries or Aquarius. Shingles laid during the New Moon have a tendency to curl at the edges.

Sauerkraut

The best-tasting sauerkraut is made just after the Full Moon in the fruitful signs of Cancer, Scorpio, or Pisces.

Select a Child's Sex

Count from the last day of menstruation to the first day of the next cycle and divide the interval between the two dates in half. Pregnancy in the first half produces females, but copulation should take place with the Moon in a feminine sign. Pregnancy in the latter half, up to three days before the beginning of menstruation, produces males, but copulation should take place with the Moon in a masculine sign. The three-day period before the next period again produces females.

Sell or Canvass

Begin these activities during a day favorable to your Sun sign. Otherwise, sell on days when Jupiter, Mercury, or Mars is trine, sextile, or conjunct the Moon. Avoid days when Saturn is square or opposing the Moon, for that always hinders business and

causes discord. If the Moon is passing from the first quarter to full, it is best to have the Moon swift in motion and in good aspect with Venus and/or Jupiter.

Sign Papers

Sign contracts or agreements when the Moon is increasing in a fruitful sign and on a day when the Moon is making favorable aspects to Mercury. Avoid days when Mars, Saturn, or Neptune are square or opposite the Moon.

Spray and Weed

Spray pests and weeds during the fourth quarter when the Moon is in the barren sign Leo or Aquarius and making favorable aspects to Pluto. Weed during a waning Moon in a barren sign.

Staff (Fire)

Have the Moon in the third or fourth quarter, but not full. The Moon should not be square any planets.

Staff (Hire)

The Moon should be in the first or second quarter, and preferably in the sign of Gemini or Virgo. The Moon should be conjunct, trine, or sextile Mercury or Jupiter.

Stocks (Buy)

The Moon should be in Taurus or Capricorn, and there should be a sextile or trine to Jupiter or Saturn.

Surgical Procedures

Blood flow, like ocean tides, appears to be related to Moon phases. To reduce hemorrhage after a surgery, schedule it within one week before or after a New Moon. Schedule surgery to occur during the increase of the Moon if possible, as wounds heal better and vitality is greater than during the decrease of the Moon. Avoid surgery within one week before or after the Full

Moon. Select a date when the Moon is past the sign governing the part of the body involved in the operation. For example, abdominal operations should be done when the Moon is in Sagittarius, Capricorn, or Aquarius. The further removed the Moon sign is from the sign ruling the afflicted part of the body, the better.

For successful operations, avoid times when the Moon is applying to any aspect of Mars. (This tends to promote inflammation and complications.) See the Lunar Aspectarian on odd pages 137–159 to find days with negative Mars aspects and positive Venus and Jupiter aspects. Never operate with the Moon in the same sign as a person's Sun sign or Ascendant. Let the Moon be in a fixed sign and avoid square or opposing aspects. The Moon should not be void-of-course. Cosmetic surgery should be done in the increase of the Moon, when the Moon is not square or in opposition to Mars. Avoid days when the Moon is square or opposing Saturn or the Sun

Travel (Air)

Start long trips when the Moon is making favorable aspects to the Sun For enjoyment, aspects to Jupiter are preferable; for visiting, look for favorable aspects to Mercury. To prevent accidents, avoid squares or oppositions to Mars, Saturn, Uranus, or Pluto. Choose a day when the Moon is in Sagittarius or Gemini and well aspected to Mercury, Jupiter, or Uranus. Avoid adverse aspects of Mars, Saturn, or Uranus.

Visit

On setting out to visit a person, let the Moon be in aspect with any retrograde planet, for this ensures that the person you're visiting will be at home. If you desire to stay a long time in a place, let the Moon be in good aspect to Saturn. If you desire to leave the place quickly, let the Moon be in a cardinal sign.

Wean Children

To wean a child successfully, do so when the Moon is in Sagittarius, Capricorn, Aquarius, or Pisces—signs that do not rule vital human organs. By observing this astrological rule, much trouble for parents and child may be avoided.

Weight (Reduce)

If you want to lose weight, the best time to get started is when the Moon is in the third or fourth quarter and in the barren sign of Virgo. Review the section on How to Use the Moon Tables and Lunar Aspectarian beginning on page 136 to help you select a date that is favorable to begin your weight-loss program.

Wine and Drink Other Than Beer

Start brewing when the Moon is in Pisces or Taurus. Sextiles or trines to Venus are favorable, but avoid aspects to Mars or Saturn.

Write

Write for pleasure or publication when the Moon is in Gemini. Mercury should be making favorable aspects to Uranus and Neptune.

How to Use the Moon Tables and Lunar Aspectarian

Timing activities is one of the most important things you can do to ensure success. In many Eastern countries, timing by the planets is so important that practically no event takes place without first setting up a chart for it. Weddings have occurred in the middle of the night because the influences were at the best then. You may not want to take it that far, but you can still make use of the influences of the Moon whenever possible. It's easy and it works!

Llewellyn's **Moon Sign Book** has information to help you plan just about any activity: weddings, fishing, making purchases, cutting your hair, traveling, and more. We provide the guidelines you need to pick the best day out of the several from which you have to choose. The Moon Tables are the **Moon Sign Book's** primary method for choosing dates. Following are instructions, examples, and directions on how to read the Moon Tables. More advanced information on using the tables containing the Lunar Aspectarian and favorable and unfavorable days (found on odd-numbered pages opposite the Moon Tables), Moon void-of-course and retrograde information to choose the dates best for you is also included.

The Five Basic Steps

Step 1: Directions for Choosing Dates

Look up the directions for choosing dates for the activity that you wish to begin, then go to step 2.

Step 2: Check the Moon Tables

You'll find two tables for each month of the year beginning on page 136. The Moon Tables (on the left-hand pages) include the day, date, and sign the Moon is in; the element and nature of the sign; the Moon's phase; and when it changes sign or phase. If there is a time listed after a date, that time is the time when the Moon moves into that zodiac sign. Until then, the Moon is considered to be in the sign for the previous day.

The abbreviation Full signifies Full Moon and New signifies New Moon. The times listed with dates indicate when the Moon changes sign. The times listed after the phase indicate when the Moon changes phase.

Turn to the month you would like to begin your activity. You will be using the Moon's sign and phase information most often when you begin choosing your own dates. Use the Time Zone Map on page 164 and the Time Zone Conversions table on page 165 to convert time to your own time zone.

When you find dates that meet the criteria for the correct Moon phase and sign for your activity, you may have completed the process. For certain simple activities, such as getting a haircut, the phase and sign information is all that is needed. If the directions for your activity include information on certain lunar aspects, however, you should consult the Lunar Aspectarian. An example of this would be if the directions told you not to perform a certain activity when the Moon is square (Q) Jupiter.

Step 3: Check the Lunar Aspectarian

On the pages opposite the Moon Tables you will find tables containing the Lunar Aspectarian and Favorable and Unfavorable Days. The Lunar Aspectarian gives the aspects (or angles) of the Moon to other planets. Some aspects are favorable, while others are not. To use the Lunar Aspectarian, find the planet that the directions list as favorable for your activity, and run down the column to the date desired. For example, you should avoid aspects to Mars if you are planning surgery. So you would look for Mars across the top and then run down that column looking for days where there are no aspects to Mars (as signified by empty boxes). If you want to find a **favorable** aspect (sextile (X) or trine (T)) to Mercury, run your finger down the column under Mercury until you find an X or T. **Adverse** aspects to planets are squares (Q) or oppositions (O). A conjunction (C) is sometimes beneficial, sometimes not, depending on the activity or planets involved.

Step 4: Favorable and Unfavorable Days

The tables listing favorable and unfavorable days are helpful when you want to choose your personal best dates because your Sun sign is taken into consideration. The twelve Sun signs are listed on the right side of the tables. Once you have determined which days meet your criteria for phase, sign, and aspects, you can determine whether or not those days are positive for you by checking the favorable and unfavorable days for your Sun sign.

To find out if a day is positive for you, find your Sun sign and then look down the column. If it is marked F, it is very favorable. The Moon is in the same sign as your Sun on a favorable day. If it is marked f, it is slightly favorable; U is very unfavorable; and u means slightly unfavorable. A day marked very unfavorable (U) indicates that the Moon is in the sign opposing your Sun

Once you have selected good dates for the activity you are about to begin, you can go straight to "Using What You've Learned," beginning on the next page. To learn how to fine-tune your selections even further, read on.

Step 5: Void-of-Course Moon and Retrogrades

This last step is perhaps the most advanced portion of the procedure. It is generally considered poor timing to make decisions, sign important papers, or start special activities during a Moon void-of-course period or during a Mercury retrograde. Once you have chosen the best date for your activity based on steps one through four, you can check the Void-of-Course tables, beginning on page 76, to find out if any of the dates you have chosen have void periods.

The Moon is said to be void-of-course after it has made its last aspect to a planet within a particular sign, but before it has moved into the next sign. Put simply, the Moon is "resting" during the void-of-course period, so activities initiated at this time generally don't come to fruition. You will notice that there are many void periods during the year, and it is nearly impossible to avoid all of them. Some people choose to ignore these altogether and do not take them into consideration when planning activities.

Next, you can check the Retrograde Planets tables on page 160 to see what planets are retrograde during your chosen date(s).

A planet is said to be retrograde when it appears to move backward in the sky as viewed from Earth. Generally, the farther a planet is away from the Sun, the longer it can stay retrograde. Some planets will retrograde for several months at a time. Avoiding retrogrades is not as important in lunar planning as avoiding the Moon void-of-course, with the exception of the planet Mercury.

East Coast may be, for example, under the influence of a Virgo Moon, while those of you living on the West Coast will still have a Leo Moon influence.

We follow a commonly held belief among astrologers: whatever sign the Moon is in at the start of a day—12:00 am Eastern Time—is considered the dominant influence of the day. That sign is indicated in the Moon Tables. If the date you select for an activity shows the Moon changing signs, you can decide how important the sign change may be for your specific election and adjust your election date and time accordingly.

Use Common Sense

Some activities depend on outside factors. Obviously, you can't go out and plant when there is a foot of snow on the ground. You should adjust to the conditions at hand. If the weather was bad during the first quarter, when it was best to plant crops, do it during the second quarter while the Moon is in a fruitful sign. If the Moon is not in a fruitful sign during the first or second quarter, choose a day when it is in a semi-fruitful sign. The best advice is to choose either the sign or phase that is most favorable, when the two don't coincide.

To Summarize

First, look up the activity under the proper heading, then look for the information given in the tables. Choose the best date considering the number of positive factors in effect. If most of the dates are favorable, there is no problem choosing the one that will fit your schedule. However, if there aren't any really good dates, pick the ones with the least number of negative influences. Please keep in mind that the information found here applies in the broadest sense to the events you want to plan or are considering. To be the most effective, when you use electional astrology, you should also consider your own birth chart in relation to a chart drawn for the time or times you have under consideration. The best advice we can offer you is: read the entire introduction to each section.

January Moon Table

Date	Sign	Element	Nature	Phase
1 Wed 11:00 pm	Aries	Fire	Barren	1st
2 Thu	Aries	Fire	Barren	2nd 11:45 pm
3 Fri	Aries	Fire	Barren	2nd
4 Sat 11:15 am	Taurus	Earth	Semi-fruitful	2nd
5 Sun	Taurus	Earth	Semi-fruitful	2nd
6 Mon 9:11 pm	Gemini	Air	Barren	2nd
7 Tue	Gemini	Air	Barren	2nd
8 Wed	Gemini	Air	Barren	2nd
9 Thu 3:43 am	Cancer	Water	Fruitful	2nd
10 Fri	Cancer	Water	Fruitful	Full 2:21 pm
11 Sat 7:16 am	Leo	Fire	Barren	3rd
12 Sun	Leo	Fire	Barren	3rd
13 Mon 9:06 am	Virgo	Earth	Barren	3rd
14 Tue	Virgo	Earth	Barren	3rd
15 Wed 10:43 am	Libra	Air	Semi-fruitful	3rd
16 Thu	Libra	Air	Semi-fruitful	3rd
17 Fri 1:20 pm	Scorpio	Water	Fruitful	4th 7:58 am
18 Sat	Scorpio	Water	Fruitful	4th
19 Sun 5:41 pm	Sagittarius	Fire	Barren	4th
20 Mon	Sagittarius	Fire	Barren	4th
21 Tue	Sagittarius	Fire	Barren	4th
22 Wed 12:00 am	Capricorn	Earth	Semi-fruitful	4th
23 Thu	Capricorn	Earth	Semi-fruitful	4th
24 Fri 8:20 am	Aquarius	Air	Barren	New 4:42 pm
25 Sat	Aquarius	Air	Barren	1st
26 Sun 6:44 pm	Pisces	Water	Fruitful	1st
27 Mon	Pisces	Water	Fruitful	1st
28 Tue	Pisces	Water	Fruitful	1st
29 Wed 6:51 am	Aries	Fire	Barren	1st
30 Thu	Aries	Fire	Barren	1st
31 Fri 7:28 pm	Taurus	Earth	Semi-fruitful	1st

January Aspectarian/Favorable & Unfavorable Days

Date	Sun	Mercury	Venus	Mars	Jupiter	Saturn	Uranus	Neptune	Pluto
1				T		X			X
2	Q	Q			Q				
3			X			Q			Q
4							C		
5	T	T			T			X	
6			Q			T			T
7				O					
8			T					Q	
9					O		X		
10	O	O				O		T	O
11				T				Q	
12									
13			O	Q				T	
14					T	T		O	T
15	T	T							
16				X	Q				
17	Q	Q	T			Q	O		Q
18					X			T	
19	X					X			X
20		X	Q	C				Q	
21									
22			X		C		T		
23						C		X	C
24	C							Q	
25		C		X					
26									
27					X		X		
28			C	Q		X		C	X
29									
30	X			T	Q				
31		X				Q			Q

Date	Aries	Taurus	Gemini	Cancer	Leo	Virgo	Libra	Scorpio	Sagittarius	Capricorn	Aquarius	Pisces
1		f	u	f		U		f	u	f		F
2	F		f	u	f		U		f	u	f	
3	F		f	u	f		U		f	u	f	
4	F		f	u	f		U		f	u	f	
5		F		f	u	f		U		f	u	f
6		F		f	u	f		U		f	u	f
7	f		F		f	u	f		U		f	u
8	f		F		f	u	f		U		f	u
9	f		F		f	u	f		U		f	u
10	u	f		F		f	u	f		U		f
11	u	f		F		f	u	f		U		f
12	f	u	f		F		f	u	f		U	
13	f	u	f		F		f	u	f		U	
14		f	u	f		F		f	u	f		U
15		f	u	f		F		f	u	f		U
16	U		f	u	f		F		f	u	f	
17	U		f	u	f		F		f	u	f	
18		U		f	u	f		F		f	u	f
19		U		f	u	f		F		f	u	f
20	f		U		f	u	f		F		f	u
21	f		U		f	u	f		F		f	u
22	u	f		U		f	u	f		F		f
23	u	f		U		f	u	f		F		f
24	u	f		U		f	u	f		F		f
25	f	u	f		U		f	u	f		F	
26	f	u	f		U		f	u	f		F	
27		f	u	f		U		f	u	f		F
28		f	u	f		U		f	u	f		F
29		f	u	f		U		f	u	f		F
30	F		f	u	f		U		f	u	f	
31	F		f	u	f		U		f	u	f	

February Moon Table

Date	Sign	Element	Nature	Phase
1 Sat	Taurus	Earth	Semi-fruitful	2nd 8:42 pm
2 Sun	Taurus	Earth	Semi-fruitful	2nd
3 Mon 6:29 am	Gemini	Air	Barren	2nd
4 Tue	Gemini	Air	Barren	2nd
5 Wed 2:03 pm	Cancer	Water	Fruitful	2nd
6 Thu	Cancer	Water	Fruitful	2nd
7 Fri 5:45 pm	Leo	Fire	Barren	2nd
8 Sat	Leo	Fire	Barren	2nd
9 Sun 6:39 pm	Virgo	Earth	Barren	Full 2:33 am
10 Mon	Virgo	Earth	Barren	3rd
11 Tue 6:37 pm	Libra	Air	Semi-fruitful	3rd
12 Wed	Libra	Air	Semi-fruitful	3rd
13 Thu 7:37 pm	Scorpio	Water	Fruitful	3rd
14 Fri	Scorpio	Water	Fruitful	3rd
15 Sat 11:07 pm	Sagittarius	Fire	Barren	4th 5:17 pm
16 Sun	Sagittarius	Fire	Barren	4th
17 Mon	Sagittarius	Fire	Barren	4th
18 Tue 5:37 am	Capricorn	Earth	Semi-fruitful	4th
19 Wed	Capricorn	Earth	Semi-fruitful	4th
20 Thu 2:42 pm	Aquarius	Air	Barren	4th
21 Fri	Aquarius	Air	Barren	4th
22 Sat	Aquarius	Air	Barren	4th
23 Sun 1:37 am	Pisces	Water	Fruitful	New 10:32 am
24 Mon	Pisces	Water	Fruitful	1st
25 Tue 1:47 pm	Aries	Fire	Barren	1st
26 Wed	Aries	Fire	Barren	1st
27 Thu	Aries	Fire	Barren	1st
28 Fri 2:30 am	Taurus	Earth	Semi-fruitful	1st
29 Sat	Taurus	Earth	Semi-fruitful	1st

February Aspectarian/Favorable & Unfavorable Days

Date	Sun	Mercury	Venus	Mars	Jupiter	Saturn	Uranus	Neptune	Pluto
1	Q				T		C		
2			X			T		X	T
3		Q							
4	T							Q	
5		T	Q	O			X		
6					O			T	
7			T			O	Q		O
8									
9	O			T			T		
10		O			T			O	
11				Q		T			T
12			O		Q				
13	T			X		Q			Q
14		T		X			O		
15	Q						X	T	X
16		Q	T						
17								Q	
18	X			C			T		
19		X	Q	C			X		
20						C	Q		C
21			X						
22									
23	C	C		X			X		
24						X		C	
25						X			X
26			Q						
27			C		Q	Q			Q
28	X	X		T			C		
29					T			X	

Date	Aries	Taurus	Gemini	Cancer	Leo	Virgo	Libra	Scorpio	Sagittarius	Capricorn	Aquarius	Pisces
1		F		f	u	f		U		f	u	f
2		F		f	u	f		U		f	u	f
3		F		f	u	f		U		f	u	f
4	f		F		f	u	f		U		f	u
5	f		F		f	u	f		U		f	u
6	u	f		F		f	u	f		U		f
7	u	f		F		f	u	f		U		f
8	f	u	f		F		f	u	f		U	
9	f	u	f		F		f	u	f		U	
10		f	u	f		F		f	u	f		U
11		f	u	f		F		f	u	f		U
12	U		f	u	f		F		f	u	f	
13	U		f	u	f		F		f	u	f	
14		U		f	u	f		F		f	u	f
15		U		f	u	f		F		f	u	f
16	f		U		f	u	f		F		f	u
17	f		U		f	u	f		F		f	u
18	f		U		f	u	f		F		f	u
19	u	f		U		f	u	f		F		f
20	u	f		U		f	u	f		F		f
21	f	u	f		U		f	u	f		F	
22	f	u	f		U		f	u	f		F	
23		f	u	f		U		f	u	f		F
24		f	u	f		U		f	u	f		F
25		f	u	f		U		f	u	f		F
26	F		f	u	f		U		f	u	f	
27	F		f	u	f		U		f	u	f	
28		F		f	u	f		U		f	u	f
29		F		f	u	f		U		f	u	f

March Moon Table

Date	Sign	Element	Nature	Phase
1 Sun 2:21 pm	Gemini	Air	Barren	1st
2 Mon	Gemini	Air	Barren	2nd 2:57 pm
3 Tue 11:25 pm	Cancer	Water	Fruitful	2nd
4 Wed	Cancer	Water	Fruitful	2nd
5 Thu	Cancer	Water	Fruitful	2nd
6 Fri 4:27 am	Leo	Fire	Barren	2nd
7 Sat	Leo	Fire	Barren	2nd
8 Sun 6:47 am	Virgo	Earth	Barren	2nd
9 Mon	Virgo	Earth	Barren	Full 1:48 pm
10 Tue 6:03 am	Libra	Air	Semi-fruitful	3rd
11 Wed	Libra	Air	Semi-fruitful	3rd
12 Thu 5:28 am	Scorpio	Water	Fruitful	3rd
13 Fri	Scorpio	Water	Fruitful	3rd
14 Sat 7:09 am	Sagittarius	Fire	Barren	3rd
15 Sun	Sagittarius	Fire	Barren	3rd
16 Mon 12:25 pm	Capricorn	Earth	Semi-fruitful	4th 5:34 am
17 Tue	Capricorn	Earth	Semi-fruitful	4th
18 Wed 9:16 pm	Aquarius	Air	Barren	4th
19 Thu	Aquarius	Air	Barren	4th
20 Fri	Aquarius	Air	Barren	4th
21 Sat 8:33 am	Pisces	Water	Fruitful	4th
22 Sun	Pisces	Water	Fruitful	4th
23 Mon 8:58 pm	Aries	Fire	Barren	4th
24 Tue	Aries	Fire	Barren	New 5:28 am
25 Wed	Aries	Fire	Barren	1st
26 Thu 9:37 am	Taurus	Earth	Semi-fruitful	1st
27 Fri	Taurus	Earth	Semi-fruitful	1st
28 Sat 9:38 pm	Gemini	Air	Barren	1st
29 Sun	Gemini	Air	Barren	1st
30 Mon	Gemini	Air	Barren	1st
31 Tue 7:43 am	Cancer	Water	Fruitful	1st

March Aspectarian/Favorable & Unfavorable Days

Date	Sun	Mercury	Venus	Mars	Jupiter	Saturn	Uranus	Neptune	Pluto
1		Q				T			T
2	Q								
3		T	X					Q	
4				O				X	
5	T				O			T	O
6			Q			O	Q		
7									
8		O	T					T	
9	O			T	T			O	T
10						T			
11				Q	Q				Q
12		T	O				Q	O	
13	T			X	X			T	X
14		Q				X			
15								Q	
16	Q	X					T		
17			T					X	
18	X			C	C	C			C
19							Q		
20			Q						
21		C					X		
22			X					C	
23				X	X	X			X
24	C								
25					Q				Q
26				Q			Q	C	
27		X							
28			C	T	T	T		X	T
29	X	Q							
30								Q	
31								X	

Date	Aries	Taurus	Gemini	Cancer	Leo	Virgo	Libra	Scorpio	Sagittarius	Capricorn	Aquarius	Pisces
1	F		f	u	f		U		f	u	f	
2	f		F		f	u	f		U		f	u
3	f		F		f	u	f		U		f	u
4	u	f		F		f	u	f		U		f
5	u	f		F		f	u	f		U		f
6	u	f		F		f	u	f		U		f
7	f	u	f		F		f	u	f		U	
8	f	u	f		F		f	u	f		U	
9		f	u	f		F		f	u	f		U
10		f	u	f		F		f	u	f		U
11	U		f	u	f		F		f	u	f	
12	U		f	u	f		F		f	u	f	
13		U		f	u	f		F		f	u	f
14		U		f	u	f		F		f	u	f
15	f		U		f	u	f		F		f	u
16	f		U		f	u	f		F		f	u
17	u	f		U		f	u	f		F		f
18	u	f		U		f	u	f		F		f
19	f	u	f		U		f	u	f		F	
20	f	u	f		U		f	u	f		F	
21	f	u	f		U		f	u	f		F	
22		f	u	f		U		f	u	f		F
23		f	u	f		U		f	u	f		F
24	F		f	u	f		U		f	u	f	
25	F		f	u	f		U		f	u	f	
26	F		f	u	f		U		f	u	f	
27		F		f	u	f		U		f	u	f
28		F		f	u	f		U		f	u	f
29	f		F		f	u	f		U		f	u
30	f		F		f	u	f		U		f	u
31	f		F		f	u	f		U		f	u

April Moon Table

Date	Sign	Element	Nature	Phase
1 Wed	Cancer	Water	Fruitful	2nd 6:21 am
2 Thu 2:26 pm	Leo	Fire	Barren	2nd
3 Fri	Leo	Fire	Barren	2nd
4 Sat 5:18 pm	Virgo	Earth	Barren	2nd
5 Sun	Virgo	Earth	Barren	2nd
6 Mon 5:16 pm	Libra	Air	Semi-fruitful	2nd
7 Tue	Libra	Air	Semi-fruitful	Full 10:35 pm
8 Wed 4:17 pm	Scorpio	Water	Fruitful	3rd
9 Thu	Scorpio	Water	Fruitful	3rd
10 Fri 4:35 pm	Sagittarius	Fire	Barren	3rd
11 Sat	Sagittarius	Fire	Barren	3rd
12 Sun 8:05 pm	Capricorn	Earth	Semi-fruitful	3rd
13 Mon	Capricorn	Earth	Semi-fruitful	3rd
14 Tue	Capricorn	Earth	Semi-fruitful	4th 6:56 pm
15 Wed 3:37 am	Aquarius	Air	Barren	4th
16 Thu	Aquarius	Air	Barren	4th
17 Fri 2:29 pm	Pisces	Water	Fruitful	4th
18 Sat	Pisces	Water	Fruitful	4th
19 Sun	Pisces	Water	Fruitful	4th
20 Mon 3:00 am	Aries	Fire	Barren	4th
21 Tue	Aries	Fire	Barren	4th
22 Wed 3:36 pm	Taurus	Earth	Semi-fruitful	New 10:26 pm
23 Thu	Taurus	Earth	Semi-fruitful	1st
24 Fri	Taurus	Earth	Semi-fruitful	1st
25 Sat 3:20 am	Gemini	Air	Barren	1st
26 Sun	Gemini	Air	Barren	1st
27 Mon 1:28 pm	Cancer	Water	Fruitful	1st
28 Tue	Cancer	Water	Fruitful	1st
29 Wed 9:06 pm	Leo	Fire	Barren	1st
30 Thu	Leo	Fire	Barren	2nd 4:38 pm

April Aspectarian/Favorable & Unfavorable Days

Date	Sun	Mercury	Venus	Mars	Jupiter	Saturn	Uranus	Neptune	Pluto
1	Q	T						T	
2			X	O	O	O	Q		O
3	T								
4			Q						
5								T	
6		O	T		T	T		O	T
7	O			T					
8					Q	Q			Q
9			Q					O	T
10		T			X	X			X
11			O	X					
12	T								Q
13		Q						T	
14	Q				C			X	C
15		X	T			C	Q		
16				C					
17	X								
18			Q					X	
19					X			C	X
20						X			
21		C	X	X					
22	C				Q	Q			Q
23							C		
24				Q	T			X	T
25						T			
26			C	T				Q	
27		X							
28	X							X	
29					O			T	O
30	Q	Q				O	Q		X

Date	Aries	Taurus	Gemini	Cancer	Leo	Virgo	Libra	Scorpio	Sagittarius	Capricorn	Aquarius	Pisces
1	u	f		F		f	u	f		U		f
2	u	f		F		f	u	f		U		f
3	f	u	f		F		f	u	f		U	
4	f	u	f		F		f	u	f		U	
5		f	u	f		F		f	u	f		U
6		f	u	f		F		f	u	f		U
7	U		f	u	f		F		f	u	f	
8	U		f	u	f		F		f	u	f	
9		U		f	u	f		F		f	u	f
10		U		f	u	f		F		f	u	f
11	f		U		f	u	f		F		f	u
12	f		U		f	u	f		F		f	u
13	u	f		U		f	u	f		F		f
14	u	f		U		f	u	f		F		f
15	u	f		U		f	u	f		F		f
16	f	u	f		U		f	u	f		F	
17	f	u	f		U		f	u	f		F	
18		f	u	f		U		f	u	f		F
19		f	u	f		U		f	u	f		F
20		f	u	f		U		f	u	f		F
21	F		f	u	f		U		f	u	f	
22	F		f	u	f		U		f	u	f	
23		F		f	u	f		U		f	u	f
24		F		f	u	f		U		f	u	f
25		F		f	u	f		U		f	u	f
26	f		F		f	u	f		U		f	u
27	f		F		f	u	f		U		f	u
28	u	f		F		f	u	f		U		f
29	u	f		F		f	u	f		U		f
30	f	u	f		F		f	u	f		U	

May Moon Table

Date	Sign	Element	Nature	Phase
1 Fri	Leo	Fire	Barren	2nd
2 Sat 1:35 am	Virgo	Earth	Barren	2nd
3 Sun	Virgo	Earth	Barren	2nd
4 Mon 3:09 am	Libra	Air	Semi-fruitful	2nd
5 Tue	Libra	Air	Semi-fruitful	2nd
6 Wed 3:05 am	Scorpio	Water	Fruitful	2nd
7 Thu	Scorpio	Water	Fruitful	Full 6:45 am
8 Fri 3:15 am	Sagittarius	Fire	Barren	3rd
9 Sat	Sagittarius	Fire	Barren	3rd
10 Sun 5:39 am	Capricorn	Earth	Semi-fruitful	3rd
11 Mon	Capricorn	Earth	Semi-fruitful	3rd
12 Tue 11:39 am	Aquarius	Air	Barren	3rd
13 Wed	Aquarius	Air	Barren	3rd
14 Thu 9:24 pm	Pisces	Water	Fruitful	4th 10:03 am
15 Fri	Pisces	Water	Fruitful	4th
16 Sat	Pisces	Water	Fruitful	4th
17 Sun 9:36 am	Aries	Fire	Barren	4th
18 Mon	Aries	Fire	Barren	4th
19 Tue 10:10 pm	Taurus	Earth	Semi-fruitful	4th
20 Wed	Taurus	Earth	Semi-fruitful	4th
21 Thu	Taurus	Earth	Semi-fruitful	4th
22 Fri 9:36 am	Gemini	Air	Barren	New 1:39 pm
23 Sat	Gemini	Air	Barren	1st
24 Sun 7:09 pm	Cancer	Water	Fruitful	1st
25 Mon	Cancer	Water	Fruitful	1st
26 Tue	Cancer	Water	Fruitful	1st
27 Wed 2:33 am	Leo	Fire	Barren	1st
28 Thu	Leo	Fire	Barren	1st
29 Fri 7:40 am	Virgo	Earth	Barren	2nd 11:30 pm
30 Sat	Virgo	Earth	Barren	2nd
31 Sun 10:38 am	Libra	Air	Semi-fruitful	2nd

May Aspectarian/Favorable & Unfavorable Days

Date	Sun	Mercury	Venus	Mars	Jupiter	Saturn	Uranus	Neptune	Pluto
1			X	O					
2	T	T						T	
3			Q		T			O	T
4						T			
5			T	T	Q				Q
6						Q	O		
7	O	O		Q	X			T	X
8						X			
9			O					Q	
10				X			T		
11	T						X		
12		T			C	C			C
13							Q		
14	Q		T						
15		Q		C			X		
16		Q						C	X
17	X				X	X			
18		X							
19			X		Q				Q
20				X		Q	C		
21								X	T
22	C			Q	T	T			
23			C						
24		C						Q	
25				T			X		
26					O			T	O
27	X					O	Q		
28			X						
29	Q	X					T		
30			Q	O				O	
31		Q			T	T			T

Date	Aries	Taurus	Gemini	Cancer	Leo	Virgo	Libra	Scorpio	Sagittarius	Capricorn	Aquarius	Pisces
1	f	u	f		F		f	u	f		U	
2		f	u	f		F		f	u	f		U
3		f	u	f		F		f	u	f		U
4		f	u	f		F		f	u	f		U
5	U		f	u	f		F		f	u	f	
6	U		f	u	f		F		f	u	f	
7		U		f	u	f		F		f	u	f
8		U		f	u	f		F		f	u	f
9	f		U		f	u	f		F		f	u
10	f		U		f	u	f		F		f	u
11	u	f		U		f	u	f		F		f
12	u	f		U		f	u	f		F		f
13	f	u	f		U		f	u	f		F	
14	f	u	f		U		f	u	f		F	
15		f	u	f		U		f	u	f		F
16		f	u	f		U		f	u	f		F
17		f	u	f		U		f	u	f		F
18	F		f	u	f		U		f	u	f	
19	F		f	u	f		U		f	u	f	
20		F		f	u	f		U		f	u	f
21		F		f	u	f		U		f	u	f
22		F		f	u	f		U		f	u	f
23	f		F		f	u	f		U		f	u
24	f		F		f	u	f		U		f	u
25	u	f		F		f	u	f		U		f
26	u	f		F		f	u	f		U		f
27	f	u	f		F		f	u	f		U	
28	f	u	f		F		f	u	f		U	
29	f	u	f		F		f	u	f		U	
30		f	u	f		F		f	u	f		U
31		f	u	f		F		f	u	f		U

June Moon Table

Date	Sign	Element	Nature	Phase
1 Mon	Libra	Air	Semi-fruitful	2nd
2 Tue 12:06 pm	Scorpio	Water	Fruitful	2nd
3 Wed	Scorpio	Water	Fruitful	2nd
4 Thu 1:17 pm	Sagittarius	Fire	Barren	2nd
5 Fri	Sagittarius	Fire	Barren	Full 3:12 pm
6 Sat 3:44 pm	Capricorn	Earth	Semi-fruitful	3rd
7 Sun	Capricorn	Earth	Semi-fruitful	3rd
8 Mon 8:54 pm	Aquarius	Air	Barren	3rd
9 Tue	Aquarius	Air	Barren	3rd
10 Wed	Aquarius	Air	Barren	3rd
11 Thu 5:32 am	Pisces	Water	Fruitful	3rd
12 Fri	Pisces	Water	Fruitful	3rd
13 Sat 5:03 pm	Aries	Fire	Barren	4th 2:24 am
14 Sun	Aries	Fire	Barren	4th
15 Mon	Aries	Fire	Barren	4th
16 Tue 5:35 am	Taurus	Earth	Semi-fruitful	4th
17 Wed	Taurus	Earth	Semi-fruitful	4th
18 Thu 5:00 pm	Gemini	Air	Barren	4th
19 Fri	Gemini	Air	Barren	4th
20 Sat	Gemini	Air	Barren	4th
21 Sun 2:02 am	Cancer	Water	Fruitful	New 2:41 am
22 Mon	Cancer	Water	Fruitful	1st
23 Tue 8:33 am	Leo	Fire	Barren	1st
24 Wed	Leo	Fire	Barren	1st
25 Thu 1:05 pm	Virgo	Earth	Barren	1st
26 Fri	Virgo	Earth	Barren	1st
27 Sat 4:16 pm	Libra	Air	Semi-fruitful	1st
28 Sun	Libra	Air	Semi-fruitful	2nd 4:16 am
29 Mon 6:48 pm	Scorpio	Water	Fruitful	2nd
30 Tue	Scorpio	Water	Fruitful	2nd

June Aspectarian/Favorable & Unfavorable Days

Date	Sun	Mercury	Venus	Mars	Jupiter	Saturn	Uranus	Neptune	Pluto
1	T		T						
2		T			Q	Q			Q
3				T			O	T	
4					X	X			X
5	O		O	Q					
6								Q	
7		O		X				T	
8					C	C		X	C
9			T					Q	
10	T								
11			Q					X	
12		T		C				C	
13	Q				X	X			X
14		Q	X						
15	X				Q				Q
16						Q			
17		X					C	X	
18				X	T	T			T
19			C						
20				Q				Q	
21	C						X		
22		C			O			T	O
23			X	T			O		
24								Q	
25	X		Q						
26		X						T	
27					O	T	T	O	T
28	Q	Q	T						
29					Q	Q			Q
30	T	T					O		

Date	Aries	Taurus	Gemini	Cancer	Leo	Virgo	Libra	Scorpio	Sagittarius	Capricorn	Aquarius	Pisces
1	U		f	u	f		F		f	u	f	
2	U		f	u	f		F		f	u	f	
3		U		f	u	f		F		f	u	f
4		U		f	u	f		F		f	u	f
5	f		U		f	u	f		F		f	u
6	f		U		f	u	f		F		f	u
7	u	f		U		f	u	f		F		f
8	u	f		U		f	u	f		F		f
9	f	u	f		U		f	u	f		F	
10	f	u	f		U		f	u	f		F	
11	f	u	f		U		f	u	f		F	
12		f	u	f		U		f	u	f		F
13		f	u	f		U		f	u	f		F
14	F		f	u	f		U		f	u	f	
15	F		f	u	f		U		f	u	f	
16	F		f	u	f		U		f	u	f	
17		F		f	u	f		U		f	u	f
18		F		f	u	f		U		f	u	f
19	f		F		f	u	f		U		f	u
20	f		F		f	u	f		U		f	u
21	u	f		F		f	u	f		U		f
22	u	f		F		f	u	f		U		f
23	u	f		F		f	u	f		U		f
24	f	u	f		F		f	u	f		U	
25	f	u	f		F		f	u	f		U	
26		f	u	f		F		f	u	f		U
27		f	u	f		F		f	u	f		U
28	U		f	u	f		F		f	u	f	
29	U		f	u	f		F		f	u	f	
30		U		f	u	f		F		f	u	f

July Moon Table

Date	Sign	Element	Nature	Phase
1 Wed 9:21 pm	Sagittarius	Fire	Barren	2nd
2 Thu	Sagittarius	Fire	Barren	2nd
3 Fri	Sagittarius	Fire	Barren	2nd
4 Sat 12:48 am	Capricorn	Earth	Semi-fruitful	2nd
5 Sun	Capricorn	Earth	Semi-fruitful	Full 12:44 am
6 Mon 6:08 am	Aquarius	Air	Barren	3rd
7 Tue	Aquarius	Air	Barren	3rd
8 Wed 2:13 pm	Pisces	Water	Fruitful	3rd
9 Thu	Pisces	Water	Fruitful	3rd
10 Fri	Pisces	Water	Fruitful	3rd
11 Sat 1:06 am	Aries	Fire	Barren	3rd
12 Sun	Aries	Fire	Barren	4th 7:29 pm
13 Mon 1:34 pm	Taurus	Earth	Semi-fruitful	4th
14 Tue	Taurus	Earth	Semi-fruitful	4th
15 Wed	Taurus	Earth	Semi-fruitful	4th
16 Thu 1:19 am	Gemini	Air	Barren	4th
17 Fri	Gemini	Air	Barren	4th
18 Sat 10:24 am	Cancer	Water	Fruitful	4th
19 Sun	Cancer	Water	Fruitful	4th
20 Mon 4:16 pm	Leo	Fire	Barren	New 1:33 pm
21 Tue	Leo	Fire	Barren	1st
22 Wed 7:40 pm	Virgo	Earth	Barren	1st
23 Thu	Virgo	Earth	Barren	1st
24 Fri 9:54 pm	Libra	Air	Semi-fruitful	1st
25 Sat	Libra	Air	Semi-fruitful	1st
26 Sun	Libra	Air	Semi-fruitful	1st
27 Mon 12:12 am	Scorpio	Water	Fruitful	2nd 8:33 am
28 Tue	Scorpio	Water	Fruitful	2nd
29 Wed 3:25 am	Sagittarius	Fire	Barren	2nd
30 Thu	Sagittarius	Fire	Barren	2nd
31 Fri 7:58 am	Capricorn	Earth	Semi-fruitful	2nd

July Aspectarian/Favorable & Unfavorable Days

Date	Sun	Mercury	Venus	Mars	Jupiter	Saturn	Uranus	Neptune	Pluto
1					X	X		T	X
2			O	T					
3								Q	
4		O		Q				T	
5	O				C			X	C
6			T	X		C			
7								Q	
8									
9		T	Q					X	
10	T				X	X		C	X
11		Q	X	C					
12	Q				Q				
13						Q			Q
14		X						C	
15	X				T	T		X	T
16				X					
17			C					Q	
18									
19		C		Q				X	
20	C				O	O		T	O
21			X	T				Q	
22									
23		X						T	
24			Q		T	T		O	T
25	X	Q		O					
26			T		Q	Q			Q
27	Q							O	
28		T			X			T	X
29	T					X			
30			O	T				Q	
31									

Date	Aries	Taurus	Gemini	Cancer	Leo	Virgo	Libra	Scorpio	Sagittarius	Capricorn	Aquarius	Pisces
1		U		f	u	f		F		f	u	f
2	f		U		f	u	f		F		f	u
3	f		U		f	u	f		F		f	u
4	u	f		U		f	u	f		F		f
5	u	f		U		f	u	f		F		f
6	u	f		U		f	u	f		F		f
7	f	u	f		U		f	u	f		F	
8	f	u	f		U		f	u	f		F	
9		f	u	f		U		f	u	f		F
10		f	u	f		U		f	u	f		F
11	F		f	u	f		U		f	u	f	
12	F		f	u	f		U		f	u	f	
13	F		f	u	f		U		f	u	f	
14		F		f	u	f		U		f	u	f
15		F		f	u	f		U		f	u	f
16	f		F		f	u	f		U		f	u
17	f		F		f	u	f		U		f	u
18	f		F		f	u	f		U		f	u
19	u	f		F		f	u	f		U		f
20	u	f		F		f	u	f		U		f
21	f	u	f		F		f	u	f		U	
22	f	u	f		F		f	u	f		U	
23		f	u	f		F		f	u	f		U
24		f	u	f		F		f	u	f		U
25	U		f	u	f		F		f	u	f	
26	U		f	u	f		F		f	u	f	
27	U			f	u	f		F		f	u	f
28	U			f	u	f		F		f	u	f
29	U			f	u	f		F		f	u	f
30	f		U		f	u	f		F		f	u
31	f		U		f	u	f		F		f	u

August Moon Table

Date	Sign	Element	Nature	Phase
1 Sat	Capricorn	Earth	Semi-fruitful	2nd
2 Sun 2:11 pm	Aquarius	Air	Barren	2nd
3 Mon	Aquarius	Air	Barren	Full 11:59 am
4 Tue 10:28 pm	Pisces	Water	Fruitful	3rd
5 Wed	Pisces	Water	Fruitful	3rd
6 Thu	Pisces	Water	Fruitful	3rd
7 Fri 9:05 am	Aries	Fire	Barren	3rd
8 Sat	Aries	Fire	Barren	3rd
9 Sun 9:28 pm	Taurus	Earth	Semi-fruitful	3rd
10 Mon	Taurus	Earth	Semi-fruitful	3rd
11 Tue	Taurus	Earth	Semi-fruitful	4th 12:45 pm
12 Wed 9:46 am	Gemini	Air	Barren	4th
13 Thu	Gemini	Air	Barren	4th
14 Fri 7:35 pm	Cancer	Water	Fruitful	4th
15 Sat	Cancer	Water	Fruitful	4th
16 Sun	Cancer	Water	Fruitful	4th
17 Mon 1:38 am	Leo	Fire	Barren	4th
18 Tue	Leo	Fire	Barren	New 10:42 pm
19 Wed 4:20 am	Virgo	Earth	Barren	1st
20 Thu	Virgo	Earth	Barren	1st
21 Fri 5:16 am	Libra	Air	Semi-fruitful	1st
22 Sat	Libra	Air	Semi-fruitful	1st
23 Sun 6:16 am	Scorpio	Water	Fruitful	1st
24 Mon	Scorpio	Water	Fruitful	1st
25 Tue 8:49 am	Sagittarius	Fire	Barren	2nd 1:58 pm
26 Wed	Sagittarius	Fire	Barren	2nd
27 Thu 1:37 pm	Capricorn	Earth	Semi-fruitful	2nd
28 Fri	Capricorn	Earth	Semi-fruitful	2nd
29 Sat 8:37 pm	Aquarius	Air	Barren	2nd
30 Sun	Aquarius	Air	Barren	2nd
31 Mon	Aquarius	Air	Barren	2nd

August Aspectarian/Favorable & Unfavorable Days

Date	Sun	Mercury	Venus	Mars	Jupiter	Saturn	Uranus	Neptune	Pluto
1				Q	C		T	X	
2		O				C			C
3	O							Q	
4			T	X					
5								X	
6					X			C	X
7		T	Q			X			
8	T				Q				
9			C		Q				Q
10		Q	X				C		
11	Q				T			X	T
12						T			
13		X							
14	X			X				Q	
15			C				X		
16				Q	O	O		T	O
17								Q	
18	C			T					
19		C						T	
20			X		T	T		O	T
21									
22			Q	O	Q				Q
23	X	X				Q			
24			T		X		O	T	X
25	Q					X			
26		Q						Q	
27	T			T					
28		T			C		T		
29			O	Q		C		X	C
30								Q	
31									

Date	Aries	Taurus	Gemini	Cancer	Leo	Virgo	Libra	Scorpio	Sagittarius	Capricorn	Aquarius	Pisces
1	u	f		U		f	u	f		F		f
2	u	f		U		f	u	f		F		f
3	f	u	f		U		f	u	f		F	
4	f	u	f		U		f	u	f		F	
5		f	u	f		U		f	u	f		F
6		f	u	f		U		f	u	f		F
7		f	u	f		U		f	u	f		F
8	F		f	u	f		U		f	u	f	
9	F		f	u	f		U		f	u	f	
10		F		f	u	f		U		f	u	f
11		F		f	u	f		U		f	u	f
12		F		f	u	f		U		f	u	f
13	f		F		f	u	f		U		f	u
14	f		F		f	u	f		U		f	u
15	u	f		F		f	u	f		U		f
16	u	f		F		f	u	f		U		f
17	f	u	f		F		f	u	f		U	
18	f	u	f		F		f	u	f		U	
19	f	u	f		F		f	u	f		U	
20		f	u	f		F		f	u	f		U
21		f	u	f		F		f	u	f		U
22	U		f	u	f		F		f	u	f	
23	U		f	u	f		F		f	u	f	
24		U		f	u	f		F		f	u	f
25		U		f	u	f		F		f	u	f
26	f		U		f	u	f		F		f	u
27	f		U		f	u	f		F		f	u
28	u	f		U		f	u	f		F		f
29	u	f		U		f	u	f		F		f
30	f	u	f		U		f	u	f		F	
31	f	u	f		U		f	u	f		F	

September Moon Table

Date	Sign	Element	Nature	Phase
1 Tue 5:34 am	Pisces	Water	Fruitful	2nd
2 Wed	Pisces	Water	Fruitful	Full 1:22 am
3 Thu 4:22 pm	Aries	Fire	Barren	3rd
4 Fri	Aries	Fire	Barren	3rd
5 Sat	Aries	Fire	Barren	3rd
6 Sun 4:43 am	Taurus	Earth	Semi-fruitful	3rd
7 Mon	Taurus	Earth	Semi-fruitful	3rd
8 Tue 5:28 pm	Gemini	Air	Barren	3rd
9 Wed	Gemini	Air	Barren	3rd
10 Thu	Gemini	Air	Barren	4th 5:26 am
11 Fri 4:23 am	Cancer	Water	Fruitful	4th
12 Sat	Cancer	Water	Fruitful	4th
13 Sun 11:32 am	Leo	Fire	Barren	4th
14 Mon	Leo	Fire	Barren	4th
15 Tue 2:37 pm	Virgo	Earth	Barren	4th
16 Wed	Virgo	Earth	Barren	4th
17 Thu 2:56 pm	Libra	Air	Semi-fruitful	New 7:00 am
18 Fri	Libra	Air	Semi-fruitful	1st
19 Sat 2:33 pm	Scorpio	Water	Fruitful	1st
20 Sun	Scorpio	Water	Fruitful	1st
21 Mon 3:32 pm	Sagittarius	Fire	Barren	1st
22 Tue	Sagittarius	Fire	Barren	1st
23 Wed 7:16 pm	Capricorn	Earth	Semi-fruitful	2nd 9:55 pm
24 Thu	Capricorn	Earth	Semi-fruitful	2nd
25 Fri	Capricorn	Earth	Semi-fruitful	2nd
26 Sat 2:08 am	Aquarius	Air	Barren	2nd
27 Sun	Aquarius	Air	Barren	2nd
28 Mon 11:34 am	Pisces	Water	Fruitful	2nd
29 Tue	Pisces	Water	Fruitful	2nd
30 Wed 10:47 pm	Aries	Fire	Barren	2nd

September Aspectarian/Favorable & Unfavorable Days

Date	Sun	Mercury	Venus	Mars	Jupiter	Saturn	Uranus	Neptune	Pluto
1				X					
2	O				X		X	C	
3		O	T			X			X
4									
5					Q	Q			Q
6			Q	C					
7	T				T		C	X	
8			X			T			T
9		T							
10	Q							Q	
11		Q		X			X		
12	X				O			T	O
13				Q		O			
14		X	C				Q		
15				T					
16						T		T	O
17	C					T			T
18		C	X		Q				
19				O		Q			Q
20			Q		X		O	T	
21	X					X			X
22			T						
23	Q	X		T				Q	
24								T	
25		Q		Q	C	C		X	C
26	T							Q	
27									
28		T	O	X					
29					X		X		
30						X		C	X

Date	Aries	Taurus	Gemini	Cancer	Leo	Virgo	Libra	Scorpio	Sagittarius	Capricorn	Aquarius	Pisces
1	f	u	f		U		f	u	f		F	
2		f	u	f		U		f	u	f		F
3		f	u	f		U		f	u	f		F
4	F		f	u	f		U		f	u	f	
5	F		f	u	f		U		f	u	f	
6	F		f	u	f		U		f	u	f	
7		F		f	u	f		U		f	u	f
8		F		f	u	f		U		f	u	f
9	f		F		f	u	f		U		f	u
10	f		F		f	u	f		U		f	u
11	f		F		f	u	f		U		f	u
12	u	f		F		f	u	f		U		f
13	u	f		F		f	u	f		U		f
14	f	u	f		F		f	u	f		U	
15	f	u	f		F		f	u	f		U	
16		f	u	f		F		f	u	f		U
17		f	u	f		F		f	u	f		U
18	U		f	u	f		F		f	u	f	
19	U		f	u	f		F		f	u	f	
20		U		f	u	f		F		f	u	f
21		U		f	u	f		F		f	u	f
22	f		U		f	u	f		F		f	u
23	f		U		f	u	f		F		f	u
24	u	f		U		f	u	f		F		f
25	u	f		U		f	u	f		F		f
26	f	u	f		U		f	u	f		F	
27	f	u	f		U		f	u	f		F	
28	f	u	f		U		f	u	f		F	
29		f	u	f		U		f	u	f		F
30		f	u	f		U		f	u	f		F

October Moon Table

Date	Sign	Element	Nature	Phase
1 Thu	Aries	Fire	Barren	Full 5:05 pm
2 Fri	Aries	Fire	Barren	3rd
3 Sat 11:12 am	Taurus	Earth	Semi-fruitful	3rd
4 Sun	Taurus	Earth	Semi-fruitful	3rd
5 Mon	Taurus	Earth	Semi-fruitful	3rd
6 Tue 12:03 am	Gemini	Air	Barren	3rd
7 Wed	Gemini	Air	Barren	3rd
8 Thu 11:45 am	Cancer	Water	Fruitful	3rd
9 Fri	Cancer	Water	Fruitful	4th 8:40 pm
10 Sat 8:24 pm	Leo	Fire	Barren	4th
11 Sun	Leo	Fire	Barren	4th
12 Mon	Leo	Fire	Barren	4th
13 Tue 12:56 am	Virgo	Earth	Barren	4th
14 Wed	Virgo	Earth	Barren	4th
15 Thu 1:54 am	Libra	Air	Semi-fruitful	4th
16 Fri	Libra	Air	Semi-fruitful	New 3:31 pm
17 Sat 1:05 am	Scorpio	Water	Fruitful	1st
18 Sun	Scorpio	Water	Fruitful	1st
19 Mon 12:43 am	Sagittarius	Fire	Barren	1st
20 Tue	Sagittarius	Fire	Barren	1st
21 Wed 2:44 am	Capricorn	Earth	Semi-fruitful	1st
22 Thu	Capricorn	Earth	Semi-fruitful	1st
23 Fri 8:17 am	Aquarius	Air	Barren	2nd 9:23 am
24 Sat	Aquarius	Air	Barren	2nd
25 Sun 5:18 pm	Pisces	Water	Fruitful	2nd
26 Mon	Pisces	Water	Fruitful	2nd
27 Tue	Pisces	Water	Fruitful	2nd
28 Wed 4:45 am	Aries	Fire	Barren	2nd
29 Thu	Aries	Fire	Barren	2nd
30 Fri 5:19 pm	Taurus	Earth	Semi-fruitful	2nd

October Aspectarian/Favorable & Unfavorable Days

Date	Sun	Mercury	Venus	Mars	Jupiter	Saturn	Uranus	Neptune	Pluto
1	O								
2				C	Q				Q
3			T			Q			
4		O						C	
5					T	T		X	T
6			Q						
7	T			X				Q	
8									
9	Q	T	X		O		X	T	
10				Q		O			O
11		Q						Q	
12	X			T					
13		X	C					T	
14					T	T		O	T
15									
16	C			O	Q	Q			Q
17		C						O	
18			X		X	X		T	X
19									
20	X		Q	T				Q	
21		X						T	
22			T	Q	C			X	C
23	Q	Q				C			
24				X				Q	
25	T	T							
26								X	
27					X	X		C	X
28			O						
29				C	Q				
30		O				Q			Q
31	O							C	

Date	Aries	Taurus	Gemini	Cancer	Leo	Virgo	Libra	Scorpio	Sagittarius	Capricorn	Aquarius	Pisces
1	F		f	u	f		U		f	u	f	
2	F		f	u	f		U		f	u	f	
3	F		f	u	f		U		f	u	f	
4		F		f	u	f		U		f	u	f
5		F		f	u	f		U		f	u	f
6	f		F		f	u	f		U		f	u
7	f		F		f	u	f		U		f	u
8	f		F		f	u	f		U		f	u
9	u	f		F		f	u	f		U		f
10	u	f		F		f	u	f		U		f
11	f	u	f		F		f	u	f		U	
12	f	u	f		F		f	u	f		U	
13		f	u	f		F		f	u	f		U
14		f	u	f		F		f	u	f		U
15	U		f	u	f		F		f	u	f	
16	U		f	u	f		F		f	u	f	f
17		U		f	u	f		F		f	u	f
18		U		f	u	f		F		f	u	f
19	f		U		f	u	f		F		f	u
20	f		U		f	u	f		F		f	u
21	u	f		U		f	u	f		F		f
22	u	f		U		f	u	f		F		f
23	u	f		U		f	u	f		F		f
24	f	u	f		U		f	u	f		F	
25	f	u	f		U		f	u	f		F	U
26		f	u	f		U		f	u	f		F
27		f	u	f		U		f	u	f		F
28		f	u	f		U		f	u	f		F
29	F		f	u	f		U		f	u	f	
30	F		f	u	f		U		f	u	f	
31		F		f	u	f		U		f	u	f

November Moon Table

Date	Sign	Element	Nature	Phase
1 Sun	Taurus	Earth	Semi-fruitful	3rd
2 Mon 5:00 am	Gemini	Air	Barren	3rd
3 Tue	Gemini	Air	Barren	3rd
4 Wed 4:45 pm	Cancer	Water	Fruitful	3rd
5 Thu	Cancer	Water	Fruitful	3rd
6 Fri	Cancer	Water	Fruitful	3rd
7 Sat 2:18 am	Leo	Fire	Barren	3rd
8 Sun	Leo	Fire	Barren	4th 8:46 am
9 Mon 8:30 am	Virgo	Earth	Barren	4th
10 Tue	Virgo	Earth	Barren	4th
11 Wed 11:09 am	Libra	Air	Semi-fruitful	4th
12 Thu	Libra	Air	Semi-fruitful	4th
13 Fri 11:19 am	Scorpio	Water	Fruitful	4th
14 Sat	Scorpio	Water	Fruitful	4th
15 Sun 10:47 am	Sagittarius	Fire	Barren	New 12:07 am
16 Mon	Sagittarius	Fire	Barren	1st
17 Tue 11:35 am	Capricorn	Earth	Semi-fruitful	1st
18 Wed	Capricorn	Earth	Semi-fruitful	1st
19 Thu 3:25 pm	Aquarius	Air	Barren	1st
20 Fri	Aquarius	Air	Barren	1st
21 Sat 11:06 pm	Pisces	Water	Fruitful	2nd 11:45 pm
22 Sun	Pisces	Water	Fruitful	2nd
23 Mon	Pisces	Water	Fruitful	2nd
24 Tue 10:05 am	Aries	Fire	Barren	2nd
25 Wed	Aries	Fire	Barren	2nd
26 Thu 10:43 pm	Taurus	Earth	Semi-fruitful	2nd
27 Fri	Taurus	Earth	Semi-fruitful	2nd
28 Sat	Taurus	Earth	Semi-fruitful	2nd
29 Sun 11:16 am	Gemini	Air	Barren	2nd
30 Mon	Gemini	Air	Barren	Full 4:30 am

November Aspectarian/Favorable & Unfavorable Days

Date	Sun	Mercury	Venus	Mars	Jupiter	Saturn	Uranus	Neptune	Pluto
1					T	T		X	T
2		T							
3				X				Q	
4		T							
5	T		Q	Q				X	
6		Q			O	O		T	O
7							Q		
8	Q		X	T					
9		X					T		
10	X				T			O	T
11						T			
12			C	O					
13		C			Q	Q			Q
14							O	T	X
15	C				X	X			
16				T				Q	
17			X						
18		X		Q				T	X
19	X		Q		C	C			C
20		Q		X				Q	
21	Q								
22			T					X	
23		T			X			C	X
24	T					X			
25				C					
26					Q	Q			Q
27			O				C		
28								X	T
29		O			T	T			
30	O			X				Q	

Date	Aries	Taurus	Gemini	Cancer	Leo	Virgo	Libra	Scorpio	Sagittarius	Capricorn	Aquarius	Pisces
1	F			f	u	f		U		f	u	f
2	F			f	u	f		U		f	u	f
3	f		F		f	u	f		U		f	u
4	f		F		f	u	f		U		f	u
5	u	f		F		f	u	f		U		f
6	u	f		F		f	u	f		U		f
7	f	u	f		F		f	u	f		U	
8	f	u	f		F		f	u	f		U	
9	f	u	f		F		f	u	f		U	
10		f	u	f		F		f	u	f		U
11		f	u	f		F		f	u	f		U
12	U		f	u	f		F		f	u	f	
13	U		f	u	f		F		f	u	f	f
14		U		f	u	f		F		f	u	f
15		U		f	u	f		F		f	u	f
16	f		U		f	u	f		F		f	u
17	f		U		f	u	f		F		f	u
18	u	f		U		f	u	f		F		f
19	u	f		U		f	u	f		F		f
20	f	u	f		U		f	u	f		F	
21	f	u	f		U		f	u	f		F	
22		f	u	f		U		f	u	f		F
23		f	u	f		U		f	u	f		F
24		f	u	f		U		f	u	f		F
25	F		f	u	f		U		f	u	f	
26	F		f	u	f		U		f	u	f	f
27		F		f	u	f		U		f	u	f
28		F		f	u	f		U		f	u	f
29		F		f	u	f		U		f	u	f
30	f		F		f	u	f		U		f	u

December Moon Table

Date	Sign	Element	Nature	Phase
1 Tue 10:33 pm	Cancer	Water	Fruitful	3rd
2 Wed	Cancer	Water	Fruitful	3rd
3 Thu	Cancer	Water	Fruitful	3rd
4 Fri 7:53 am	Leo	Fire	Barren	3rd
5 Sat	Leo	Fire	Barren	3rd
6 Sun 2:46 pm	Virgo	Earth	Barren	3rd
7 Mon	Virgo	Earth	Barren	4th 7:37 pm
8 Tue 7:01 pm	Libra	Air	Semi-fruitful	4th
9 Wed	Libra	Air	Semi-fruitful	4th
10 Thu 8:59 pm	Scorpio	Water	Fruitful	4th
11 Fri	Scorpio	Water	Fruitful	4th
12 Sat 9:39 pm	Sagittarius	Fire	Barren	4th
13 Sun	Sagittarius	Fire	Barren	4th
14 Mon 10:35 pm	Capricorn	Earth	Semi-fruitful	New 11:17 am
15 Tue	Capricorn	Earth	Semi-fruitful	1st
16 Wed	Capricorn	Earth	Semi-fruitful	1st
17 Thu 1:27 am	Aquarius	Air	Barren	1st
18 Fri	Aquarius	Air	Barren	1st
19 Sat 7:39 am	Pisces	Water	Fruitful	1st
20 Sun	Pisces	Water	Fruitful	1st
21 Mon 5:32 pm	Aries	Fire	Barren	2nd 6:41 pm
22 Tue	Aries	Fire	Barren	2nd
23 Wed	Aries	Fire	Barren	2nd
24 Thu 5:55 am	Taurus	Earth	Semi-fruitful	2nd
25 Fri	Taurus	Earth	Semi-fruitful	2nd
26 Sat 6:33 pm	Gemini	Air	Barren	2nd
27 Sun	Gemini	Air	Barren	2nd
28 Mon	Gemini	Air	Barren	2nd
29 Tue 5:28 am	Cancer	Water	Fruitful	Full 10:28 pm
30 Wed	Cancer	Water	Fruitful	3rd

December Aspectarian/Favorable & Unfavorable Days

Date	Sun	Mercury	Venus	Mars	Jupiter	Saturn	Uranus	Neptune	Pluto
1									
2							X		
3			T	Q				T	O
4		T			O	O	Q		
5	T		Q	T					
6									
7	Q	Q						T	O
8			X		T	T			T
9		X							
10	X			O	Q	Q			Q
11							O		
12			C		X	X		T	X
13									
14	C	C		T				Q	
15							T		
16				Q				X	C
17			X		C	C	Q		
18			X						
19	X	X	Q					X	
20								C	
21	Q	Q			X	X			X
22			T						
23				C					Q
24	T	T			Q	Q	C		
25								X	
26					T	T			T
27									
28			O	X				Q	
29	O						X		
30		O						T	
31				Q	O	O			O

Date	Aries	Taurus	Gemini	Cancer	Leo	Virgo	Libra	Scorpio	Sagittarius	Capricorn	Aquarius	Pisces
1	f		F		f	u	f		U		f	u
2	u	f		F		f	u	f		U		f
3	u	f		F		f	u	f		U		f
4	u	f		F		f	u	f		U		f
5	f	u	f		F		f	u	f		U	
6	f	u	f		F		f	u	f		U	
7		f	u	f		F		f	u	f		U
8		f	u	f		F		f	u	f		U
9	U		f	u	f		F		f	u	f	
10	U		f	u	f		F		f	u	f	f
11		U		f	u	f		F		f	u	f
12		U		f	u	f		F		f	u	f
13	f		U		f	u	f		F		f	u
14	f		U		f	u	f		F		f	u
15	u	f		U		f	u	f		F		f
16	u	f		U		f	u	f		F		f
17	f	u	f		U		f	u	f		F	
18	f	u	f		U		f	u	f		F	
19	f	u	f		U		f	u	f		F	
20		f	u	f		U		f	u	f		F
21		f	u	f		U		f	u	f		F
22	F		f	u	f		U		f	u	f	
23	F		f	u	f		U		f	u	f	
24	F		f	u	f		U		f	u	f	u
25		F		f	u	f		U		f	u	f
26		F		f	u	f		U		f	u	f
27	f		F		f	u	f		U		f	u
28	f		F		f	u	f		U		f	u
29	f		F		f	u	f		U		f	u
30	u	f		F		f	u	f		U		f
31	u	f		F		f	u	f		U		f

2020 Retrograde Planets

Planet	Begin	Eastern	Pacific	End	Eastern	Pacific
Uranus	8/11/19	10:27 pm	7:27 pm	1/10/20	8:49 pm	5:49 pm
Mercury	2/16	7:54 pm	4:54 pm	3/9	11:49 pm	8:49 pm
Pluto	4/25	2:54 pm	11:54 am	10/4	9:32 am	6:32 am
Saturn	5/11		9:09 pm	9/28		10:11 pm
Saturn	5/12	12:09 am		9/29	1:11 am	
Venus	5/13		11:45 pm	6/24		11:48 pm
Venus	5/14	2:45 am		6/25	2:48 am	
Jupiter	5/14	10:32 am	7:32 am	9/12	8:41 pm	5:41 pm
Mercury	6/17		9:59 pm	7/12	4:26 am	1:26 am
Mercury	6/18	12:59 am		7/12	4:26 am	1:26 am
Neptune	6/22		9:31 pm	11/28	7:36 pm	4:36 pm
Neptune	6/23	12:31 am		11/28	7:36 pm	4:36 pm
Uranus	8/5	10:25 am	7:25 am	1/14/21	3:36 am	12:36 am
Mars	9/9	6:22 pm	3:22 pm	11/13	7:36 pm	4:36 pm
Mercury	10/13	9:05 pm	6:05 pm	11/3	12:50 pm	9:50 am

Eastern Time in plain type, Pacific Time in bold type

Egg-Setting Dates

To Have Eggs by this Date	Sign	Qtr.	Date to Set Eggs
Jan 4, 11:15 am–Jan 6, 9:11 pm	Taurus	2nd	Dec 14, 2019
Jan 9, 3:43 am–Jan 10, 2:21 pm	Cancer	2nd	Dec 19, 2019
Jan 26, 6:44 pm–Jan 29, 6:51 am	Pisces	1st	Jan 05, 2020
Jan 31, 7:28 am–Feb 3, 6:29 am	Taurus	1st	Jan 10
Feb 5, 2:03 pm–Feb 7, 5:45 pm	Cancer	2nd	Jan 15
Feb 23, 10:32 am–Feb 25, 1:47 pm	Pisces	1st	Feb 02
Feb 28, 2:30 am–Mar 1, 2:21 pm	Taurus	1st	Feb 07
Mar 3, 11:25 pm–Mar 6, 4:27 am	Cancer	2nd	Feb 11
Mar 26, 9:37 am–Mar 28, 9:38 pm	Taurus	1st	Mar 05
Mar 31, 7:43 am–Apr 2, 2:26 pm	Cancer	1st	Mar 10
Apr 6, 5:16 pm–Apr 7, 10:35 pm	Libra	2nd	Mar 16
Apr 22, 10:26 pm–Apr 25, 3:20 am	Taurus	1st	Apr 01
Apr 27, 1:28 pm–Apr 29, 9:06 pm	Cancer	1st	Apr 06
May 4, 3:09 am–May 6, 3:05 am	Libra	2nd	Apr 13
May 24, 7:09 pm–May 27, 2:33 am	Cancer	1st	May 03
May 31, 10:38 am–Jun 2, 12:06 pm	Libra	2nd	May 10
Jun 21, 2:41 am–Jun 23, 8:33 am	Cancer	1st	May 31
Jun 27, 4:16 pm–Jun 29, 6:48 pm	Libra	1st	Jun 06
Jul 20, 1:33 pm–Jul 20, 4:16 pm	Cancer	1st	Jun 29
Jul 24, 9:54 pm–Jul 27, 12:12 am	Libra	1st	Jul 03
Aug 21, 5:16 am–Aug 23, 6:16 am	Libra	1st	Jul 31
Sep 1, 5:34 am–Sep 2, 1:22 am	Pisces	2nd	Aug 11
Sep 17, 2:56 pm–Sep 19, 2:33 pm	Libra	1st	Aug 27
Sep 28, 11:34 am–Sep 30, 10:47 pm	Pisces	2nd	Sep 07
Oct 16, 3:31 pm–Oct 17, 1:05 am	Libra	1st	Sep 25
Oct 25, 5:18 pm–Oct 28, 4:45 am	Pisces	2nd	Oct 04
Oct 30, 5:19 pm–Oct 31, 10:49 am	Taurus	2nd	Oct 09
Nov 21, 11:06 pm–Nov 24, 10:05 am	Pisces	1st	Oct 31
Nov 26, 10:43 pm–Nov 29, 11:16 am	Taurus	2nd	Nov 05
Dec 19, 7:39 am–Dec 21, 5:32 pm	Pisces	1st	Nov 28
Dec 24, 5:55 am–Dec 26, 6:33 pm	Taurus	2nd	Dec 03
Dec 29, 5:28 am–Dec 29, 10:28 pm	Cancer	2nd	Dec 08

Dates to Hunt and Fish

Date	Quarter	Sign
Jan 9, 3:43 am–Jan 11, 7:16 am	2nd	Cancer
Jan 17, 1:20 pm–Jan 19, 5:41 pm	4th	Scorpio
Jan 26, 6:44 pm–Jan 29, 6:51 am	1st	Pisces
Feb 5, 2:03 pm–Feb 7, 5:45 pm	2nd	Cancer
Feb 13, 7:37 pm–Feb 15, 11:07 pm	3rd	Scorpio
Feb 23, 1:37 am–Feb 25, 1:47 pm	4th	Pisces
Mar 3, 11:25 pm–Mar 6, 4:27 am	2nd	Cancer
Mar 12, 5:28 am–Mar 14, 7:09 am	3rd	Scorpio
Mar 14, 7:09 am–Mar 16, 12:25 pm	3rd	Sagittarius
Mar 21, 8:33 am–Mar 23, 8:58 pm	4th	Pisces
Mar 31, 7:43 am–Apr 2, 2:26 pm	1st	Cancer
Apr 8, 4:17 pm–Apr 10, 4:35 pm	3rd	Scorpio
Apr 10, 4:35 pm–Apr 12, 8:05 pm	3rd	Sagittarius
Apr 17, 2:29 pm–Apr 20, 3:00 am	4th	Pisces
Apr 27, 1:28 pm–Apr 29, 9:06 pm	1st	Cancer
May 6, 3:05 am–May 8, 3:15 am	2nd	Scorpio
May 8, 3:15 am–May 10, 5:39 am	3rd	Sagittarius
May 14, 9:24 pm–May 17, 9:36 am	4th	Pisces
May 24, 7:09 pm–May 27, 2:33 am	1st	Cancer
Jun 2, 12:06 pm–Jun 4, 1:17 pm	2nd	Scorpio
Jun 4, 1:17 pm–Jun 6, 3:44 pm	2nd	Sagittarius
Jun 11, 5:32 am–Jun 13, 5:03 pm	3rd	Pisces
Jun 21, 2:02 am–Jun 23, 8:33 am	4th	Cancer
Jun 29, 6:48 pm–Jul 1, 9:21 pm	2nd	Scorpio
Jul 1, 9:21 pm–Jul 4, 12:48 am	2nd	Sagittarius
Jul 8, 2:13 pm–Jul 11, 1:06 am	3rd	Pisces
Jul 11, 1:06 am–Jul 13, 1:34 pm	3rd	Aries
Jul 18, 10:24 am–Jul 20, 4:16 pm	4th	Cancer
Jul 27, 12:12 am–Jul 29, 3:25 am	1st	Scorpio
Jul 29, 3:25 am–Jul 31, 7:58 am	2nd	Sagittarius
Aug 4, 10:28 pm–Aug 7, 9:05 am	3rd	Pisces
Aug 7, 9:05 am–Aug 9, 9:28 pm	3rd	Aries
Aug 14, 7:35 am–Aug 17, 1:38 am	4th	Cancer
Aug 23, 6:16 am–Aug 25, 8:49 am	1st	Scorpio
Sep 1, 5:34 am–Sep 3, 4:22 pm	2nd	Pisces
Sep 3, 4:22 pm–Sep 6, 4:43 am	3rd	Aries
Sep 11, 4:23 am–Sep 13, 11:32 am	4th	Cancer
Sep 19, 2:33 pm–Sep 21, 3:32 pm	1st	Scorpio
Sep 28, 11:34 am–Sep 30, 10:47 pm	2nd	Pisces
Sep 30, 10:47 pm–Oct 3, 11:12 am	2nd	Aries
Oct 8, 11:45 am–Oct 10, 8:24 pm	3rd	Cancer
Oct 17, 1:05 am–Oct 19, 12:43 pm	1st	Scorpio
Oct 25, 5:18 pm–Oct 28, 4:45 am	2nd	Pisces
Oct 28, 4:45 am–Oct 30, 5:19 pm	2nd	Aries
Nov 4, 4:45 pm–Nov 7, 2:18 am	3rd	Cancer
Nov 13, 11:19 am–Nov 15, 10:47 am	4th	Scorpio
Nov 21, 11:06 am–Nov 24, 10:05 am	1st	Pisces
Nov 24, 10:05 am–Nov 26, 10:43 pm	2nd	Aries
Dec 1, 10:33 pm–Dec 4, 7:53 am	3rd	Cancer
Dec 10, 8:59 pm–Dec 12, 9:39 pm	4th	Scorpio
Dec 19, 7:39 am–Dec 21, 5:32 pm	1st	Pisces
Dec 29, 5:28 am–Dec 31, 1:58 pm	2nd	Cancer

Dates to Destroy Weeds and Pests

Date	Sign	Qtr.
Jan 11 7:16 am–Jan 13 9:06 am	Leo	3rd
Jan 13 9:06 am–Jan 15 10:43 am	Virgo	3rd
Jan 19 5:41 pm–Jan 22 12:00 am	Sagittarius	4th
Jan 24 8:20 am–Jan 24 4:42 pm	Aquarius	4th
Feb 9 2:33 am–Feb 9 6:39 pm	Leo	3rd
Feb 9 6:39 pm–Feb 11 6:37 pm	Virgo	3rd
Feb 15 11:07 pm–Feb 18 5:37 am	Sagittarius	4th
Feb 20 2:42 pm–Feb 23 1:37 am	Aquarius	4th
Mar 9 1:48 pm–Mar 10 6:03 am	Virgo	3rd
Mar 14 7:09 am–Mar 16 5:34 am	Sagittarius	3rd
Mar 16 5:34 am–Mar 16 12:25 pm	Sagittarius	4th
Mar 18 9:16 pm–Mar 21 8:33 am	Aquarius	4th
Mar 23 8:58 pm–Mar 24 5:28 am	Aries	4th
Apr 10 4:35 am–Apr 12 8:05 pm	Sagittarius	3rd
Apr 15 3:37 am–Apr 17 2:29 pm	Aries	4th
Apr 20 3:00 am–Apr 22 3:36 pm	Aries	4th
May 8 3:15 am–May 10 5:39 am	Sagittarius	3rd
May 12 11:39 am–May 14 10:03 pm	Aquarius	4th
May 14 10:03 am–May 14 9:24 pm	Aquarius	4th
May 17 9:36 am–May 19 10:10 pm	Aries	4th
May 22 9:36 am–May 22 1:39 pm	Gemini	4th
Jun 5 3:12 pm–Jun 6 3:44 pm	Sagittarius	3rd
Jun 8 8:54 pm–Jun 11 5:32 am	Aquarius	3rd
Jun 13 5:03 pm–Jun 16 5:35 am	Aries	4th
Jun 18 5:00 pm–Jun 21 2:02 am	Gemini	4th
Jul 6 6:08 am–Jul 8 2:13 pm	Aquarius	3rd
Jul 11 1:06 am–Jul 12 7:29 pm	Aries	3rd
Jul 12 7:29 pm–Jul 13 1:34 pm	Aries	4th
Jul 16 1:19 am–Jul 18 10:24 am	Gemini	4th
Aug 3 11:59 am–Aug 4 10:28 pm	Aquarius	3rd
Aug 7 9:05 am–Aug 9 9:28 pm	Aries	3rd
Aug 12 9:46 am–Aug 14 7:35 pm	Gemini	4th
Aug 17 1:38 am–Aug 18 10:42 pm	Leo	4th
Sep 3 4:22 pm–Sep 6 4:43 am	Aries	3rd
Sep 8 5:28 pm–Sep 10 5:26 am	Gemini	3rd
Sep 10 5:26 am–Sep 11 4:23 am	Gemini	4th
Sep 13 11:32 am–Sep 15 2:37 pm	Leo	4th
Sep 15 2:37 pm–Sep 17 7:00 am	Virgo	4th
Oct 1 5:05 pm–Oct 3 11:12 am	Aries	3rd
Oct 6 12:03 am–Oct 8 11:45 am	Gemini	3rd
Oct 10 8:24 pm–Oct 13 12:56 am	Leo	4th
Oct 13 12:56 am–Oct 15 1:54 am	Virgo	4th
Nov 2 5:00 am–Nov 4 4:45 pm	Gemini	3rd
Nov 7 2:18 am–Nov 8 8:46 am	Leo	3rd
Nov 8 8:46 am–Nov 9 8:30 am	Leo	4th
Nov 9 8:30 am–Nov 11 11:09 am	Virgo	4th
Nov 30 4:30 am–Dec 1 10:33 pm	Gemini	3rd
Dec 4 7:53 am–Dec 6 2:46 pm	Leo	3rd
Dec 6 2:46 pm–Dec 7 7:37 pm	Virgo	3rd
Dec 7 7:37 pm–Dec 8 7:01 pm	Virgo	4th
Dec 12 9:39 pm–Dec 14 11:17 am	Sagittarius	4th

Time Zone Map

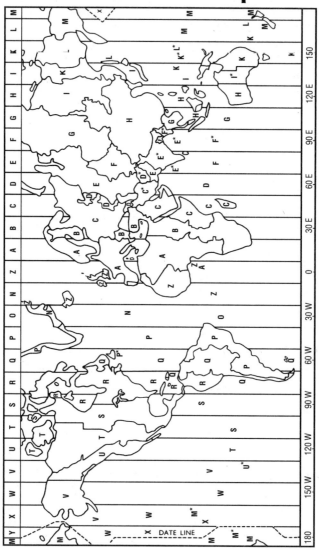

Time Zone Conversions

(R) EST—Used in book
(S) CST—Subtract 1 hour
(T) MST—Subtract 2 hours
(U) PST—Subtract 3 hours
(V) Subtract 4 hours
(V*) Subtract 4½ hours
(U*) Subtract 3½ hours
(W) Subtract 5 hours
(X) Subtract 6 hours
(Y) Subtract 7 hours
(Q) Add 1 hour
(P) Add 2 hours
(P*) Add 2½ hours
(O) Add 3 hours
(N) Add 4 hours
(Z) Add 5 hours
(A) Add 6 hours
(B) Add 7 hours
(C) Add 8 hours
(C*) Add 8½ hours

(D) Add 9 hours
(D*) Add 9½ hours
(E) Add 10 hours
(E*) Add 10½ hours
(F) Add 11 hours
(F*) Add 11½ hours
(G) Add 12 hours
(H) Add 13 hours
(I) Add 14 hours
(I*) Add 14½ hours
(K) Add 15 hours
(K*) Add 15½ hours
(L) Add 16 hours
(L*) Add 16½ hours
(M) Add 17 hours
(M*) Add 18 hours
(P*) Add 2½ hours

Important!

All times given in the *Moon Sign Book* are set in Eastern Time. The conversions shown here are for standard times only. Use the time zone conversions map and table to calculate the difference in your time zone. You must make the adjustment for your time zone and adjust for Daylight Saving Time where applicable.

Weather, Economic & Lunar Forecasts

Forecasting the Weather

by Kris Brandt Riske

Astrometeorology—astrological weather forecasting—reveals seasonal and weekly weather trends based on the cardinal ingresses (Summer and Winter Solstices, and Spring and Autumn Equinoxes) and the four monthly lunar phases. The planetary alignments and the longitudes and latitudes they influence have the strongest effect, but the zodiacal signs are also involved in creating weather conditions.

The components of a thunderstorm, for example, are heat, wind, and electricity. A Mars-Jupiter configuration generates the necessary heat and Mercury adds wind and electricity. A severe thunderstorm, and those that produce tornados, usually involve Mercury, Mars, Uranus, or Neptune. The zodiacal signs add their energy to the planetary mix to increase or decrease the chance for weather phenomena and their severity.

In general, the fire signs (Aries, Leo, Sagittarius) indicate heat and dryness, both of which peak when Mars, the planet with a similar nature, is in these signs. Water signs (Cancer, Scorpio, Pisces) are conducive to precipitation, and air signs (Gemini, Libra, Aquarius) are conducive to cool temperatures and wind. Earth signs (Taurus, Virgo, Capricorn) vary from wet to dry, heat to cold. The signs and their prevailing weather conditions are listed here:

Aries: Heat, dry, wind
Taurus: Moderate temperatures, precipitation
Gemini: Cool temperatures, wind, dry
Cancer: Cold, steady precipitation
Leo: Heat, dry, lightning
Virgo: Cold, dry, windy
Libra: Cool, windy, fair
Scorpio: Extreme temperatures, abundant precipitation
Sagittarius: Warm, fair, moderate wind
Capricorn: Cold, wet, damp
Aquarius: Cold, dry, high pressure, lightning
Pisces: Wet, cool, low pressure

Take note of the Moon's sign at each lunar phase. It reveals the prevailing weather conditions for the next six to seven days. The same is true of Mercury and Venus. These two influential weather planets transit the entire zodiac each year, unless retrograde patterns add their influence.

Planetary Influences

People relied on astrology to forecast weather for thousands of years. They were able to predict drought, floods, and temperature variations through interpreting planetary alignments. In recent years there has been a renewed interest in astrometeorology.

A weather forecast can be composed for any date—tomorrow, next week, or a thousand years in the future. According to astrometeorology, each planet governs certain weather phenomena. When certain planets are aligned with other planets, weather—precipitation, cloudy or clear skies, tornados, hurricanes, and other conditions—are generated.

Sun and Moon

The Sun governs the constitution of the weather and, like the Moon, it serves as a trigger for other planetary configurations that result in weather events. When the Sun is prominent in a cardinal ingress or lunar phase chart, the area is often warm and sunny. The Moon can bring or withhold moisture, depending upon its sign placement.

Mercury

Mercury is also a triggering planet, but its main influence is wind direction and velocity. In its stationary periods, Mercury reflects high winds, and its influence is always prominent in major weather events, such as hurricanes and tornadoes, when it tends to lower the temperature.

Venus

Venus governs moisture, clouds, and humidity. It brings warming trends that produce sunny, pleasant weather if in positive aspect to other planets. In some signs—Libra, Virgo, Gemini, Sagittarius—Venus is drier. It is at its wettest when placed in Cancer, Scorpio, Pisces, or Taurus.

Mars

Mars is associated with heat, drought, and wind, and can raise the temperature to record-setting levels when in a fire sign (Aries, Leo, Sagittarius). Mars is also the planet that provides the spark that generates thunderstorms and is prominent in tornado and hurricane configurations.

Jupiter

Jupiter, a fair-weather planet, tends toward higher temperatures when in Aries, Leo, or Sagittarius. It is associated with high-pressure systems and is a contributing factor at times to dryness. Storms are often amplified by Jupiter.

Saturn

Saturn is associated with low-pressure systems, cloudy to overcast skies, and excessive precipitation. Temperatures drop when Saturn is involved. Major winter storms always have a strong Saturn influence, as do storms that produce a slow, steady downpour for hours or days.

Uranus

Like Jupiter, Uranus indicates high-pressure systems. It reflects descending cold air and, when prominent, is responsible for a jet stream that extends far south. Uranus can bring drought in winter, and it is involved in thunderstorms, tornados, and hurricanes.

Neptune

Neptune is the wettest planet. It signals low-pressure systems and is dominant when hurricanes are in the forecast. When Neptune is strongly placed, flood danger is high. It's often associated with winter thaws. Temperatures, humidity, and cloudiness increase where Neptune influences weather.

Pluto

Pluto is associated with weather extremes, as well as unseasonably warm temperatures and drought. It reflects the high winds involved in major hurricanes, storms, and tornados.

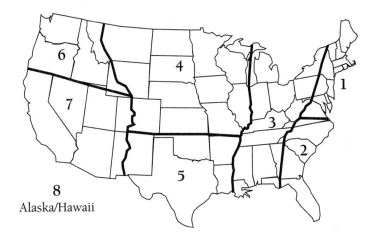

Weather Forecast for 2020

by Kris Brandt Riske

Winter

Winter 2020 in Zone 1 will be seasonal in temperature and precipitation. The westernmost part of the zone, however, will be cooler and windy. Zone 2 will experience many cool, windy, and cloudy days with above-average precipitation in southern parts of the zone.

Much of Zone 3 will experience a higher level of precipitation, both in frequency and quantity. The most southern areas of the zone will, however, see precipitation levels that are more seasonal. Eastern and northern areas, in particular, will see higher levels. This zone will be generally seasonal in temperature with variably cloudy skies.

Zones 4 and 5, the central states in the continental United States, will vary somewhat in weather from west to east. The eastern areas will be mostly partly cloudy to cloudy with temperatures seasonal to below. Storms will be frequent in the central areas of these zones with very cold temperatures at times and high winds. Western areas will also see high winds but more seasonal temperatures and precipitation.

Cold temperatures will be frequent in the northwest—Zone 6—along with above average precipitation and overcast skies. In Zone 7, temperatures will range from seasonal to above and dryness, even drought, will be the norm. Windy conditions will prevail here as well.

In Zone 8, Alaska can expect generally seasonal temperatures and precipitation, but there will also be weeks of very cold temperatures. Hawaii will tend to sunny skies and temperatures ranging from seasonal to above. Precipitation will be seasonal to below.

2nd Quarter Moon, January 1–9

Zone 1: The zone is windy and cool.

Zone 2: Northern areas are fair to partly cloudy, central and southern skies are partly cloudy to cloudy with precipitation, and temperatures are seasonal to below.

Zone 3: The zone is seasonal with precipitation central and east, skies are partly cloudy to cloudy, and temperatures are seasonal to below.

Zone 4: Cloudy skies dominate, temperatures are seasonal, abundant precipitation is possible in western and central areas, eastern areas are mostly fair, and the zone is windy.

Zone 5: Cloudy skies accompany temperatures seasonal to below, and abundant precipitation is possible central and east.

Zone 6: Central and western areas are windy, the zone is variably cloudy with more cloudiness central and east, eastern areas are stormy with high winds, and much of the zone sees precipitation.

Zone 7: Western and central areas are windy with precipitation, eastern skies are cloudy with scattered precipitation, and temperatures are seasonal.

Zone 8: In Alaska, cloudy skies bring precipitation to western areas which then moves into central parts of the zone; eastern areas are cold; and central and western areas are seasonal and windy. Hawaii is cloudy and seasonal with scattered precipitation.

Full Moon, January 10–16

Zone 1: The zone is variably cloudy with temperatures ranging from seasonal to above; northern areas see precipitation.

Zone 2: Central parts of the zone are windy with precipitation, skies are variably cloudy, and temperatures are seasonal to above.

Zone 3: Much of the zone is cloudy, northern areas are windy, temperatures are seasonal to above, and northern areas see scattered precipitation.

Zone 4: Scattered precipitation west and central moves into eastern areas of the zone under variably cloudy skies and temperatures seasonal to below; eastern areas are cold.

Zone 5: Western parts of the zone are cloudy with scattered precipitation, eastern areas are windy, and temperatures are seasonal to above.

Zone 6: Precipitation in western areas moves into central parts of the zone, some abundant, much of the zone is cloudy, and the entire zone is windy.

Zone 7: Skies are variably cloudy and windy, western and central areas see precipitation, some abundant, and temperatures are seasonal.

Zone 8: Western Alaska sees precipitation; central areas are windy; eastern parts of the zone see precipitation, some abundant; and temperatures are seasonal. Much of Hawaii sees showers and is variably cloudy and seasonal.

4th Quarter Moon, January 17–23

Zone 1: Northern areas see precipitation, and the zone is variably cloudy and seasonal.

Zone 2: Temperatures are seasonal, skies are partly cloudy, and winds in northern areas move into central and southern areas, bringing scattered precipitation and a chance for thunderstorms central and south.

Zone 3: The zone is seasonal and windy with variably cloudy skies and showers.

Zone 4: Western areas are cloudy and windy, with weather moving into central parts of the zone under variably cloudy skies and seasonal to below seasonal temperatures. Western and central areas see high levels of precipitation.

Zone 5: Temperatures are seasonal to below, skies are windy and cloudy, and much of the zone sees scattered precipitation.

Zone 6: Skies are variably cloudy and eastern areas are windy with more cloudiness and precipitation.

Zone 7: Fair to partly cloudy skies accompany seasonal temperatures. Eastern areas see more cloudiness and precipitation.

Zone 8: Central Alaska sees precipitation that moves into eastern areas, some abundant, and temperatures are seasonal. Central and eastern Hawaii see precipitation, and the state is variably cloudy, seasonal, and humid.

New Moon, January 24–31

Zone 1: Temperatures are seasonal to below and the zone is cloudy and windy with precipitation.

Zone 2: Northern areas see precipitation and the zone is variably cloudy and windy with temperatures seasonal to below.

Zone 3: Much of the zone is windy, seasonal, and fair to partly cloudy with scattered precipitation west and precipitation east.

Zone 4: Precipitation west moves across the zone as the week unfolds, with abundant downfall in central areas and possible flooding; skies are partly cloudy to cloudy and windy.

Zone 5: Abundant precipitation west and central and temperatures seasonal to above could result in thawing and flooding; the zone is also very windy.

Zone 6: Fair to partly cloudy skies are windy and temperatures are seasonal.

Zone 7: The zone is mostly fair with increasing cloudiness, wind, and precipitation as the week unfolds.

Zone 8: Alaska is windy and cloudy in central areas, mostly fair west and east, and seasonal to below. Hawaii's eastern skies are cloudy and windy, and temperatures are seasonal to below.

2nd Quarter Moon, February 1–7

Zone 1: Precipitation in southern areas moves into northern parts of the zone. Some downfall is heavy with windy, stormy conditions, and skies are partly cloudy to cloudy.

Zone 2: Northern areas are cloudy and see precipitation. Central and southern areas see abundant precipitation with thunderstorms and possibly tornados; conditions are windy with seasonal temperatures.

Zone 3: Western and central areas are cloudy. Central and eastern areas could see abundant downfall resulting in flooding, as well as thunderstorms and possibly tornados, and temperatures range from seasonal to above.

Zone 4: Central parts of the zone are windy with a chance for precipitation, eastern areas are cloudy, and temperatures are seasonal to below.

Zone 5: Skies are fair to partly cloudy, temperatures are seasonal to below, and western and central areas are windy.

Zone 6: Central and eastern areas are partly cloudy to cloudy, western areas are stormy and windy, and temperatures are seasonal.

Zone 7: The zone is partly cloudy to cloudy and windy with seasonal temperatures.

Zone 8: In Alaska, precipitation west moves into central parts of the state and skies are partly cloudy to cloudy with seasonal temperatures. Hawaii's temperatures are seasonal, skies are variably cloudy, and western and central areas see precipitation.

Full Moon, February 8–14

Zone 1: The zone is variably cloudy and windy with temperatures seasonal to below, and northern areas see precipitation.

Zone 2: Windy skies and seasonal temperatures accompany scattered precipitation central and south.

Zone 3: Western areas are windy, temperatures are seasonal, thunderstorms and tornados are possible, and central parts of the zone see precipitation with fog in low-lying areas.

Zone 4: Temperatures are seasonal to below, skies are partly cloudy to cloudy and windy, and much of the zone sees precipitation.

Zone 5: Western parts of the zone see precipitation, eastern areas are windy, skies are variably cloudy, and temperatures are seasonal.

Zone 6: Much of the zone is cloudy with precipitation, which is abundant in western and central areas, and temperatures are seasonal.

Zone 7: Western and central areas are windy, eastern parts of the zone see precipitation, skies are variably cloudy, and temperatures are seasonal to above.

Zone 8: Western Alaska is windy, skies are partly cloudy to cloudy. Western and central parts of the zone see precipitation, and eastern areas see strong winds later in the week; temperatures are seasonal to below. Much of Hawaii sees precipitation under partly cloudy to cloudy skies and temperatures are seasonal to below.

4th Quarter Moon, February 15–22

Zone 1: The zone is windy and gusty and seasonal and skies are fair to partly cloudy.

Zone 2: Skies are very windy and fair to partly cloudy with scattered precipitation.

Zone 3: Windy and cold with precipitation east, skies are partly cloudy and zonal temperatures are seasonal to below.

Zone 4: The zone is mostly fair to partly cloudy and windy with temperatures seasonal to below. Stormy conditions are possible in the northeastern part of the zone.

Zone 5: Western skies are fair to partly cloudy, central and eastern parts of the zone are partly cloudy to cloudy with scattered precipitation, western and central areas are windy, and temperatures are seasonal to below.

Zone 6: Central areas are windy, eastern areas are windy with precipitation, skies are partly cloudy to cloudy with more cloudiness in central and eastern areas, and temperatures range from seasonal to below.

Zone 7: Eastern areas are cloudy with precipitation and the zone is windy with temperatures ranging from seasonal to above.

Zone 8: Western Alaska is windy, central areas see precipitation, and temperatures are seasonal. Hawaii is seasonal to above, western areas are windy, and eastern parts of the state see precipitation.

New Moon, February 23–March 1

Zone 1: Skies are windy and partly cloudy to cloudy and temperatures are seasonal to below.

Zone 2: The zone is windy with potential for stormy conditions, temperatures are seasonal to below, and thunderstorms with tornado potential are possible central and south.

Zone 3: Skies are cloudy and overcast across the zone with scattered precipitation. Stormy conditions are possible central and east, and temperatures are seasonal to below.

Zone 4: The zone is windy west, precipitation west and central moves into eastern areas, skies are cloudy in central and eastern areas, and temperatures are seasonal to below.

Zone 5: Western areas are windy, temperatures are seasonal to below, central and eastern areas see precipitation and storms, and skies are mostly cloudy.

Zone 6: Skies are fair to partly cloudy and windy, with more cloudiness east, and high winds. Temperatures are seasonal.

Zone 7: Skies are partly cloudy to cloudy, temperatures are seasonal to above, and eastern parts of the zone see scattered precipitation under windy skies.

Zone 8: Western and central parts of Alaska are windy; western areas are stormy; central and eastern areas are cloudy with precipitation, some abundant; and temperatures are seasonal to below. Hawaii is windy with temperatures ranging from seasonal to above.

2nd Quarter Moon, March 2–8

Zone 1: Temperatures range from seasonal to below, the zone is cloudy, and southern areas see precipitation.

Zone 2: The zone is cloudy with locally heavy precipitation and stormy conditions, and temperatures are seasonal to below.

Zone 3: Precipitation across the zone accompanies windy conditions, eastern areas are stormy, the zone is cloudy, and temperatures are seasonal.

Zone 4: The zone is seasonal and fair to partly cloudy west and central, cloudy east, and some areas are windy with precipitation, some locally heavy.

Zone 5: Skies are partly cloudy to cloudy and windy central with temperatures seasonal to below.

Zone 6: The zone is windy with temperatures seasonal to above and precipitation west and central.

Zone 7: Western coastal areas see scattered precipitation; precipitation in southern coastal areas moves into the central mountains; central and eastern areas are seasonal with fair to partly cloudy skies; and temperatures are seasonal to above.

Zone 8: Western and central parts of Alaska see precipitation, with some stormy conditions central, skies are variably cloudy, and temperatures are seasonal. Temperatures in Hawaii are seasonal to above, western areas are cloudy with thunderstorms and heavy precipitation, much of the state sees showers, and the state is partly cloudy to cloudy.

Full Moon, March 9–15

Zone 1: The zone is cloudy and seasonal with scattered precipitation.

Zone 2: Skies are variably cloudy, temperatures are seasonal, and much of the zone sees precipitation, some locally heavy.

Zone 3: The zone is very windy with scattered precipitation and seasonal temperatures; central areas see strong thunderstorms.

Zone 4: Windy conditions accompany seasonal temperatures, western areas are cooler as a front moves through, much of the zone sees precipitation, and skies are partly cloudy to cloudy.

Zone 5: The zone is partly cloudy with scattered precipitation and seasonal temperatures, and western areas could see abundant downfall.

Zone 6: Western and central areas see precipitation, with abundant downfall possible east. The entire zone is windy and temperatures are seasonal.

Zone 7: Skies are fair to partly cloudy with more cloudiness east, precipitation west, and wind across much of the zone; temperatures are seasonal.

Zone 8: Alaska is seasonal with variable cloudiness and scattered precipitation. Hawaii is windy with temperatures seasonal to above.

4th Quarter Moon, March 16–23

Zone 1: The zone has a chance for precipitation and temperatures are seasonal to above under partly cloudy skies.

Zone 2: Partly cloudy to cloudy skies accompany windy conditions and precipitation, temperatures are seasonal to below, and central and southern areas see strong thunderstorms with tornado potential.

Zone 3: The zone is windy with thunderstorms with tornado potential, temperatures are seasonal to below, and much of the zone sees precipitation.

Zone 4: Western areas are stormy, cloudy, and windy; precipitation moves east across the zone during the week; temperatures are seasonal to below; and central areas are cold.

Zone 5: Cloudy skies prevail across the zone, with precipitation central and east. Conditions are windy, temperatures are seasonal to below, and thunderstorms with tornados are possible.

Zone 6: Western areas are windy with precipitation, some abundant. Central and eastern areas also see abundant precipitation, skies are cloudy, and temperatures are seasonal to below.

Zone 7: Temperatures are seasonal to above, the zone is windy, and skies are fair to partly cloudy with more cloudiness east.

Zone 8: Alaska is windy with abundant precipitation east, windy west and into central areas with precipitation, variable clouds, and seasonal temperatures. Hawaii is windy west with abundant precipitation east, humid, and seasonal to above.

Spring 2020

Zone 1 residents will experience above-average precipitation and periods of warm temperatures, which could trigger melt runoff and flooding. Temperatures in the southern part of Zone 2 will see temperatures seasonal to below, along with precipitation levels that are average to above.

Zone 3 will see wet weather during the spring months, along with periods of abundant precipitation. Strong thunderstorms with tornados are possible. Partly cloudy to cloudy skies can be expected, and eastern areas will be especially cool, with the remainder of the zone more seasonal.

In Zones 4 and 5, skies will be partly cloudy to cloudy with heavy precipitation in western parts of the zone along with overcast skies. Temperatures will be seasonal in eastern areas but below seasonal, with cold spells, in western and central parts of the zone. These zones can expect some major storms.

High winds will be the norm in Zone 6, where temperatures will range from seasonal to above. Zone 7 will also see high winds and temperatures seasonal to above. Dryness, and even drought, could be an issue. Eastern areas of the zone, however, see more cloudiness and precipitation.

In Zone 8, temperatures will be seasonal to below in eastern Alaska, along with high winds and limited precipitation. Central areas of the state will see abundant precipitation, which could trigger flooding. Western parts of the state will be seasonal. Western Hawaii will see precipitation that ranges from seasonal to above, along with higher humidity and cloudiness. Much of the state will be seasonal in temperature and precipitation.

New Moon, March 24–31

Zone 1: The zone is partly cloudy to cloudy and seasonal with scattered precipitation and windy; conditions are stormy later in the week.

Zone 2: Thunderstorms, possibly with tornados and precipitation, occur across the zone, along with windy conditions, variably cloudy skies, and temperatures that range from seasonal to above.

Zone 3: Skies are partly cloudy to cloudy, central and eastern areas are windy with thunderstorms with tornado potential, and much of the zone sees precipitation.

Zone 4: Precipitation moves east across the Plains, skies are cloudy and windy, central and eastern areas are stormy, and temperatures are seasonal to below.

Zone 5: Western parts of the zone are windy with thunderstorms, central areas are cloudy with precipitation, eastern areas are stormy, and temperatures are seasonal to above.

Zone 6: The zone is cloudy with precipitation, western and central areas are windy, eastern areas see abundant precipitation and stormy conditions, and temperatures are seasonal to below.

Zone 7: Much of the zone is cloudy with precipitation, which could be abundant in eastern areas, skies are windy and stormy, and temperatures are seasonal to above but cooler north.

Zone 8: Central areas of Alaska are stormy with abundant precipitation, skies are variably cloudy, and temperatures are seasonal. Hawaii is humid and cloudy with temperatures seasonal to above, and central and eastern areas see abundant precipitation.

2nd Quarter Moon, April 1–6

Zone 1: The zone is seasonal with partly cloudy skies and scattered precipitation.

Zone 2: Temperatures are seasonal to above, thunderstorms with tornados are possible, and skies are fair to partly cloudy with more cloudiness central and south.

Zone 3: Abundant precipitation is possible in central and western areas, some locations see strong storms with tornado potential, skies are variably cloudy, and temperatures are seasonal to above.

Zone 4: Much of the zone is windy with precipitation, skies are variably cloudy, thunderstorms with tornados are possible, and temperatures are seasonal to above.

Zone 5: Temperatures are seasonal to above, central and eastern areas see precipitation, eastern areas are windy, and strong thunderstorms with tornados are possible.

Zone 6: The zone sees scattered precipitation east and west, temperatures are seasonal to above, and skies are variably cloudy, with more cloudiness east.

Zone 7: Eastern areas are cloudy with precipitation, temperatures are seasonal to above, stormy conditions are possible in southern coastal areas and central mountains with much cloudiness, and northern coastal areas and eastern mountains are fair to partly cloudy.

Zone 8: Central and eastern Alaska see precipitation, skies are variably cloudy, and temperatures are seasonal. Central and eastern parts of Hawaii see showers, temperatures are seasonal to below, and skies are fair to partly cloudy.

Full Moon, April 7–13

Zone 1: Skies are fair to partly cloudy and temperatures are seasonal to above.

Zone 2: Much of the zone sees precipitation and wind, temperatures are seasonal to above, and strong thunderstorms with tornados are possible.

Zone 3: Central and eastern areas are cloudy with precipitation, western areas are partly cloudy, and temperatures are seasonal to above.

Zone 4: Thunderstorms with tornados are possible west, which is windy and partly cloudy to cloudy, central and eastern areas are fair to partly cloudy, and temperatures are seasonal to above.

Zone 5: Western parts of the zone are cloudy and windy with precipitation, central and eastern areas are fair to partly cloudy, and temperatures are seasonal to above.

Zone 6: Much of the zone is windy and stormy under variably cloudy skies, eastern areas see abundant precipitation, and temperatures are seasonal to below.

Zone 7: Windy and stormy conditions prevail across much of the zone, with variable cloudiness and temperatures seasonal to above.

Zone 8: Western and central Alaska see precipitation, some abundant. Skies are variably cloudy and windy central, and temperatures are seasonal. Hawaii is windy with scattered precipitation and temperatures are seasonal to above.

4th Quarter Moon, April 14–21

Zone 1: The zone is windy and fair to partly cloudy with scattered precipitation and temperatures seasonal to above.

Zone 2: Temperatures are seasonal to above and skies are fair to partly cloudy.

Zone 3: Western skies are partly cloudy to cloudy with scattered precipitation, central and eastern areas are fair to partly cloudy, and the zone is seasonal to below.

Zone 4: The zone is windy with scattered precipitation and thunderstorms with possible tornados, skies are partly cloudy to cloudy, and temperatures are seasonal to below.

Zone 5: Skies are partly cloudy to cloudy and windy with thunderstorms with tornado potential. Temperatures are seasonal to below.

Zone 6: The zone sees precipitation under cloudy skies, with abundant downfall east, and temperatures are seasonal.

Zone 7: Much of the zone sees precipitation and cloudy skies with abundant downfall east. Western and central areas are windy, and temperatures seasonal to above.

Zone 8: Alaska is cloudy with precipitation west and central, stormy central, windy west, with temperatures seasonal to below. Hawaii is windy, stormy, and cloudy west with temperatures seasonal to above.

New Moon, April 22–29

Zone 1: Precipitation prevails across the zone, with southern areas seeing abundant downfall with flood potential. The zone is windy and partly cloudy to cloudy with temperatures seasonal to below.

Zone 2: The zone is cloudy and overcast with abundant precipitation and flood potential north; temperatures are seasonal to above.

Zone 3: Western areas of the zone are windy, central and eastern areas see precipitation, eastern areas see abundant precipitation with flood potential, skies are partly cloudy to cloudy to overcast, and temperatures are seasonal to below.

Zone 4: Much of the zone is windy, skies are fair to partly cloudy, and temperatures are seasonal to above.

Zone 5: Temperatures range from seasonal to above and skies are fair to partly cloudy and windy.

Zone 6: Temperatures are seasonal to above. Central and eastern areas see precipitation, some abundant, along with mostly cloudy skies; much of the zone is windy.

Zone 7: Western and central areas see precipitation, some abundant. Under overcast skies, eastern areas are windy, and temperatures are seasonal to above.

Zone 8: Alaska is windy central and east with precipitation central and seasonal temperatures. Central Hawaii is windy, and temperatures across the state are seasonal to above.

2nd Quarter Moon, April 30–May 6

Zone 1: The zone is windy with storms and possible tornados, skies are variably cloudy, and temperatures are seasonal to above.

Zone 2: Temperatures are seasonal and the zone is partly cloudy to cloudy.

Zone 3: Western and central areas are windy with precipitation, temperatures are seasonal, and skies are partly cloudy to cloudy.

Zone 4: Temperatures range from seasonal to above, precipitation and thunderstorms with tornado potential are possible across the zone, and skies are cloudy.

Zone 5: The zone is partly cloudy to cloudy with more cloudiness east, scattered precipitation, and temperatures seasonal to below.

Zone 6: Central and eastern areas of the zone are windy with a chance for precipitation and temperatures are seasonal to above.

Zone 7: Western and central parts of the zone are windy, skies are fair to partly cloudy, and temperatures are seasonal to above.

Zone 8: Western parts of Alaska see precipitation, skies are cloudy, and temperatures are seasonal. Hawaii is seasonal and fair to partly cloudy.

Full Moon, May 7–13

Zone 1: Southern areas of the zone are stormy, skies are partly cloudy to cloudy and windy, and temperatures are seasonal.

Zone 2: Much of the zone sees precipitation with potential for strong thunderstorms, conditions are windy, skies are partly cloudy to cloudy, and temperatures are seasonal to below.

Zone 3: The zone is windy with scattered thunderstorms and showers, temperatures are seasonal, and skies are partly cloudy to cloudy.

Zone 4: Thunderstorms and scattered showers accompany partly cloudy to cloudy skies and temperatures seasonal to above.

Zone 5: Western and central parts of the zone are fair to partly cloudy, eastern areas are cloudy, and temperatures are seasonal.

Zone 6: Western areas see abundant precipitation, skies are partly cloudy to cloudy, temperatures are seasonal, and eastern areas are windy.

Zone 7: Northern coastal areas see precipitation, eastern areas are very windy with scattered precipitation, and temperatures are seasonal to below.

Zone 8: Alaska is windy with precipitation central and west and seasonal temperatures. Hawaii is windy with showers and temperatures seasonal to above.

4th Quarter Moon, May 14–21

Zone 1: Cloudy skies yield precipitation across the zone, which is windy and seasonal.

Zone 2: Scattered showers, wind, and seasonal temperatures accompany variably cloudy skies and thunderstorms.

Zone 3: Western areas see scattered precipitation and the zone is seasonal and partly cloudy.

Zone 4: The zone is windy west and partly cloudy with thunderstorms; eastern areas see showers, some abundant; and the zone is seasonal to above.

Zone 5: Western skies are windy and fair to partly cloudy, eastern areas could see abundant downfall under variably cloudy skies, and temperatures are seasonal to above.

Zone 6: The zone is fair to partly cloudy and windy with temperatures seasonal to above.

Zone 7: Fair to partly cloudy skies dominate and temperatures are seasonal to above.

Zone 8: Alaska is windy, partly cloudy to cloudy, and seasonal with scattered showers. Hawaii's temperatures are seasonal; central and eastern areas are windy with scattered showers.

New Moon, May 22–28

Zone 1: Northern areas see showers, southern areas see abundant downfall, skies are cloudy, and temperatures are seasonal.

Zone 2: Thunderstorms with tornado potential accompany variably cloudy and windy skies and temperatures are seasonal to above.

Zone 3: The zone is windy, with thunderstorms with tornado potential and temperatures that are seasonal to above.

Zone 4: Temperatures are seasonal to above, conditions are humid, skies are variably cloudy, and the zone sees scattered showers.

Zone 5: Temperatures range from seasonal to above, skies are partly cloudy, and conditions are humid.

Zone 6: Western and central parts of the zone are windy and stormy and much of the zone sees showers and thunderstorms; temperatures are seasonal and skies are variably cloudy.

Zone 7: Western and central areas are cloudy with scattered precipitation; eastern areas are fair to partly cloudy with a chance for showers and thunderstorms.

Zone 8: Western and central parts of Alaska see precipitation, some abundant with potential for flooding, high winds, and seasonal temperatures. Hawaii is humid and variably cloudy with temperatures seasonal to above and abundant precipitation in central areas.

2nd Quarter Moon, May 29–June 4

Zone 1: The zone is windy, humid, seasonal, and fair to partly cloudy.

Zone 2: Variably cloudy skies accompany windy conditions, scattered thunderstorms, and temperatures seasonal to above.

Zone 3: The zone is cloudy with precipitation west and central, scattered thunderstorms east, temperatures seasonal to above, and windy conditions.

Zone 4: Western areas have a chance for precipitation and thunderstorms, skies across the zone are mostly cloudy, central and eastern areas see precipitation, and temperatures are seasonal to above.

Zone 5: Western and central skies are fair to partly cloudy and windy, eastern areas are cloudy with strong winds, showers, and thunderstorms with tornados; temperatures are seasonal to above.

Zone 6: Temperatures are seasonal to above, central and eastern areas are windy with showers and scattered thunderstorms, and skies are variably cloudy.

Zone 7: Western and central parts of the zone are windy, eastern areas are humid, skies are fair to partly cloudy, and temperatures are seasonal to above.

Zone 8: Alaska is variably cloudy and seasonal with scattered precipitation. Hawaii is fair to partly cloudy and seasonal.

Full Moon, June 5–12

Zone 1: Temperatures are seasonal, skies are partly cloudy and windy, and the zone is humid with scattered showers.

Zone 2: Partly cloudy skies and seasonal temperatures accompany windy conditions and scattered showers.

Zone 3: Skies are partly cloudy to cloudy, eastern areas are windy with showers, and temperatures are seasonal to above.

Zone 4: Western and central parts of the zone are stormy with temperatures seasonal to above; some precipitation is abundant and could cause flooding.

Zone 5: Abundant precipitation and thunderstorms could trigger flooding west and central, conditions are very windy, temperatures are seasonal to above, and skies are partly cloudy to cloudy.

Zone 6: Stormy conditions yield abundant precipitation, and skies are windy and cloudy with temperatures seasonal to above.

Zone 7: Skies are fair to partly cloudy, temperatures are seasonal to above, and eastern areas see showers and thunderstorms.

Zone 8: Much of Alaska is stormy with significant cloud cover and precipitation. Hawaii is cloudy and seasonal with showers and thunderstorms.

4th Quarter Moon, June 13–20

Zone 1: Skies are fair to partly cloudy, temperatures are seasonal, and the zone is windy with scattered showers.

Zone 2: Northern areas are windy with scattered showers, central and southern areas have a chance for precipitation, temperatures are seasonal to above, and skies are fair to partly cloudy.

Zone 3: The zone sees thunderstorms and showers, eastern areas are windy, temperatures are seasonal, and skies are fair to partly cloudy.

Zone 4: Thunderstorms, possibly with tornados, dominate in this zone, along with abundant precipitation, seasonal temperatures, windy conditions, and partly cloudy to cloudy skies.

Zone 5: Central and eastern areas see abundant precipitation, conditions are windy and humid, skies are partly cloudy to cloudy, and temperatures range from seasonal to above.

Zone 6: Windy conditions, seasonal temperatures, and partly cloudy to cloudy skies dominate in this zone, with precipitation in western and central areas.

Zone 7: The zone is windy with variably cloudiness, seasonal to above temperatures, and precipitation east.

Zone 8: Alaska is stormy with precipitation and high winds, partly cloudy to cloudy skies, and seasonal temperatures. Hawaii is windy with showers and temperatures seasonal to above.

Summer 2020

Summer 2020 in Zone 1 will be somewhat cool and cloudy with seasonal precipitation. Damp days will also be experienced—altogether, not ideal summer weather for many people. Zone 2, though, is likely to be much warmer than Zone 1, humid and steamy, with precipitation seasonal to below.

Weather in Zone 3 will be typical of most everyone's image of summer. Precipitation will be seasonal and at times above average. The Gulf states are especially prone to tropical storms and hurricanes.

Zones 4 and 5 will see thunderstorms with tornado potential in their central regions. Precipitation could be significant across much of these zones and the western areas will also experience cloudiness and cooler temperatures.

Zone 6 will have precipitation and cloudiness in central and eastern areas and windy conditions west. Storms will be prominent in areas of Zone 7. Eastern parts of the zone will see cloudiness and cooler temperatures overall.

In Zone 8, summer weather in Alaska will be windy and cool east, windy and stormy at times in central areas with abundant downfall, and seasonal west. Hawaii can expect periods of high temperatures and high humidity with seasonal precipitation throughout the summer months.

New Moon, June 21–27
Zone 1: Skies are windy and partly cloudy to cloudy, temperatures are seasonal to below, and showers dominate.
Zone 2: The zone sees precipitation with thunderstorms central and south, skies are partly cloudy to cloudy and windy, and temperatures are seasonal.
Zone 3: Temperatures are seasonal to below, skies are windy and

partly cloudy to cloudy with much cloudiness east, and eastern areas see precipitation, some locally heavy, and strong thunderstorms with tornado potential.

Zone 4: Temperatures are seasonal to above, and eastern areas are partly cloudy and windy with scattered showers.

Zone 5: The zone is windy and seasonal to above, with scattered thunderstorms west and partly cloudy skies.

Zone 6: Western areas see precipitation, central parts of the zone see scattered showers, eastern areas see precipitation, some abundant. Skies are partly cloudy to cloudy and temperatures are seasonal.

Zone 7: The zone has a chance for showers west and central, skies are partly cloudy to cloudy, temperatures are seasonal, and eastern areas are humid.

Zone 8: Western and central Alaska could see abundant precipitation and the state is windy. In Hawaii, thunderstorms, wind, and showers accompany temperatures seasonal to above.

2nd Quarter Moon, June 28–July 3

Zone 1: Precipitation across the zone is accompanied by windy conditions, temperatures seasonal to above, partly cloudy to cloudy skies, and abundant downfall in some locations.

Zone 2: The zone is partly cloudy to cloudy with precipitation, windy conditions, and temperatures seasonal to above.

Zone 3: Eastern areas see precipitation under fair to partly cloudy skies and temperatures seasonal to above.

Zone 4: Western parts of the zone see showers, central and eastern areas see scattered showers, temperatures are seasonal to above, and skies are partly cloudy.

Zone 5: Precipitation in western areas with cloudy skies and scattered showers across the zone, and temperatures are seasonal.

Zone 6: Western areas and much of the zone see precipitation, temperatures are seasonal, and skies are partly cloudy to cloudy and windy.

Zone 7: Precipitation in western and central areas is accompanied

by wind, eastern areas are humid with scattered precipitation, skies are partly cloudy to cloudy, and temperatures are seasonal.

Zone 8: Central Alaska sees precipitation and the state is windy and partly cloudy to cloudy with temperatures seasonal to below. Central parts of Hawaii see showers and wind, and temperatures are seasonal.

Full Moon, July 4–11

Zone 1: The zone is seasonal, windy, and partly cloudy to cloudy.

Zone 2: Windy conditions accompany temperatures seasonal to above with a chance for showers.

Zone 3: Eastern areas are windy and temperatures are seasonal to above.

Zone 4: Skies are fair to partly cloudy with scattered showers; temperatures are seasonal to above.

Zone 5: Temperatures are seasonal to above and skies are partly cloudy to cloudy with scattered showers.

Zone 6: Much of the zone is windy, skies are partly cloudy, and temperatures are seasonal to above.

Zone 7: Partly cloudy to cloudy and windy skies accompany scattered showers and thunderstorms, and temperatures are seasonal to above.

Zone 8: Alaska is cloudy with precipitation central and east and seasonal temperatures. Hawaii's temperatures are seasonal to above and skies are partly cloudy with showers.

4th Quarter Moon, July 12–19

Zone 1: Temperatures are seasonal to above, under windy and partly cloudy to cloudy skies with scattered precipitation.

Zone 2: Northern parts of the zone are cloudy with showers, central and southern areas see showers, the zone is windy, and temperatures are seasonal to above.

Zone 3: Much of the zone sees scattered showers under fair to partly cloudy and windy skies, temperatures are seasonal to above, and central and southern areas are cloudy with thunderstorms.

Zone 4: Western areas see showers, central areas are windy with thunderstorms. Heavy precipitation is possible east, along with thunderstorms and tornados, with temperatures seasonal to above.

Zone 5: Temperatures are seasonal to above and the zone is windy with thunderstorms and showers and variably cloudy skies. Eastern areas see strong thunderstorms; central and eastern areas could experience abundant precipitation.

Zone 6: Skies are partly cloudy to cloudy, temperatures are seasonal to above, and much of the zone sees precipitation.

Zone 7: Western and central areas see showers, skies are partly cloudy to cloudy, eastern areas are humid, and temperatures are seasonal to above.

Zone 8: Western and central regions of Alaska are cloudy and windy with abundant precipitation possible central; temperatures are seasonal. Hawaii is seasonal, variably cloudy, and humid, with seasonal to above temperatures.

New Moon, July 20–26

Zone 1: The zone is cloudy with potential for abundant downfall, temperatures are seasonal to below, and a tropical storm or hurricane is possible.

Zone 2: Precipitation across the zone accompanies cloudy skies, high winds, temperatures seasonal to below, and a possible tropical storm or hurricane.

Zone 3: Temperatures are seasonal to above, western skies are partly cloudy to cloudy, central and eastern areas are windy with potential for abundant downfall.

Zone 4: Western areas are windy, central parts of the zone see thunderstorms and showers, eastern areas are fair to partly cloudy, western and central areas are partly cloudy to cloudy, and temperatures are seasonal to above.

Zone 5: Western and central parts of the zone are windy with a chance for thunderstorms and temperatures seasonal to above.

Zone 6: Temperatures are seasonal and western areas see showers under partly cloudy to cloudy skies.

Zone 7: Some areas to the west see abundant precipitation, western and central areas are partly cloudy to cloudy, and eastern areas are fair to partly cloudy.

Zone 8: Alaska is fair to partly cloudy, windy west, and seasonal. In Hawaii, temperatures are seasonal to above and skies are fair to partly cloudy.

2nd Quarter Moon, July 27–August 2

Zone 1: Skies are fair to partly cloudy and windy and temperatures are seasonal.

Zone 2: Temperatures are seasonal to above, skies are partly cloudy to cloudy and windy, and the zone sees showers and thunderstorms.

Zone 3: Skies are fair to partly cloudy and windy with more cloudiness east, and temperatures are seasonal to above.

Zone 4: Temperatures are seasonal to above and skies are fair to partly cloudy.

Zone 5: Western skies are cloudy, central and eastern skies are partly cloudy, central and eastern areas see scattered thunderstorms, temperatures are seasonal to above, and the zone is humid.

Zone 6: The zone is partly cloudy to cloudy and windy, with showers and thunderstorms; temperatures are seasonal.

Zone 7: Western parts of the zone are windy, central areas see scattered thunderstorms, temperatures are seasonal to above, eastern skies are partly cloudy to cloudy, and the zone is humid with scattered thunderstorms.

Zone 8: Eastern Alaska sees abundant precipitation with partly cloudy to cloudy skies; central and western parts of the state are windy and temperatures are seasonal. Hawaii sees showers and thunderstorms with abundant precipitation possible in central areas; temperatures are seasonal to above and the zone is humid.

Full Moon, August 3–10

Zone 1: The zone is cloudy, overcast, and gusty, possibly because of a tropical storm or hurricane, and temperatures are seasonal to below.

Zone 2: Temperatures are seasonal to below; northern areas are stormy; and the zone is windy, variably cloudy, and humid, with thunderstorms and precipitation, possibly because of a tropical storm or hurricane.

Zone 3: Temperatures are seasonal to below; central and eastern areas are stormy, windy, and gusty; and the zone sees thunderstorms, some strong with tornado potential.

Zone 4: Western parts of the zone are overcast with precipitation, central and eastern areas are mostly fair with scattered precipitation, and temperatures are seasonal.

Zone 5: Western areas see precipitation under cloudy skies, central and eastern areas are fair to partly cloudy, and temperatures are seasonal.

Zone 6: Much of the zone is cloudy with precipitation, eastern areas see locally heavy downfall, and temperatures are seasonal to above.

Zone 7: Western parts of the zone are cloudy with precipitation that then moves into central areas. Eastern areas are humid with thunderstorms and showers, some locally heavy. Temperatures are seasonal to above.

Zone 8: Alaska is windy west and central with scattered precipitation and temperatures seasonal to below. Hawaii is windy with scattered showers and thunderstorms and temperatures are seasonal to above.

4th Quarter Moon, August 11–17

Zone 1: The zone is windy and humid with thunderstorms, and temperatures are seasonal to below.

Zone 2: Windy skies accompany thunderstorms, humidity and temperatures are high, and central and southern areas have potential for abundant downfall.

Zone 3: Western skies are cloudy and the weather moves into central and eastern parts of the zone, bringing thunderstorms with tornado potential. Much of the zone is humid or damp from abundant downfall, and temperatures are seasonal to above.

Zone 4: Strong thunderstorms with tornado potential are active in western parts of the zone, moving into central and eastern areas; skies are overcast; much of the zone sees high winds and gusts; and temperatures are seasonal to above.

Zone 5: Skies are fair to partly cloudy, strong thunderstorms could trigger tornados, eastern areas are overcast, and central and eastern parts of the zone are windy with strong gusts.

Zone 6: The zone is partly cloudy to cloudy, windy, and seasonal, and central and eastern areas see showers.

Zone 7: Western and central parts of the zone are variably cloudy with precipitation, temperatures are seasonal to above, and eastern areas are windy.

Zone 8: Alaska is seasonal, partly cloudy to cloudy, and windy, with showers west moving into central areas. Hawaii is fair to partly cloudy and seasonal, with scattered showers.

New Moon, August 18–24

Zone 1: The zone is variably cloudy, temperatures are seasonal, winds are gusty, and thunderstorms with tornados are possible.

Zone 2: Skies are partly cloudy to cloudy, windy, and gusty. Central and southern areas see showers and thunderstorms, and humidity accompanies temperatures seasonal to above.

Zone 3: Western and central areas see precipitation, eastern areas are windy and humid with gusts under fair to partly cloudy skies, and temperatures are seasonal to above.

Zone 4: Abundant precipitation is possible in western areas, eastern areas are cloudy and windy with precipitation, and much of the zone is stormy with temperatures seasonal to below.

Zone 5: Western areas, which see abundant downfall, are windy with showers and thunderstorms that move into central parts of the zone; skies are cloudy, eastern skies are mostly fair, and temperatures are seasonal.

Zone 6: The zone is windy with scattered thunderstorms and showers, skies are partly cloudy, and temperatures are seasonal to above.

Zone 7: Western and central parts of the zone are windy, cloudy, and stormy. Eastern areas are partly cloudy to cloudy, and showers and strong thunderstorms are possible across the zone, which is humid and windy with seasonal temperatures.

Zone 8: Western Alaska is windy with showers, central and eastern areas see showers, skies are variably cloudy, and temperatures are seasonal. Eastern areas of Hawaii see showers and are windy; western and central areas see precipitation with gusty winds.

2nd Quarter Moon, August 25–September 1

Zone 1: Showers and scattered thunderstorms, some that yield abundant downfall, accompany windy and humid conditions and temperatures seasonal to above.

Zone 2: The zone is windy, partly cloudy to cloudy, and seasonal, with showers and thunderstorms.

Zone 3: Western areas are partly cloudy to cloudy with scattered showers, central areas are windy and gusty with thunderstorms and showers, western areas see scattered precipitation under partly cloudy skies, and temperatures are seasonal to above.

Zone 4: Skies are partly cloudy to cloudy with a chance for showers and temperatures are seasonal to above.

Zone 5: Partly cloudy skies accompany humidity and temperatures seasonal to above.

Zone 6: Windy, cloudy, and stormy conditions west move into central and eastern areas, abundant precipitation is possible central and east, and temperatures range from seasonal to above.

Zone 7: Western areas are windy and stormy, conditions that move into central parts of the zone, eastern areas see thunderstorms and variably cloudy skies, and temperatures are seasonal to above with humidity.

Zone 8: Alaska is windy west and central with temperatures seasonal to above. Hawaii's skies are fair to partly cloudy and the state is windy with temperatures seasonal to above.

Full Moon, September 2–9

Zone 1: The zone is seasonal and windy with scattered showers and thunderstorms.

Zone 2: Showers and thunderstorms across the zone—some with abundant downfall—accompany humidity and variably cloudy skies, with seasonal temperatures.

Zone 3: Eastern and central areas are cloudy with showers and thunderstorms, temperatures are seasonal, and skies are partly cloudy to cloudy.

Zone 4: Skies are partly cloudy to cloudy and windy and the zone sees showers and thunderstorms with temperatures that are seasonal to above.

Zone 5: Skies are partly cloudy to cloudy in central and eastern areas with scattered precipitation, mostly fair in western areas, and temperatures are seasonal.

Zone 6: Much of the zone sees showers and thunderstorms, western areas see heavy precipitation, skies are partly cloudy to cloudy, and temperatures are seasonal.

Zone 7: Northern coastal areas see showers that move into the central mountains, the zone is windy, southern coastal areas are windy, eastern areas see showers and thunderstorms, and temperatures are seasonal to above.

Zone 8: Alaska is windy and partly cloudy to cloudy with showers west. Hawaii is windy with temperatures seasonal to above and showers and thunderstorms.

4th Quarter Moon, September 10–16

Zone 1: Partly cloudy and windy skies yield scattered precipitation and temperatures are seasonal to above.

Zone 2: Temperatures are seasonal and the zone is partly cloudy and windy with scattered precipitation.

Zone 3: Western areas are windy with showers, skies are partly cloudy, conditions are humid, and temperatures are seasonal to above.

Zone 4: Skies are partly cloudy to cloudy with showers central and thunderstorms east, and temperatures are seasonal to below.

Zone 5: Precipitation central and east under partly cloudy to cloudy skies accompanies temperatures seasonal to below.

Zone 6: Skies are partly cloudy with scattered showers and temperatures seasonal to above.

Zone 7: The zone is windy with partly cloudy to cloudy skies and scattered showers; temperatures are seasonal to below.

Zone 8: Alaska is windy and stormy, and partly cloudy to cloudy, with temperatures seasonal to below. Hawaii is windy and partly cloudy to cloudy with scattered showers central and seasonal temperatures.

New Moon, September 17–22

Zone 1: The zone is windy and seasonal with showers south and fair to partly cloudy skies.

Zone 2: Skies are windy and partly cloudy to cloudy with abundant precipitation, thunderstorms, and humidity; temperatures are seasonal to below.

Zone 3: Partly cloudy skies and windy conditions accompany temperatures seasonal to below and abundant precipitation east.

Zone 4: The zone is windy and partly cloudy to cloudy with scattered precipitation and temperatures seasonal to above.

Zone 5: Strong winds in central and eastern areas accompany variably cloudy skies, showers, and thunderstorms; temperatures are seasonal to above.

Zone 6: Western and central parts of the zone see precipitation, skies are partly cloudy to cloudy, and temperatures are seasonal to below.

Zone 7: Skies are partly cloudy to cloudy, western and central parts of the zone see showers, much of the zone experiences strong winds, and temperatures are seasonal to below.

Zone 8: Eastern Alaska is very windy, the state sees scattered precipitation, and temperatures are seasonal to below. Scattered showers in western and central Hawaii accompany seasonal temperatures across the state.

Autumn 2020

Zone 1 will see an above average number of storms during the autumn months, as well as unseasonably cold temperatures. Precipitation levels will be average to above with some periods of substantial downfall. Zone 2 will be cooler north and warmer south, generally seasonal with dampness in northern coastal areas. Temperatures will be seasonal and interior locations will be warmer and dryer. High winds and stormy conditions will prevail.

In Zone 3, which will also experience temperatures that are

seasonal to below, strong thunderstorms with tornado potential will be seen throughout the zone, more commonly in southern areas. Temperatures will be seasonal to below.

In Zones 4 and 5, temperatures will range from seasonal to below and dryness will be the norm. Eastern areas will see more precipitation than the rest of the zone.

Western parts of Zone 6 will be windy and coastal areas will see abundant precipitation. Temperatures will be seasonal and precipitation seasonal to below. Zone 7 will be much the same as Zone 6, with temperatures ranging from seasonal to below. High winds will add to dryness in Zone 7.

In Zone 8, western and central Alaska will be windy and cold with precipitation levels seasonal to above, much cloudiness, and some major storms. Eastern parts of the state will be seasonal in temperature and precipitation levels will be average to below. Temperatures in Hawaii will be seasonal to below, and the state will see much cloudiness. Precipitation in western and central areas will be seasonal to above.

2nd Quarter Moon, September 23–30

Zone 1: Northern areas see abundant precipitation, southern areas see scattered showers, skies are partly cloudy to cloudy and windy, and temperatures are seasonal.

Zone 2: The zone is windy and humid, temperatures are seasonal to above, and the zone sees showers and strong thunderstorms with tornado potential.

Zone 3: Temperatures range from seasonal to above, the zone is humid, western areas are windy with scattered showers and thunderstorms that move into central and southern parts of the zone.

Zone 4: High winds in central and eastern parts of the zone accompany showers and strong thunderstorms with tornado potential, and temperatures seasonal to above.

Zone 5: Thunderstorms with tornado potential are possible, the

zone is windy, eastern areas are partly cloudy to cloudy, and temperatures are seasonal to above.

Zone 6: The zone is windy and mostly cloudy, much of the zone sees precipitation, some abundant, and temperatures are seasonal to above.

Zone 7: Western and central parts of the zone see precipitation, skies are partly cloudy to cloudy, eastern skies are fair, and temperatures are seasonal to above.

Zone 8: Alaska is variably cloudy, temperatures are seasonal to below, and precipitation west is abundant. Hawaii is partly cloudy to cloudy, with showers west and central, seasonal temperatures, and humid conditions.

Full Moon, October 1–8

Zone 1: The zone sees high winds, showers, and thunderstorms, some with abundant downfall north, and temperatures seasonal to above.

Zone 2: The zone is windy, stormy, and partly cloudy to cloudy with strong thunderstorms and temperatures seasonal to above.

Zone 3: Showers and thunderstorms across the zone accompany partly cloudy to cloudy skies, strong winds, and temperatures seasonal to above.

Zone 4: Skies are fair to partly cloudy and windy central and east, western areas are cloudy, eastern areas see showers and thunderstorms that could be strong with tornados.

Zone 5: Fair to partly cloudy skies are windy, with strong thunderstorms and showers across much of the zone.

Zone 6: Western skies are cloudy with strong winds, showers, and thunderstorms with tornado potential that move into central and eastern areas.

Zone 7: Skies are partly cloudy to cloudy and windy, northern coastal areas see showers that move into the central and eastern mountains, eastern areas are windy with showers and thunderstorms, and temperatures are seasonal to above.

Zone 8: Alaska is partly cloudy to cloudy, windy, and seasonal, with abundant precipitation and overcast skies central. Hawaii has seasonal to above temperatures and is windy with showers and partly cloudy to cloudy skies.

4th Quarter Moon, October 9–15

Zone 1: Skies are fair to partly cloudy, temperatures are seasonal, and southern areas are very windy with showers.

Zone 2: Northern areas are windy, skies are partly cloudy, central and southern parts of the zone are humid, temperatures are seasonal, and thunderstorms with tornado potential are likely.

Zone 3: Much of the zone sees showers, skies are partly cloudy to cloudy, western skies are overcast, temperatures are seasonal, and the zone is windy with thunderstorms, possibly with tornados.

Zone 4: Seasonal temperatures, partly cloudy to cloudy skies, showers and thunderstorms central and east accompany very windy and stormy conditions, and temperatures are seasonal to below.

Zone 5: Partly cloudy to cloudy and windy skies yield scattered showers and thunderstorms with tornado potential under temperatures seasonal to above.

Zone 6: The zone is windy with partly cloudy to cloudy skies and scattered precipitation; temperatures are seasonal to above.

Zone 7: Northern coastal areas are windy with precipitation, skies are fair to partly cloudy, and temperatures are seasonal to above.

Zone 8: Alaska is seasonal and partly cloudy to cloudy with precipitation east. Hawaii is windy, partly cloudy, and seasonal to below.

New Moon, October 16–22

Zone 1: The zone is cloudy and windy with precipitation, stormy conditions south, and seasonal temperatures.

Zone 2: Northern areas are windy with thunderstorms, seasonal temperatures, partly cloudy to cloudy skies, and scattered showers.

Zone 3: Showers and scattered thunderstorms accompany partly cloudy to cloudy and windy skies and seasonal temperatures.

Zone 4: Thunderstorms with tornado potential are possible across the zone, which is windy with partly cloudy to cloudy skies and temperatures seasonal to above; central and eastern areas see showers.

Zone 5: Temperatures are seasonal to above and the zone is windy and partly cloudy to cloudy with thunderstorms, while eastern areas see abundant downfall.

Zone 6: Showers across the zone, some bringing abundant downfall, accompany partly cloudy to cloudy skies and temperatures seasonal to below.

Zone 7: Temperatures are seasonal to above, northern coastal areas are windy with showers, central parts of the zone see thunderstorms, and eastern areas are cloudy and cool with showers.

Zone 8: Alaska is seasonal to below, skies are windy and partly cloudy to cloudy, and eastern areas see abundant precipitation. In Hawaii, partly cloudy to cloudy skies bring thunderstorms and abundant precipitation to eastern areas.

2nd Quarter Moon, October 23–30

Zone 1: Partly cloudy to cloudy and windy skies accompany strong thunderstorms and temperatures seasonal to above.

Zone 2: The zone is windy with scattered thunderstorms, temperatures seasonal to above, and variable cloudiness.

Zone 3: Skies are partly cloudy and windy with scattered precipitation north, central and southern areas see strong thunderstorms with tornado potential and high winds, and temperatures are seasonal.

Zone 4: Temperatures are seasonal to below, skies are partly cloudy to cloudy, and eastern areas see precipitation, some abundant.

Zone 5: Western parts of the zone see some abundant precipitation, skies are windy, central areas see strong thunderstorms, and temperatures are seasonal to below.

Zone 6: Western areas are windy with thunderstorms, central areas see precipitation, skies are partly cloudy to cloudy, and temperatures are seasonal to above.

Zone 7: Western and central areas are windy with showers and thunderstorms, skies are partly cloudy to cloudy, temperatures are seasonal to above, and eastern areas see scattered showers.

Zone 8: Alaska is windy and seasonal with partly cloudy to cloudy skies and scattered precipitation. Hawaii's temperatures are seasonal to above and humid with scattered showers and thunderstorms.

Full Moon, October 31–November 7

Zone 1: The zone is seasonally windy with partly cloudy to cloudy skies and precipitation south.

Zone 2: Much of the zone sees showers, some with abundant precipitation, skies are breezy and humid, and temperatures are seasonal to above.

Zone 3: Temperatures are seasonal to below, skies partly cloudy to cloudy, and much of the zone has potential for abundant downfall.

Zone 4: Scattered precipitation across much of the zone with abundant downfall east and windy conditions accompanies partly cloudy to cloudy skies and seasonal temperatures.

Zone 5: The zone sees variably cloudy skies and seasonal temperatures with scattered showers and thunderstorms.

Zone 6: Temperatures are seasonal, skies are partly cloudy to cloudy, and precipitation falls west, some abundant, and scattered central and east.

Zone 7: Northern coastal areas see scattered precipitation, central and eastern areas are mostly fair to partly cloudy.

Zone 8: Alaska is windy and stormy central and into eastern areas; temperatures are seasonal to below. Hawaii sees scattered thunderstorms and showers, skies are partly cloudy and windy, and temperatures are seasonal to above.

4th Quarter Moon, November 8–14

Zone 1: The zone is windy and seasonal with scattered precipitation.

Zone 2: Temperatures are seasonal to above and the zone is windy with scattered showers and thunderstorms with potential for abundant downfall central and south.

Zone 3: Scattered showers and thunderstorms accompany windy, humid, and damp conditions. Temperatures are seasonal to above, but cooler west, with variable clouds and more cloudiness east.

Zone 4: Western areas are windy with scattered showers and thunderstorms, partly cloudy to cloudy skies with more cloudiness east, and seasonal temperatures.

Zone 5: Scattered showers and thunderstorms accompany seasonal temperatures and partly cloudy to cloudy and windy skies with more cloudiness and gusts east.

Zone 6: Much of the zone is stormy and windy, with abundant precipitation possible central and east and seasonal temperatures.

Zone 7: Temperatures are seasonal, skies are partly cloudy to cloudy, and the zone has a chance for showers.

Zone 8: Alaska is fair to partly cloudy, seasonal to below, and windy and stormy east. Temperatures in Hawaii are seasonal to above, with a chance for showers; skies are fair to partly cloudy.

New Moon, November 15–20

Zone 1: Abundant downfall results from stormy conditions and cloudy skies north, southern areas are partly cloudy with scattered precipitation, and temperatures are seasonal to below.

Zone 2: Skies are partly cloudy and windy with scattered precipitation, temperatures are seasonal to above, and southern areas are windy and humid.

Zone 3: Fair to partly cloudy skies are windy with scattered thunderstorms central and east, and seasonal temperatures.

Zone 4: Skies are partly cloudy to cloudy with scattered precipitation, temperatures are seasonal to below, and central parts of the zone are stormy, with abundant downfall in some areas.

Zone 5: Skies are partly cloudy to cloudy and windy with precipitation and temperatures seasonal to below.

Zone 6: Much of the zone sees precipitation, some abundant, and skies are windy and variably cloudy with temperatures seasonal to below.

Zone 7: Western areas are windy with precipitation, central parts of the zone see scattered showers, eastern areas are windy and stormy with abundant precipitation, skies are partly cloudy to cloudy, and temperatures are seasonal.

Zone 8: Eastern Alaska is windy central areas see precipitation, temperatures are seasonal, and skies are partly cloudy to cloudy. Hawaii is variably cloudy with showers across much of the state.

2nd Quarter Moon, November 21–29

Zone 1: Skies are partly cloudy to cloudy and windy with scattered precipitation; temperatures are seasonal.

Zone 2: Northern and central areas see scattered precipitation, skies are variably cloudy to cloudy, southern areas see thunderstorms, and temperatures are seasonal to above.

Zone 3: The zone is very windy and partly cloudy to cloudy with thunderstorms and temperatures seasonal to above.

Zone 4: Central areas are stormy with precipitation and temperatures seasonal to below; skies are partly cloudy to cloudy.

Zone 5: Western and central areas see precipitation that moves into eastern areas later in the week, skies are partly cloudy to cloudy and windy, and temperatures are seasonal.

Zone 6: Much of the zone sees precipitation, some abundant in central and eastern areas, with variable cloudiness and seasonal temperatures.

Zone 7: Variable clouds and seasonal temperatures accompany precipitation across the zone.

Zone 8: Eastern areas of Alaska see abundant precipitation, temperatures are seasonal, and skies are partly cloudy to cloudy. Hawaii is fair to partly cloudy with scattered showers and temperatures seasonal to above.

Full Moon, November 30–December 6

Zone 1: Precipitation south moves into northern parts of the zone as the week progresses, skies are partly cloudy to cloudy, and temperatures are seasonal to below.

Zone 2: Much of the zone sees precipitation under windy and stormy conditions with temperatures seasonal to below.

Zone 3: The zone is cloudy and windy with scattered precipitation west and central and precipitation east, some abundant; temperatures are seasonal.

Zone 4: Much of the zone sees scattered precipitation under windy and partly cloudy to cloudy skies, central and western areas see high winds with precipitation, and temperatures are seasonal to below.

Zone 5: The zone is very windy and stormy with variable cloudiness and temperatures seasonal to below.

Zone 6: Temperatures are seasonal to below and stormy conditions accompany wind and variable cloudiness.

Zone 7: Skies are fair to partly cloudy west and central, eastern areas see precipitation with partly cloudy to cloudy skies, and temperatures are seasonal to below.

Zone 8: Alaska is windy and cloudy with precipitation and temperatures seasonal to below. Hawaii is windy and variably cloudy with showers and seasonal temperatures.

4th Quarter Moon, December 7–13

Zone 1: The zone is cloudy and windy with precipitation south, some abundant.

Zone 2: Central and southern areas see precipitation, which is scattered in northern areas, skies are windy and partly cloudy to cloudy, southern areas see thunderstorms, and temperatures are seasonal to above.

Zone 3: Partly cloudy to cloudy skies accompany precipitation central and east, which are windy with temperatures seasonal and above.

Zone 4: Western and central parts of the zone are windy, central areas see precipitation, some abundant, skies are partly cloudy to cloudy, and temperatures are seasonal.

Zone 5: Skies are partly cloudy to cloudy and windy with scattered precipitation and temperatures seasonal to below.

Zone 6: Precipitation west and central accompanies seasonal temperatures and partly cloudy to cloudy skies.

Zone 7: Western areas see precipitation that moves into central parts of the zone, eastern skies are windy and fair to partly cloudy, and temperatures are seasonal to below.

Zone 8: Alaska sees scattered precipitation, central and western areas are windy, temperatures are seasonal to below, and some areas see abundant downfall. Hawaii is seasonal to below, cloudy, and windy, with a chance for showers.

New Moon, December 14–20

Zone 1: Scattered precipitation is heavier north, skies are windy and cloudy, and temperatures are seasonal to below.

Zone 2: The zone is windy with strong thunderstorms central and south, variably cloudy skies, and seasonal temperatures.

Zone 3: Western and central areas are windy with precipitation and scattered precipitation east, and seasonal temperatures.

Zone 4: Skies are partly cloudy to cloudy and windy with scattered precipitation, and temperatures are seasonal to above.

Zone 5: Temperatures are seasonal to below, eastern areas see precipitation, and skies are partly cloudy to cloudy.

Zone 6: Scattered precipitation accompanies very windy and partly cloudy to cloudy skies, temperatures are seasonal but cooler east with precipitation.

Zone 7: Much of the zone sees precipitation under partly cloudy to cloudy skies. Temperatures are seasonal and eastern parts of the zone are fair to partly cloudy and windy.

Zone 8: Central Alaska sees abundant precipitation, skies are windy and variably cloudy, and temperatures are seasonal to below. Hawaii is windy, humid, and seasonal. Abundant downfall is possible in western areas and skies are partly cloudy to cloudy.

2nd Quarter Moon, December 21–29

Zone 1: Partly cloudy to cloudy skies with precipitation accompany temperatures seasonal to below and windy skies.

Zone 2: Central and southern areas are windy, the zone sees scattered precipitation, temperatures are seasonal, and skies are variably cloudy.

Zone 3: Skies are partly cloudy to cloudy, central and eastern areas are windy with precipitation, and temperatures are seasonal to below.

Zone 4: Western areas see precipitation, skies are fair to partly cloudy with scattered precipitation central and east, and temperatures are seasonal.

Zone 5: West and central areas see precipitation, some abundant, temperatures are seasonal to above, and skies are partly cloudy to cloudy.

Zone 6: Western areas see precipitation, some abundant, skies are windy, partly cloudy to cloudy, and temperatures are seasonal.

Zone 7: Skies are variably cloudy and windy, western areas see precipitation, and temperatures are seasonal.

Zone 8: Central Alaska is windy and the state is partly cloudy to cloudy with scattered precipitation; temperatures are seasonal to below. Hawaii is windy central and east with scattered showers, thunderstorms, and temperatures seasonal to above.

Economic Forecast for 2020

by Christeen Skinner

Before considering the correlation between lunar positions and economic activity, we must first start with the Sun and, specifically, the sunspot cycle.

The sunspot cycle has an average length of 11.2 years, with peaks of activity tending to coincide with high stock market prices, and low numbers of sunspots with low prices. The number of visible sunspots has been decreasing since apparent maxima in 2014. If minima is reached, as anticipated, in 2019 or 2020, we should expect depressed prices in all markets through these years.

Sunspot cycles have been numbered for the last couple of hundred years, with Cycle 25 due to begin at the coming minima. Noting that the number of sunspots at maxima has diminished in the last three cycles, solar scientists are already wondering if Cycle 25 might have even fewer sunspots than Cycle 24. While this does not necessarily mean that prices will stay depressed for the next decade, it does suggest major economic difficulties ahead—not least because there is a link between solar energy and terrestrial weather.

Another major factor is that the Moon does not maintain equidistance from Earth, in some years coming closer to the planet than in other years. The fact that the closest lunar perigee takes place in 2019, potentially coinciding with solar minima, indicates exceptional conditions and the potential for noteworthy economic events. Coupled with this, several slow-moving planets form key conjunctions in the next two years. It is perhaps understandable then that 2020 is already being termed (in astrological circles at least) "The Year of the Great Financial Reset." This is in no way to suggest a repeat of the global financial crisis of 2007–2009, but it is likely, when a revised economic history of the world is written, that 2020 will warrant an entire chapter of its own. The looming crisis could yet be bigger than the last.

The combination of solar minima and closest lunar perigee has, in the past, coincided with unusual weather conditions. This brings with it the very real possibility of lower crop yields and higher food prices, which would no doubt add to financial discomfort. This, though, is not the only reason to deduce that 2020 will be a year of economic difficulty.

With the naked eye, sky watchers will observe Jupiter and Saturn moving ever closer to one another throughout 2020: their conjunction coincides with the December solstice. Before that date, we are, in effect, witnessing the close of the last cycle, which began in May 2000. There is a pattern to the regular alignment of these two planets, with a series of these conjunctions taking place in one element (Fire, Earth, Air, or Water) before moving on to another.

The penultimate conjunction of each 240-year-long series is in the new element and gives clues of things to come. The penultimate of this series began in 1981 and was in the Air sign of Libra, marking the dawn of the "yuppie" era and a period during which electronic currencies were developed. Exciting as these developments have been, it should be recalled that this was the period during which the now-named "weapons of financial destruction" were in development.

It makes astro-financial-historic sense to give attention to currencies and their structure, under-pinning, and development during 2020. The last time a similar planetary alignment took place was back in the late thirteenth century. This period saw the collapse of many of the Lombard banks and, eventually, the adoption of new coinage.

In recent years, using blockchain technology, cryptocurrencies have come to market. At the time of writing, the number of crypto-currencies is well over 2,000. By the time you read this, double or even triple that number may be in existence. Initial efforts to regulate this market might not be successful, but by the time that Saturn and Pluto form their conjunction in 2020 (another key feature of the year), it should be clear to all that such regulation is imperative.

Indeed, before the Sun arrives in Aquarius on January 21, 2020, world news might well be dominated by the need for international regulation of the crypto market. The banking industry itself—and, in particular, the banks of nations—should also be in the news as each tries to prove its trustworthiness and security. This theme will surely dominate the year. Disappointment in these corporate structures will surely also give way to the rise of cooperative banking and credit unions by the time that Jupiter and Saturn form their Aquarius (Air) conjunction on December 20.

2020 Eclipses

There are always two and sometimes as many as five solar eclipses in any year. These are not always accompanied by a lunar eclipse but, when they are, often coincide with sharp moves in the markets in the two weeks between related eclipses. January 1, 2020 comes between a solar and lunar eclipse so it is entirely possible that the year will open with dramatic moves in global markets.

Though the solar eclipse on December 26, 2019 on the anniversary of the Boxing Day Tsunami in Thailand of 2004 might not bring a repeat of that awful event, it would be wise to anticipate earth movement of some kind—something that affects world markets—to take place between that date and the first lunar eclipse of 2020 on January 10.

The chart for that event positions the Moon in Cancer, opposing an awesome stellium (grouping) of lunar north node, Sun, Mercury, Venus, Jupiter, Saturn, and Pluto all in the opposite sign of Capricorn. We might wonder what effect so many planets grouping on one side of the Sun might have on our special star.

An increase in the number and power of solar flares could occur, bringing with it the threat of disruption in satellite-dependent communications.

This rare and heavy accent of planets in Capricorn—a sign associated with prudence and with austerity, amongst other things—could also coincide with revaluations in the property market. Perhaps because banks are, at worst, collapsing or are unable or reluctant to lend, stalemate and lack of movement in this market will likely bring grave consequences for many. With the probability of prices falling, the term negative equity may be heard often.

The first solar eclipse of 2020 occurs on June 21—at the summer solstice. That this eclipse coincides with one of the four most powerful days of the year (solstice and equinox points) indicates a major turning point affecting much of human endeavor. This eclipse, viewable from Zaire through Saudi Arabia, India, and southern China, will likely bring political upheaval to these regions, followed by the establishment of a new economic order. The currencies of these regions may be particularly affected.

First Quarter

The concentration of planets in Capricorn at the December solstice in 2019 and lasting through the Sun's transit of that sign in January 2020 is rare. Such alignments mark seed moments. At the December 2019 solstice (the key chart preceding 2020) the Moon in Scorpio (its fall) opposes Vesta, the asteroid associated with trading and, most especially, with currency. This suggests deep unhappiness with currencies generally and, most likely, the desire by many people to convert local currencies into the "hard" exchange of gold, silver, or precious metal.

Indeed, by the time that Jupiter conjoins Pluto on April 4, many people may be wondering how best to make these investments. Jupiter and Pluto align approximately every twelve years.

It is, however, over two centuries since Jupiter and Pluto last made a Capricorn alignment. Though the constitution of the United States was not signed until 1776, in 1771, as Jupiter and Pluto formed their Capricorn conjunction, the seeds of this national identity were sown. Political developments in 2020 could yet give rise to the formations of other nations and even a revision of the United States. With these geo-political developments, the stage is set for fast-moving economic development.

The Full Moon and lunar eclipse on January 10 seem likely to mark an important economic moment. Market values fell after the lunar eclipse of January 31, 2018. Though the January 2020 accents a different area of the zodiac, it may well be that markets again turn downward after this date. In 2018, the low was reached at the alignment of Mars with Saturn in March. If history repeats, then the low should come on the very last day of March when these two planets come to another key geocentric conjunction.

Those fearful of the loss of value in equities will likely look for safe haven elsewhere. In recent years, the alignment of Mars and Jupiter conjoined in an Earth sign whilst Saturn made key aspect to the Galactic Center, has seen the price of gold especially move up only to fall quickly after the aspect becomes exact. If history repeats, then gold should do well, peaking in price around the March 2020 equinox.

Governments are unlikely to approve this move and it is entirely possible that talk of restrictions on the movement of these and other precious metal commodities will be a feature of the early months of the year, though any action may be insufficient to control those markets.

No doubt the collection of tax will also be of mounting concern, with an increase in penalties announced by many governments. It might be as well to anticipate the announcement of austerity measures in those countries whose mounting debt puts them under particular pressure. Such developments underline the potential for the collapse of some borders and even, perhaps, the demise of some nations entirely, whilst it might also (as with Switzerland at the end of the thirteenth century) see the inauguration of "new nations."

It is noteworthy that the planetary picture for the January lunar eclipse puts focus on Mars, then traveling through Sagittarius, and at a degree associated with flight. Whilst not wishing to forecast disaster, it is entirely possible that an event bringing focus to the air travel industry will result in a share price slump in that sector.

In any case, January 10–20 will probably prove a particularly tense time with stand-offs in many commercial arenas. For those with cash to spare, it would arguably be a promising time to make overtures to take over a failing commercial concern. Clearly it depends on the personal chart as much as that of the company. It is perhaps essential that any such assessment be undertaken before Mercury turns retrograde on February 16.

Mercury's retrograde periods have a distinct pattern or sequence. In 2020, each retrograde period is in an Air sign—as they were between June 2001 and October 2002. Readers will remember not only the events of 9/11 but also the aftershock. It was the case, however, that even prior to those attacks, Mercury's Air sign retrogrades coincided with loss of equity value—a trend that might well be repeated in 2020 as Mercury retrogrades are in these signs once more.

The New Moon of January 24 is in Aquarius with the Sun and Moon part of a midpoint picture including Mars and Saturn. This prompts an image of a brick wall, government placed restrictions, or an economic STOP sign. The freezing of assets and the inability of many to obtain commercial support (loans) suggests that this will be a difficult period for entrepreneurs.

Matters are unlikely to be much improved by the February Full Moon at 20° Leo. Those born in the early 1950s with Pluto at this degree could experience great surges of concern about their pension situation and general asset valuation. With Neptune opposing the Mars position of the New York Stock Exchange, losses experienced here would have a major effect on savings. True, Neptune will have been in this position for some months. It seems likely though that it will be in February 2020 that these losses will be felt most acutely and by those unlikely to be in a position to work or live long enough to recoup from any loss.

It is thought by some that retrograde Mercury is "bad" for commerce or negotiations. Yet this is not always the case: some long-thriving companies have Mercury retrograde at their inception or in the chart of their IPO. It does appear true, however, that it is advisable to avoid the dates around Mercury stations (two days either side) to sign important deals.

In February 2020, Mercury stations three days before the Sun moves from Aquarius to Pisces whilst Mars in Capricorn is "out of bounds" and within a degree of the lunar south node. It may be that if there is a low at the Mercury station, markets recover on the Monday following the New Moon (February 24). The chart for this lunation shows the New Moon to be at the exact midpoint of Mars and Uranus.

Some readers may know that the Mars-Uranus cycle has been termed the "crash cycle," since in the past the hard aspects (squares and oppositions) between the two planets have often marked market tops. The trine between the two planets is rather different, often marking a key staging post or break in a trend line.

This is not the only aspect to suggest a change of market direction: a square between Venus and Jupiter, accenting degrees associated with stress, further accentuates the possibility of Monday, February 24 being a day of high market drama. It should also be noted that heliocentrically, Venus, Mars, and Ceres all make

ingress at the New Moon. There is high probability of a complete change in market sentiment on February 24. That the asteroid Ceres is involved indicates the potential for sharp movement in food commodity prices.

Mercury's direct station coincides with the Full Moon on March 9. By then Mercury will have retrograded back through Pisces into Aquarius—the sign associated with advanced technology. It is entirely possible that pharmaceutical companies (Pisces-linked) using advanced technology will have the most volatile share prices through this period.

Pisces is also the sign linked to healing—especially mental and spiritual dis-ease. A strong possibility is that there will be much discussion about the therapeutic uses of certain manufactured drugs and that this will impact the share prices of those companies manufacturing these.

It would be understandable if, during this quarter, investors turn to what they perceive to be secure: gold and silver.

As stated earlier, these could reach new highs by the equinox later in March.

The New Moon on March 24 aligns with Chiron (planetoid of accountability). This lunation coincides with the anniversary of the Treaty of Rome and the "birth" of the Economic European Community. The probable considerable attention being drawn to the way in which this organization handles its finances, could be yet another reason for investors to move away from equities.

Second Quarter

The need for a fresh approach to finances—an economic "spring"—is apparent from the March equinox. Within seventy-two hours of this, one of the four most powerful dates of the year, Mars aligns with Jupiter (indicating the desire to implement new strategy) and both Vesta and Saturn move into two of the Air signs (Gemini and Aquarius respectively). The former may say something about parallel or dual approaches to foreign exchange (hard and digital currencies) whilst Saturn's move into Aquarius moves focus for governmental behavior and regulation to the need for tighter controls for non-government agencies and co-operatives of all types and sizes.

This may be no bad thing—it should be remembered that Saturn is as at home in Aquarius as it is in Capricorn. The difference, however, is that Saturn's presence in Aquarius (think back to 1991–1993) puts accent on the need to be forward-thinking while also operating within the rules and acceptable social boundaries. The sectors likely to benefit will surely be those exploring space-age technology.

That said, the first Full Moon of this quarter, on April 7, is in Libra. Analysis of the stock market crashes of the twentieth century shows each to have major planetary configurations in this zodiacal area. April 8, 2020, (a Wednesday) may be no exception.

Just after the next New Moon, on April 22, Uranus will be in conjunction with both the Sun and Moon. Uranus is known for bringing disruptive energy. That this alignment coincides with Mercury within a degree of that tender 19-degree cardinal position suggests, at the very least, considerable volatility when those still trading should ensure that they have adequate stop-losses in place.

It is more than a little interesting that analysis of the Sun's position by sign of the S&P index since 1950 shows that gain is much reduced as the Sun passes through Taurus, reminding us of the old adage "sell in May (when the Sun is in Taurus) and go away!" Certainly there may be many who choose to leave the market-place by the Full Moon on May 7.

This Full Moon, at 17° Scorpio, coincides with Venus in out of bounds position and at maximum declination. In the past, such periods have marked market tops with turning points reached as Venus turns toward zero declination.

While the study of New and Full Moons offers some insight into possible change of trend, no less important is the cycle of Mercury with Venus. It is rare for these two planets to form a conjunction on the exact day of a New Moon, but that is the case on May 22. True, there are fully 18 degrees between the Sun-Moon connection and that of Mercury and Venus. Yet all four are in Gemini, one of the signs greatly associated with commercial activity. Indeed, it is not hard to imagine frenetic trading in the last days of May—especially as Mercury is retrograde and in a sign where it is said to work well. If this is indeed the case, then we might also anticipate many trading errors or much-disputed valuations being made.

Nowhere is this more likely to be seen more than in property markets. With the lunar node moving from Cancer into Gemini in May 2020, there is the strong possibility of agreed deals falling through and of numerous instances of negative equity and other financial distresses being recorded.

Third Quarter

It is unusual for the Cancer New Moon to coincide with the June solstice and it implies an energy surge. With both at 0 degrees of the cardinal signs, the temptation by many to take action, to do more to husband their reserves and generally rebuild wealth will surely be great. This cosmic vibration should be of great benefit to those born under Aries, Cancer, Libra, or Capricorn (cardinal signs of the zodiac) particularly. With both Mercury and Venus retrograde, however, and Mercury returning to a conjunction with Vesta, a major difficulty will likely be which currency to trust and precisely where it is safe to keep money. Under the mattress? Probably not. In the bank? Maybe, but then which bank? The start of this quarter will no doubt be unsettling for investors and traders alike, as they battle with conflicting evidence and advice.

Those with cash to spare, and with entrepreneurial talent, could, however, make significant gain. True, with black market economies thriving and government crackdowns likely to be increasing by the day, a fixed purpose and ability to develop plans within a legal framework will doubtless require particular talents. Nor would this be an optimum period for launch—that event should wait a few weeks until those planets are once again in direct motion.

Around this solstice and New Moon, with the Moon both out of bounds and at maximum declination, the imagination of some could go into overdrive, giving rise to new concepts and yes, perhaps extraordinary commercial ideas.

In particular, anything to do with plastics, graphene, and sea enterprises could quickly gather momentum and, before the fourth quarter, have attracted the required investment.

Whichever timed chart is used for the United States of America, July 4, 1776, the Sun's position is 13° Cancer: the exact degree of the Full Moon (actually on July 5, 2020). In this chart, the Sun conjoins Vesta exactly, while Mercury continues its retrograde phase. This suggests a critical time for the US dollar. Though at the time of writing it seems unlikely, it might even be suggested earlier in 2020 that a new dollar be brought into existence.

Nor is the US dollar likely to be the only currency under significant pressure. Sterling (British Pound) might also attract considerable attention. No doubt much of this will be linked to developments in the fast-growing cryptocurrency sector.

An even more critical financial period could occur at the New Moon on July 20. Saturn opposes this lunation exactly. Though there is always one day in every year when the Sun and Saturn oppose one another, it's only approximately every three decades that this involves the sign of Cancer—a sign associated with property, nesting, and security of all kinds. Pressure on those ostensibly looking after savings (banks and cooperatives) will surely be considerable. It is worth noting that, simultaneously, the lunar south node conjoins the Galactic Center—yet another signal indicating market moves to the negative.

Should that trend continue, it might only cease at the Full Moon on August 3. This too promises to be a day of considerable tension. Mars and Jupiter are at right angles, with the latter at 19° Capricorn, the very degree that was evident at many of the stock market disasters of the twentieth century. That same day (a Monday and so a trading day), Uranus is at right angle to both the Sun and Moon, suggesting instability and high volatility.

This planetary picture accents aspects in the often-used chart for the United Kingdom (January 1, 1801, midnight, Westminster), indicating the potential for this to be an economically tense time for that nation. Venus aligns with the lunar north node at this Full Moon too—opposing the Galactic Center and so implicating global trade difficulties—perhaps linked to currency instability. The close conjunction of Mercury with Vesta that same day further implies attention to currency exchange. Forex dealers might be wise to defer their holidays and stay close to their desks should the potential whirlwind of economic activity manifest.

With the slow-moving planets all retrograde through this third quarter, while the inner, faster-moving planets are in direct motion, events may be such that those who would prefer to have time to think carefully and arrive at a careful strategy will find that denied to them. Investors and savers alike will presumably feel the need to alter their course as the global financial world lurches from one crisis to the next.

Though the global financial crisis of 2007–2009 is unlikely to be repeated, it is entirely possible that difficulties in the bond markets will require prompt action and dominate the news this quarter too. It will be entirely understandable if investors run for cover. In doing so, however, they might miss opportunities.

The New Moon on August 18 marks a distinct change in the cosmic weather. In this chart, the Sun, Moon, and Mercury all make promising aspect to the Lunar north node. As this is the Leo New Moon—a sign sometimes noted for optimism—it may be that low prices bring buying opportunity. The health and munitions sectors might attract attention. It is not hard to read the potential for widespread war in the planetary formations at many of the lunations in 2020.

Mars turns retrograde in a sign in which it is said to work well—Aries—on September 9. Not only could this coincide with a change of market trend, it might also be that its station at this degree picks up unresolved agreements from late 2018/2019 when Uranus was at this position. This further accents the potential for discord to manifest in war, bringing potential profit to those supplying weaponry, aid, and medical assistance.

Fourth Quarter

By far the greatest feature of this quarter of 2020 is at its end: the December solstice which coincides with the first Jupiter-Saturn conjunction in Aquarius since 1405. This alignment is also known as the great mutation: the term used when a series of Jupiter-Saturn conjunctions moves from one element to another (in this instance, from Earth to Air). The Air sequence lasts for approximately two and a half centuries—almost an exact Pluto cycle. Many people will surely be aware of "new times coming" and perhaps even sense this quarter of the year as offering an overture for the themes that will be heard most loudly in 2021.

That said, whatever the long-term promise, reminders of just how difficult the year has been—and might continue to be—will surely be obvious at the October 1 Full Moon. At 9 degrees of one of the cardinal signs, and with Chiron in close conjunction with the Full Moon, issues of accountability and how books might be balanced will likely dominate news bulletins. Since Mars is still retrograde in Aries and in square formation to both Saturn and Pluto, it might seem to some that they have hit the investment buffers. Those still in the market at this time will surely need considerable courage to stay there given their recent experience and probable breaking bleak commercial news.

Yet some investors may feel that markets won't get much lower and that the time for moving back into the market is coming—though they would be wise to do so only after taking expert advice.

The New Moon on October 16 contains another difficult planetary alignment, this time with retrograde Mars square to Jupiter. An apt image for this aspect would be of an ill-equipped army. The energy to move forward may be there, but lack of either weaponry or sustenance—or even possibly direction—implies pending failure. Certainly the Full Moon at the end of October indicates yet more economic difficulties.

As was the case at the time of the Lehman Brothers in September 2008, the Full Moon on Hallowe'en, October 31, aligns with Uranus in Taurus. We should perhaps be thankful that this event takes place on a Saturday when many markets are closed.

Even so, it is entirely possible that some markets will react to this "enraged bull" and that a collapse in some share prices will be apparent from market opening time on Monday, November 2.

So it would be wholly understandable if there was a collective sigh of relief at the New Moon on November 15 when it is realized that after months of volatility—and most probably negative movement—that recovery is on the horizon. By this date Mars will once more be in direct motion. Better still, the New Moon in Scorpio makes positive aspects to Jupiter, Saturn, and Pluto all clustered in Capricorn.

Reaction might of course be linked to the presidential election in the United States. Results here could give rise to investor confidence. Even those who have eschewed banking and other corporate type stocks might decide the time is right to return to these.

At this New Moon too, Vesta occupies 8° Virgo, picking up on an eclipse operative in 1998 and which coincided with the collapse of the Russian currency, the rouble. Though a repeat is most unlikely, it may be that currency matters are once again in the news. Turbulence in foreign exchange markets seems likely at the Full Moon on November 30. Silver prices too could attract much attention with a key turning point reached.

If the past is any indicator of the future, then the major technical giants should be in the headlines at the last New Moon of 2020. A common feature of these charts is accentuation of 23–24 degrees of the mutable signs. Developments announced around the New Moon at 23° Sagittarius may be enough to encourage some investors to increase the number of these shares held in their portfolios. Though an opposition between Vesta and Neptune highlighting the NYSE chart is likely indicative of continuing fragility, early shoots of potential revival in 2021 may be seen as 2020 draws to a close.

As 2020 ends, the aforementioned great mutation takes place. This is the term used to describe the first of a series of Jupiter-

Saturn conjunctions in a new element. As viewed from Earth, this alignment coincides with the December solstice, prompting some astrologers to consider this date to be the beginning of a new commercial age incorporating advancements in space technology. Certainly those working in space and related industries will find demand for their services rising. Investing in this sector will doubtless bring eventual reward, suiting those focused on the long-term. News of scientific breakthroughs in this area may be enough to lure even the most reluctant of investors back into the market. As the number of investors increases, so too might prices.

And yet, by the last Full Moon of 2020, Venus aligns with the lunar south node, at right angles to Neptune and opposing the position of Mars in the chart for the NYSE. This could be viewed as a cosmic signature for loss. Certainly, many people are likely to be significantly financially bruised after a year of difficult trading.

Traders have a habit of trying to ensure that the financial year ends on a high note. With Mars in positive aspect to the Galactic Center and on its way to forming a conjunction with Uranus (often marking a "top") at the inauguration of the next president of the USA, it may be that this Full Moon acts as "starter's orders" for an upward push.

It seems most likely that 2020 will go down as being one of the most challenging years in economic and financial history. This is not to say that some traders and investors cannot make gain. The art may be for investors to be extra diligent at the critical Full Moons and for traders to protect themselves when the cosmic and lunar weather blows most strongly.

Difficult and loss-making periods are beneficial for bargain hunters. Those with cash available, and focusing in two specific areas—utilities and in future technology—may not have to wait too far into 2021 to experience financial reward.

New and Full Moon Forecasts for 2020

by Sally Cragin

This year, I wanted to go into detail for each of the twelve signs for every New and Full Moon. You'll note that your sign has its own New and Full Moon listed throughout the year. Mark those on your 2020 datebook, because those are times when you should be very open to new opportunities.

Friday, January 10: Full Moon in Cancer

The "Wolf Moon" can increase our appetites. Up for more feasting? Cancer Moons fine-tune emotions, and with Venus in Aquarius, this phase encourages relationships with cerebral and humanitarian friends.

Aries: Gentle teasing may rankle. Respond with a firm kick of your hooves. **Taurus:** Self-protectiveness is in full flower, especially if a loved one aches. **Gemini:** Your emotional intelligence rocks! **Cancer:** Look back to mid-July of 2019. What project or relationship started and how does this connect to "right now"? **Leo:** Be magnanimous, but also cautious about oversharing. **Virgo:** Entertaining others? Why not—you're recovered from the holidays, right? **Libra:** Those with deep feelings need you to support them. Pace yourself. **Scorpio:** Improve your home, rather than focusing on others' sloppy emotions. **Sagittarius:** Be frank but understand others' sensitivities.**Capricorn:** Rest and restore, especially if you've witnessed drama. **Aquarius:** You may be slowed down by the indecision of others. **Pisces:** Enormous insights for authority figures.

Friday, January 24: New Moon in Aquarius

The "same-old" will not suit today or this weekend. Reach out to your more creative friends—especially those who may live at a distance. Aquarius rules electricity, so purchasing a new table lamp, or bulbs with less glare could brighten your home.

Aries: Your social side is ignited and "the more the merrier" is your credo. **Taurus:** Improve your home—brighter light? **Gemini:** You are the lovable "go-to" expert. **Cancer:** Get out of your comfort zone—your friends miss you! **Leo:** Sleep, restore yourself. This New Moon could make you feel that "less is less." **Virgo:** Indulge your curiosity and turn an acquaintanceship into something more. **Libra:** Get nerdy with structures and build something that lasts. **Scorpio:** Spend time with "old reliables" in your social circle. **Sagittarius:** Resist interference from well-meaning "parental" types. **Capricorn:** Messages may be garbled—ask for clarification. **Aquarius:** Your annual personal New Moon: dream big. 2020 sees Aquarians on top of the world. Yes, this means more responsibility. **Pisces:** You need your space; others need your solace.

Sunday, February 9: Full Moon in Leo

Much combustibility in the offing, as Venus (friendship) in Aries, and Mars (moving forward) in Sagittarius are making harmonious angles to the Moon (emotions). Have a party!

Aries: You're willing to fight for what you want or believe in. **Taurus:** Your childish side emerges. Keep things light. **Gemini:** Being quick-witted keeps you moving. **Cancer:** Are you impatient with friends and family? Or possessive? Solitude beckons. **Leo:** This is a crucial turning point. Look back to mid-August of 2019. What relationship or project began then? How has it changed? **Virgo:** You'll have tolerance for folks whom others deplore—your kindness makes a difference. **Libra:** Many friends make you happy. Have you seen them recently? **Scorpio:** Find a big learning curve, take a running start, and climb! **Sagittarius:** Your charisma is on display. Others need you to jump-start their lives. **Capricorn:** Indulge your sense of humor—lightening up becomes you. **Aquarius:** Welcome small reversals—these quickly pass. **Pisces:** You're braver than you think you are.

Sunday, February 23: New Moon in Pisces

"Behind the scenes"is highlighted and paranoia is a hazard. Since Mercury is now direct, figure that communication is what it is.

Aries: You may have difficulty reading "subtle cues." **Taurus:** Redecorate and connect with faraway friends. **Gemini:** If you get the opportunity to see how things work, you can teach yourself. Perceptions vis-a-vis humans, not so much. **Cancer:** Others love you—let them. **Leo:** Subtle cues may escape you; you need people to be straight up. **Virgo:** A turning point for a friendship or a (no-longer-needed) habit. **Libra:** Don't be petty. Be magnanimous. **Scorpio:** Walking on the wild side is one of Scorpio's delights. Who can go with you? **Sagittarius:** Your home could use sprucing up. An aquarium, more plants? **Capricorn:** Can you unite career advancement and enjoyment? Plan to attend a seminar. **Aquarius:** Look behind the curtain. Persistence pays.

Pisces: Your annual personal New Moon may find you stronger than you think you are. Time to map out the next year.

Monday, March 9: Full Moon in Virgo

This Full Moon is the "Worm Moon" for Native Americans, but it's also the spring cleaning Moon. Virgo emphasizes precision and perfectionism, and the Moon is in harmony again with Venus (affection) in Taurus, and Mars (action) in Capricorn. Good time for investments.

Aries: Virgo Moons can be useful for kicking the cobwebs, or tending to an overlooked project. **Taurus:** Takin' care of business—that's what you need to tell folks who want to distract you from a mission. **Gemini:** This Virgo Moon may prompt you to "destabilize" a situation that's baffled you. Full speed ahead! **Cancer:** Take the initiative, especially if you've been overlooked or your talents misunderstood. **Leo:** Health matters and your willingness to take care of others may clash. **Virgo:** Look back to mid-September of 2019. What projects or personalities were in your life? Did you make a fresh start? Reflect on the journey, but take decisive action for next step. **Libra:** Stick to your decision (yes, very un-Libra), and do something that requires endurance. **Scorpio:** A day for dealing with finance; where do you set limits? **Sagittarius:** Be ruthless about your expenses; purchase items for value, not convenience. **Capricorn:** Planning a trip this year? Get the dust off your hooves. **Aquarius:** Details aren't your thing, but they should be today. **Pisces:** You're the center of a big circle, which may prompt escapist desires.

Tuesday, March 24: New Moon in Aries

Aries Moons are excellent for starting projects you finish quickly—particularly projects you do solo. Saturn enters Aquarius, initiating a three-year period that will see huge expansions in electronic communication.

Aries: This is your New Moon. What projects will take a year to complete? Others may have insights into your life/work situation that could be helpful. **Taurus:** Physical exercise? Yes, even sturdy bulls need to get some air. Body first, soul follows. **Gemini:** Flexibility counts. Forgive your nearest and dearest who need to have a tantrum. **Cancer:** The last six weeks may have felt like you're moving through mud, but this New Moon should give better traction. **Leo:** What do you need to be your best? Get close to it! **Virgo:** Unreliable folks could bring out your irritable side. Solo endeavors are best. **Libra:** A day of reversals or tentative starts. Evaluate options, act later. **Scorpio:** Don't sell yourself short or be hurried. Take your time. **Sagittarius:** Seek out those who entertain you. Learn from their wisdom. **Capricorn:** Be conservative; no need to "even things up." **Aquarius:** Fast, stylish, and efficient—that's you! **Pisces:** If you need more time than you thought, turn off electronics.

Tuesday, April 7: Full Moon in Libra

Diplomacy rules during this Full Moon, also known as the "Planter's Moon." So does indecision. To quote The Clash, should you stay or should you go? With Mars (movement) entering Aquarius (on March 31), and Venus (affection) now in Gemini, our communication skills are at a high rev.

Aries: If plans go into reverse, please go with the flow. **Taurus:** Indulge with flowers—maybe a six-pack of pansies? **Gemini:** You are a superstar of charisma, as long as you can make eye contact with others. **Cancer:** Change your mind, cancel the plans, don't feel obligated. **Leo:** Justice matters, and Leo's sense of fairness is important to others. **Virgo:** You hate the small stuff, but it's all small stuff today. **Libra:** Your thinking may be muddled, but the truth will out. **Scorpio:** When others mess around, Scorpio may need to step back. **Sagittarius:** Don't be gulled by "get rich quick" thinking. **Capricorn:** Your ability to learn is why you keep moving forward. What are you improving? **Aquarius:** Superb time for getting together with your classy pals! **Pisces:** Decisions, decisions—do they matter?

Wednesday, April 22: New Moon in Taurus

Spring fever hit a couple of weeks ago, so this New Moon could increase self-protection. Taurus Moons bring out a stubborn streak, but don't get vexed over trifles. The Moon is at odds with Mars, so male/female interaction could be fraught.

Aries: Sustained growth is your theme, but don't get boxed into a corner. **Taurus:** As much as you'd prefer "same old" over "shock of the modern," this New Moon will get you thinking bigger. Great time to end old habits. **Gemini:** It's okay to be possessive and to count your pennies. **Cancer:** Your need for beauty is huge—what attire makes you feel your best? **Leo:** It's okay to be stubborn and to roar! **Virgo:** Indulge in a beautification ritual; your taste is sublime. **Libra:** Partnerships are highlighted—others help you find strength. **Scorpio:** Your analytical talents are peaking. **Sagittarius:** Find strength in your partnerships. **Capricorn:** Being more efficient in a work practice comes easily. **Aquarius:** Dissatisfaction over an appearance issue could be vexing. **Pisces:** Time to plant!

Thursday, May 7: Full Moon in Scorpio

Scorpio Moons emphasize the search for sensual pleasures. Be cautious with sharp knives, or overly enthusiastic hairdressers. Mars (action) and the Moon make an awkward angle, so others may object to your self-protective urges.

Aries: Others may unravel emotionally around you, leaving you perplexed. **Taurus:** The New Moon sent you on the right path, but this Full Moon wants you to doubt that. Hang tight! **Gemini:** The need to live with less prevails. **Cancer:** Your insights are appreciated by others who may want to be closer than you planned. **Leo:** Do others have a "hidden agenda"? Does it matter to a Leo with great self-esteem? **Virgo:** Trust your instincts and don't beat around the bush. **Libra:** Work on financial stability and simplifying. **Scorpio:** Your annual Full Moon! Ask for everything you need. **Sagittarius:** Explore your willingness to hoard. Does it bring joy? **Capricorn:** Your determination is full-throttle—full speed ahead. **Aquarius:** Turn the corner on a complicated power relationship. **Pisces:** Excellent time for therapy of any kind.

Friday, May 22: New Moon in Gemini

An excellent period for writing or communication projects. Since Gemini rules writers, self-expression could be a solace. The Moon (emotions) and Mars (action) in Pisces are at odds with one another. "Passive/aggressive" could be a theme.

Aries: Something complicated comes easily—how nice! **Taurus:** Others' restlessness could irk you. Power down. **Gemini:** This New Moon could initiate a year-long project that brings more responsibility. What could this be? Turning point on November 30. **Cancer:** Others may want you to be satisfied with less, but stick to what you know you deserve. **Leo:** You could meet someone you wish to charm. But remember the difference between roaring and purring. **Virgo:** Curiosity could be overwhelming, but remember what Pandora found in that box.

Libra: Teach yourself something new—Libran curiosity is without peer. **Scorpio:** Solidify communication with a partner; be firm about your needs. **Sagittarius:** Feeling distracted? Give yourself a pass. **Capricorn:** Find opportunities to entertain others and indulge the child within. **Aquarius:** A writing project (long overdue letter?) finds you mentally alert. **Pisces:** Laughter heals. Are you being too serious?

Friday, June 5: Full Moon in Sagittarius

Sagittarius Moons encourage risk-taking. Move your body! The Moon, Venus (affection) in Gemini, and Mars (action) in Pisces are in an awkward angle, but could prompt romantic revelations during this sweet "Strawberry Moon."

Aries: Fire sign Full Moons are your comfort zone—and make you fearless. Show your courage. **Taurus:** Embrace speed bumps; going fast isn't for you now. **Gemini:** Starts, not finishes come easily. Rein in your "needs." **Cancer:** Forget personal dignity, giggle at naughty jokes, and wink at others. **Leo:** You may need to adjudicate a sticky matter—perhaps a misinterpreted text? **Virgo:** Not naturally a risk-taker, Virgo will dance on a razor's edge during this phase. **Libra:** Reach out to those who haven't heard from you. **Scorpio:** Another excellent time to work on finances. **Sagittarius:** Your official "Full Moon" and a significant interlude for giant leaps in your personal life and career. **Capricorn:** Get support from faraway friends and associates. Remind them how great you are. **Aquarius:** Getting out of your comfort zone nourishes. **Pisces:** Could be accident-prone. Move slowly.

Sunday, June 21: New Moon in Cancer

Cancer Moons emphasize home pleasures and feeding the body and soul—with the Summer Solstice, this New Moon could make us all feel fragile. The Moon is cozying up to Mars (action) in Pisces, so romance is in the air.

Aries: Sometimes the "awkward silence" is preferable to saying the wrong thing. **Taurus:** A vulnerable time for others, but for you, home is best. Make it cozy. **Gemini:** Take on projects that take a long (and pleasurable) time to complete. **Cancer:** Your personal New Moon. Initiate a project that takes a year to complete. Stretch yourself! **Leo:** The lion's den may need some alterations, especially if you're embarking on a new fitness regimen. **Virgo:** You might come off as a "tough guy" (or gal) if others are over-sensitive. But you're the voice of reality. **Libra:** A tough skin is helpful; good thing you're a diplomat. **Scorpio:** Your sensual needs come first—how lovely is that! **Sagittarius:** Be grateful you're not a prisoner of emotions, as you see others to be. **Capricorn:** Discouragement could come easily, but brush this aside. **Aquarius:** You're the star of the show, but others may want the spotlight. **Pisces:** Cooking and domestic pleasures light up your life.

Sunday, July 5: Full Moon in Capricorn

Decisiveness comes easily with the "Buck Moon." However, others may think you're more emphatic than you mean to be. Mars (taking action) in Aries makes an awkward angle to the Moon. Maternal or sororal relationships could be spikey.

Aries: Slow and steady wins the race. **Taurus:** If you've had financial anxiety, this lunar phase can help you unravel it. **Gemini:** Don't know which direction to go? Why go anywhere? **Cancer:** Push your limits, get active, and stick with the folks who know you best. **Leo:** You'll be attracted to someone (or some activity) that's not your usual type. Indulge! **Virgo:** That super practical side your friends depend on? It's in full flower. **Libra:** Home improvement: tend to details that require logical thinking. **Scorpio:** Much to be learned from a short trip—getting out of the house is the hard part. **Sagittarius:** Look for a long-shot, and then pursue it! **Capricorn:** Your Full Moon initiates the start of a critical year. You'll need bravery and persistence (natural Capricorn traits). The world is your oyster—just bring your dipping sauce. **Aquarius:** Building and structures are emphasized. **Pisces:** The ability to improve your practical skills is heightened.

Monday, July 20: New Moon in Cancer

Another opportunity to dig deep into your psyche—or do what the Danes do and enjoy "hygge" (extreme coziness). Mars (action) in Aries, with Jupiter (generosity) in Capricorn are squeezing this Full Moon, so "hunkering down" is key.

Aries: Others may be shocked by what's in your heart. Choose confidants carefully. **Taurus:** Great time for messaging large groups. **Gemini:** You may reverse yourself if you commit too soon. **Cancer:** Intense (and enjoyable) self-awareness. Intuition is peaking. **Leo:** You may miss subtle cues and hints. So listen carefully. **Virgo:** Your business is at home right now. What do you need to help you recharge there? **Libra:** Others may probe, needing your approval. **Scorpio:** You may marvel at how vulnerable others are. Scorps are tough! **Sagittarius:** Deepen interactions with a partner; listening carefully helps you grow. **Capricorn:** Look back two weeks: what advancements came to you? **Aquarius:** Plan a get-together and don't self-criticize. **Pisces:** Excellent for cleaning your home—or fishtank.

Monday, August 3: Full Moon in Aquarius

The Native Americans celebrated this "Sturgeon Moon" because a food staple could be caught in droves in Lake Michigan during this Full Moon. But whether you're fishing for food or just compliments, the sky's the limit for big ideas.

Aries: Many folks need your attention—they want to share hopes and dreams. What are yours? **Taurus:** Feeling scattered? Don't worry. Give ideas time to rise to the surface. **Gemini:** Be creative and don't stay home. You need others to be at your best. **Cancer:** The urge for freedom is enormous. What makes you feel "unfettered"? Pursue. **Leo:** You could be talked out of a decision that means a lot. For now, don't listen to others. **Virgo:** Consider collaborators. Don't be hurt by carelessness. **Libra:** Working in a group moves you forward and sparks your consciousness. **Scorpio:** Be cautious about whom you share your cool idea with. **Sagittarius:** Your creative side is on fire—push yourself. **Capricorn:** Creative accounting could help you achieve an investment goal. Sharpen your pencil. **Aquarius:** Your personal "Full Moon" takes your February decisions to the next step. **Pisces:** Finishing a task is critical. Ignore distractions!

Tuesday, August 18: New Moon in Leo

This New Moon coincides with an excellent relationship with Mars (action) in Aries. Novelty, toys, amusements are worth pursuing. Leo Moons make it fun to act like a child—or to get in touch with childish interests.

Aries: Nothing can stop you—but will you burn out? Pursue comfort during this lunar phase. **Taurus:** A good day for a new hair-do, but hair-splitting is likely in even casual conversations. **Gemini:** What are you selling? Can you make it more appealing? Charge more, rather than less. **Cancer:** Venus in your Sun sign amps up your appeal to others. Enjoy the attention! **Leo:** This is your personal New Moon, and decisions you make now could unfold over the next six months. This also means that relationships and projects that are troubled could bottom out. You will prevail. **Virgo:** Being tentative isn't your style, but resisting commitment is the safe choice for now. **Libra:** Your capacity for learning something new is immense—use it. **Scorpio:** Finances are stressed—also possibly stressful! **Sagittarius:** Your positive philosophy makes a difference. **Capricorn:** Opposites attract. Loudmouths love you now! **Aquarius:** Dissatisfaction over trifles is beneath you. **Pisces:** So not your thing, but speaking up pays dividends.

Wednesday, September 2: Full Moon in Pisces

Also known as the "Corn Moon" because we're bringing in the sheaves. However, Pisces Moons can prompt the weak to indulge in substances that aren't good for them. This Full Moon is in harmony with Neptune (in Pisces), so escapism appeals to all.

Aries: Things are more complicated than you think. Don't rush. **Taurus:** Your artistic side flourishes, home-improvements bring joy. **Gemini:** You may think prospects are darker than they are, or that they require more work. **Cancer:** Make time for meditation—your perceptions are amplified. **Leo:** Visual images count more than words. Can you lose yourself in a painting or photograph? **Virgo:** Frustration is possible. Park the emotions and focus on analyzing. **Libra:** Find clarity in regards to work and health. Everything okay? **Scorpio:** Entertain and let everyone know about your cool new project! **Sagittarius:** Little things vex, but you're a big-picture person, right? **Capricorn:** Hidden talents come to the surface—give yourself time to be brilliant. **Aquarius:** Your urge to "cash in" is huge, especially if you're a natural gambler. **Pisces:** Your annual "Full Moon" could be a time of emotional engagement and opportunities from folks you're comfortable with.

Thursday, September 17: New Moon in Virgo

Virgo Moons bring perfectionism. Folks who paint in broad strokes will enjoy fine-tuning. Jupiter (generosity) and Saturn (limitations) are both in Capricorn, and all this earth can make it a good time to invest. Or clean—cleaning improves your life also!

Aries: Let others fuss about you, epecially if they're willing to help! **Taurus:** Be careful about "helping" others. They may think you're being bossy. **Gemini:** You move at a different speed than others. Don't expect them to keep up. **Cancer:** This lunar phase is excellent for setting up a health plan. **Leo:** Put into practice any ideas or ambitions that erupted during your birthday month. **Virgo:** Your personal New Moon, and an important decision time. What project or relationship do you want to focus on in the next six months? Follow your instincts and details will work themselves out. **Libra:** An audience wants to applaud you— really! **Scorpio:** Super for finishing big projects or seeing how the pieces fit. **Sagittarius:** Comments from folks who are usually affable could fog your glasses and find you in defensive mode. **Capricorn:** Don't be rushed, but do be thorough. **Aquarius:** Others may be fussy—you may find this funny. **Pisces:** Could be an emotional "low." It will pass.

Thursday, October 1: Full Moon in Aries

Since Mars in Aries is deep in a retrograde (that lasts through the year), flirtation and romantic do-si-do-ing could come with these Aries Moons. Are you fixated on someone not-your-type? Does this amuse you? Bear in mind this is the "Hunter Moon," so another could be fixating on you!

Aries: Your charisma is at full strength, but your irritability could show if your patience is tried. **Taurus:** Find a project to finish quickly, as your attention span may dwindle. **Gemini:** Loudmouths seek you out. Do they make you laugh or help your cause? **Cancer:** Most crabs are more mature than their peers, and this Full Moon may bring young 'uns to your door. **Leo:** Spend time with dear friends and family who are younger (or more jejeune!). **Virgo:** You'll resist being hurried and demand the time you need. **Libra:** Feeling vulnerable? Review diet and health choices. **Scorpio:** Children (or the childlike) seek you out or need your protection. **Sagittarius:** Take chances and move quickly. **Capricorn:** Easy to get the wrong idea—investigate if things aren't as they should be. **Aquarius:** Encourage others to be brave—you're a great cheerleader. **Pisces:** Put your shoulder to the wheel: huge effort pays off.

Friday, October 16: New Moon in Libra

A lunar phase for being the go-between. With Mercury (communication) retrograde in Scorpio/Libra from October 13 through November 3, many messed-up messages could prevail. But reviewing options is critical.

Aries: Others could read you wrong and see lack of interest in areas that affect you passionately. Be precise in your wording. **Taurus:** Bulls need to socialize. Stick with worldly, cultured pals right now. **Gemini:** You can take in much information. Fact-check before you make claims. **Cancer:** Don't hold anyone to a promise. This New Moon gives you a fresh start. **Leo:** Consider both sides and don't play favorites. **Virgo:** Your desire for grace, efficiency, and ease is strong. **Libra:** Important for long-term planning. Libra's versatility makes it hard for you to narrow focus—but make the effort now. **Scorpio:** Friends and work-family want to embrace you. It's okay to let them! **Sagittarius:** Lots of talk, lots of ideas. You're in the thick of it. **Capricorn:** Do you have insurance, or a back-up plan? Explore. **Aquarius:** You're great in groups, but today is one-on-one. **Pisces:** Take intimacy to the next step.

Saturday, October 31: Full Moon in Taurus

I've tracked the Hallowe'en lunar phases for years, and having this holiday on a weekend with a Full Moon in generous Taurus could mean maximum entertainment—or mayhem.

Aries: It's okay to ask for seconds, or thirds. Get what you need. **Taurus:** This is your Full Moon—anything you put your mind to, you can get done. Think big, bigger, biggest! **Gemini:** Others may crave intimacy with you, but you may need to keep things light. **Cancer:** This is one of those Full Moons that helps your social side. Open your doors to folks you find reliable. **Leo:** Sometimes a mask helps you discover who you really are. **Virgo:** Virgo is capable of intricate analysis—this brings great joy. **Libra:** Time for shopping! Upgrade your stuff! Your aim is true. **Scorpio:** Don't let others press your buttons. They may not mean to, but they do. **Sagittarius:** Others are blunt—don't take things personally. **Capricorn:** Take your time, strive for elegance. **Aquarius:** Stay where you're comfortable and cozy. **Pisces:** Look at your investments and do a financial reckoning.

Sunday, November 15: New Moon in Scorpio

Cut to the chase—this Scorpio Moon wants you to simplify your life. Venus (love) in Libra close behind the Moon points you toward new relationships with peers. Scorpio Moons are also useful for sensual indulgence and moving money around.

Aries: The shy or recessive folks in your life will be even more vague and mysterious. Be patient with them. **Taurus:** Intimacy and closer connections: that's what you want. **Gemini:** You may think a situation is simple, but it's not. Dig deeper than you expected. **Cancer:** Everyone has a secret, and many will want to share. You don't have to listen. **Leo:** You could surprise yourself with the complexity of your emotions. **Virgo:** Go through your tool box (however you define) and get new tools that work better. **Libra:** Are you earning what you're worth? Are you saving? Reassure yourself on those fronts. **Scorpio:** Your personal New Moon merits your attention to plans and goals for the next year. Aim high! **Sagittarius:** Take inventory—what is slowing you down? **Capricorn**: What could you learn that would save you time? **Aquarius:** Others' careless words could penetrate. **Pisces:** Stand up for what you believe in.

Monday, November 30: Full Moon in Gemini

It's been a long holiday weekend, and whether you're still stuffed with the festive bird or not, many folks in your circle have a lot more to say. With the Yule holidays around the corner, the Gemini Moon demands we all find ways to communicate clearly with near and dear ones.

Aries: Improve your communication devices. Why not upgrade? **Taurus:** Write to faraway friends, make a joke out of a recent frustration. Laughter heals. **Gemini:** Look back at late May. What happened then that connects to a current situation? **Cancer:** Sometimes the crab needs time to molt and grow another hard shell. **Leo:** Communication comes easily—work hard and find out as much as you can. This pays off. **Virgo:** Test yourself by doing some mental gymnastics. A different kind of word or number puzzle? Good distraction! **Libra:** Pursue sensual pleasures with a vengeance! **Scorpio:** Partnerships need attention. **Sagittarius:** "Low tide" emotionally. Others may accuse you of not taking things seriously. **Capricorn:** Spend time with smart people who share your droll sense of humor. **Aquarius:** An excellent time for writing, reading, or communicating. **Pisces:** Easy to get bogged down in trifles.

Monday, December 14: New Moon in Sagittarius

An excellent day for planning travel, or deciding whether to take a course, or biting the bullet and going back to school. Judging your own abilities comes easily during this New Moon. Mars (action) in Aries makes a helpful angle for changes of direction regarding health.

Aries: Your taste for eccentricity is at a high point. Seek out those friends who make you laugh. **Taurus:** The urge for travel is strong. Are you really staying home all winter? **Gemini:** You're fragile—don't push yourself. And don't get goaded. Remember: "It is what it is." **Cancer:** Get active, get moving, and don't believe everything you hear. You know the folks who like to exaggerate. **Leo:** Being on the go is preferable to cocooning—being entertained, even better. **Virgo:** Another's lack of judgment could vex. Do you need to be annoyed? Why not ignore it? **Libra:** Making new friends is easy, but you don't need to get everyone a holiday gift! **Scorpio:** Financial entangling can be sorted out. Make the time now. **Sagittarius:** Your personal "New Moon" for 2020. Find out what you believe, not what others would have you do. **Capricorn:** If you're on the edge, that's the right place. Don't be hurried. **Aquarius:** A fine day to look at sporting equipment. **Pisces:** Justice will prevail—and your sense of fairness becomes you.

Tuesday, December 29: Full Moon in Cancer

"Cold Moon." Cancer Moons can increase sensitivity. Jupiter (generosity) and Saturn (limitations) are now in Aquarius, after being in lock-step in Capricorn. Huge transformations in the works regarding power (fuel) and power (leadership). It's a great time to invest in new technology, or join an organization or group that looks to improve humanity.

Aries: If you're feeling rushed, it's not you—it's the planets. Wait until the new year to invest in big purchases. **Taurus:** Excellent time for understanding and compassion for others. Taurus's loyalty is valued. **Gemini:** Move at a slower speed. You'll notice more details that way. **Cancer:** Look back to mid-July and your personal New Moon. What happened then that has developed or deepened by now? **Leo:** A home with luxuries makes Leo purr, especially when shared with dear friends and family. **Virgo:** Sensitive folks in your circle may need you to pry. Can you help them make a significant self-discovery? **Libra:** Your body needs to feel good for you to be your best. Treat it well. **Scorpio:** Partnerships with others means dealing with their sensitivities. Play nice! **Sagittarius:** Your inner-child needs attention! **Capricorn**: Others need you to be of service to them, but you could be stretched thin. **Aquarius:** Your "do it quickly" impulse should be thwarted. Take your time. **Pisces:** Get back to basics. If you've over-indulged during the holidays, reverse direction!

2020
Moon Sign Book
Articles

Moonstruck: Moon Myths in Modern Times

by Mireille Blacke, MA, LADC, RD, CD-N

Though it's been thirty years since I sat anxiously in my general psychology class my freshman year of college, I still remember the moment clearly. The Jesuit professor was returning our first exams of the semester. This test was fairly straightforward, except for one particular question. I looked down at my graded exam—I got the question wrong! I was irritated. Then I looked around. It seemed like most of the students answered this question incorrectly, responding that the number of admissions to psychiatric wards increased during a Full Moon. This topic was not covered in our course material, but everyone knew that was true! Right?

Apparently not. Clearly, my professor had a reason to include this question on the exam. But he also touched upon something prevalent in modern society: Where do we get these notions about the Moon? Why do we believe what we do?

The Moon has been revered as sacred, mystical, and scientifically appealing across the span of human history. Moon myths, legends, and lore have persisted from our ancient past to modern times. How much of the Moon's supposed effects are fact and how much are fiction?

I'll give you one guess which myth I'm tackling first.

Myth 1: Lunacy

Obviously that test question always stuck with me, but not for the reason you might think. The truth is nearly every student in the class was convinced that the Full Moon increased psychiatric hospital admissions, despite any statistical evidence or research to back up that assertion. This belief holds true today; I hear similar sentiments from my coworkers in health care settings frequently—"It must be a Full Moon"—when overloaded emergency room, psychiatry, and other nursing staff perceive increased admissions or chaos in general.

The reason this perception is a myth and I got that test question wrong is simple: numerous studies have been conducted over the years to test the hypotheses that lunar phases (the Full Moon in particular) affect rates of births, deaths, suicides, psychiatric hospital admissions, epileptic seizures, cardiac events, episodes of violence, and other forms of human behavior, but all of them have found no statistical correlation. Anecdotal evidence—casual information collected from personal testimony in a non-scientific manner, like a friend's personal experience—does not constitute scientific proof. That was the point my psychology professor was trying to make with that test question. All of society might believe something to be true, but that by itself does not actually make the belief true.

It's not a large leap from Moon-induced lunacy, with its link to the darker side of the human psyche, to legends of the Full Moon transforming rational humans into their howling, wild counterparts: werewolves. The loss of control linked to insanity is not a far cry from primal, animal instinct, lack of inhibition, and the uncontrolled and illogical id, represented well by a crazed, blood-thirsty werewolf on the loose. I recall watching Ozzy Osbourne's "Bark at the Moon" video in my teen years, in which Ozzy portrays the dichotomous Dr. Jekyll and Mr. Hyde. Hyde morphs into a werewolf with the rise of the Full Moon (and a vat of drugs), taking away the inhibited doctor's accountability for indulgence in vices. Whether the message was from "Prince of Darkness" Ozzy Osbourne or William Shakespeare, the point was the same. Perhaps the notion of the Full Moon and werewolves is the recognition of humankind's basic, simmering urges to "let loose," and with that, the very real fear of losing control.

Myth 2: The Man in the Moon

Considering the Moon is 4.5 billion years old, there's no doubt that millions of people have seen "the man in the Moon" on the lunar surface. Looking upward at the Moon and seeing a human face gazing down upon us is a collective human experience, regardless of time period, location in the world, belief system, or race/ethnicity.

However, there is a logical explanation. Due to the perceptual phenomenon called pareidolia, humans have a tendency to interpret random patterns as familiar, particularly as faces; to our eyes, the shaded regions of the lunar surface form features of "the man in the Moon." Other cultures share this phenomenon as well, though some glimpse a large rabbit in the Moon instead of a human face. A particular Chinese legend is further explained in the following conversation between Ronald Evans at Mission Control in Houston and astronaut Michael Collins during the Apollo 11 mission in 1969:

Ronald Evans/Mission Control: "Among the large headlines concerning Apollo this morning, there's one asking that you watch for a lovely girl with a big rabbit. An ancient legend says a beautiful Chinese girl called Chango-o has been living there for 4,000 years. It seems she was banished to the Moon because she stole the pill of immortality from her husband. You might also look for her companion, a large Chinese rabbit, who is easy to spot since he is always standing on his hind feet in the shade of a cinnamon tree. The name of the rabbit is not reported."

Michael Collins/Lunar Orbiter: "OK. We'll keep a close eye out for the bunny girl" (Redd 2014).

The bunny girl and the man in the Moon wisely remained out of sight during that space mission and all others that followed, and have requested that the public respect their privacy at this time.

Myth 3: Humans Didn't Actually Land on the Moon (Apollo Moon Landings Were Faked)

One of the most common Moon myths is that the Apollo Moon landings never happened and humans didn't actually land on the Moon. Non-believers insist that technology to enable such trips during the late 1960s and early 1970s was not available then, while believers point to the differences between terrestrial material and rocks and soils returned by the Apollo teams, as well as the footprints and flags left behind. There are also some more specific points to address:

Point: The American flag is waving in a place with no wind.

Fact: The astronauts had a tough time planting the flagpole into the lunar surface, resulting in excessive pulling and shaking to keep it erect. While the Moon lacks an atmosphere, it has one-sixth of Earth's gravity, which means you can expect a shaken flagpole to produce a fluttering flag, if fleetingly.

Point: The Moon landing photos have multiple-angle shadows that could only be made in a large professional studio at that time.

Fact: One thing that space exploration is known for is documentation, so timestamps are noted on every movement the astronauts made. The Sun was close to the horizon while photos were taken on an uneven, brightly lit terrain. Shadows of different lengths would be expected in photographs taken in such a landscape.

Point: The film should have melted because the Moon's surface temperature would have fried it.

Fact: Exposed film left out on a lunar surface of 280°F would have melted, but film was kept in protective canisters. Also, the landings occurred at either lunar dawn or dusk, when temperatures were lower (Myers).

Point: Don't you need moisture to leave a footprint?

Fact: No. With friction, some fine-grained particles maintain a shape or impression like a footprint without any moisture (Myers).

Point: There was no crater left at the landing site.

Fact: As noted with the flagpole fact, the Moon is primarily made of densely packed rock. The landing films do show evidence, however, of significant dust and dirt layers being kicked up from the surface.

Point: How did that huge Moon rover fit into that tiny landing module?

Fact: Aerospace engineers are capable of many things, including clever construction and a design using light materials for a Moon rover that compactly folds-up to store easily in a tight space.

Point: Why are stars missing from all of the photographs?

Fact: In photographs taken outside at night, faint distant objects will not show up with brighter objects nearby. Try it for yourself.

Myth 4: The Moon Has a "Dark Side"

Well, don't we all?

Looking up at the Moon, you will see craters or patches of shading. Depending on if you're looking with the naked eye or using a telescope, details may vary, but the landscape will not. The same "face" will always look back at you. But what's on the other side?

The first time I heard this particular phrase was (no surprise) in reference to Pink Floyd's 1973 album title. But for many people, the phrase "dark side of the Moon" refers to a mysterious and unknown side we never see, facing away from us, seemingly cloaked in shadows.

The truth is not so foreboding. The Earth and Moon's rotation are synchronized such that the same face of the Moon is always pointed toward us. The term for the side of the Moon we see is the near side. A more accurate term for the side opposite the near side is the far side. The near side will always face toward us, and the far side will always face away. This is true from any vantage point on Earth (Plaitt).

The "dark side" term is technically inaccurate, because when the Moon's surface faces the Earth, the far side points toward the Sun and its rays. Therefore, both the near and far sides of the Moon have a day and a night. Both receive sunlight at particular points of the Moon's orbit around the Earth. Our view of the far side is blocked, even when the sun is shining on it, because the it always faces away from us.

Even though there is no actual "dark side" of the Moon, the far side still holds some mystery for us. Between both the far and near sides, we still have plenty to ponder.

Myth 5: Falling in Love Is More Likely During a Full Moon

Similar to Myth 1, there is no tangible research to support this claim. However, anecdotal evidence exists and movies like *Moonstruck* further support this widespread belief. It's likely the concept of mooning over someone (not to be confused with baring oneself and "mooning" someone) emerged from this myth.

Myth 6: The Moon Is Made of Green Cheese

While I doubt anyone ever considered this old expression to be fact, I was still curious as to its origins. Sixteenth-century English playwright and master of proverbs John Heywood is responsible for penning a poem that gave us today's "the Moon is made of green cheese." For the record, Heywood was no slouch when it came to proverbs. Some of his most famous are "haste makes waste," "a penny for your thoughts," "the more, the merrier," and "two heads are better than one." In 1546, Heywood wrote:

> *Ye fetch circumquaques to make me believe,*
> *Or thinke, that the Moone is made of greene cheese.*
> *And when ye have made me a lout in all these,*
> *It seemeth ye would make me goe to bed at noone.* (Mancini)

In this context, Heywood uses the term "greene" to mean fresh, immature, or young, and is not referring to color. In essence, the writer is stating, "You think I'm so gullible that I'd believe this! Only an idiot would believe the Moon is made of fresh cheese." In hindsight, and certainly after the Moon's composition was determined in the twentieth century, modern minds may have thought those in the sixteenth century fell for a complete impossibility, but it seems clear that even in Heywood's time, no one really thought the Moon was made of green cheese.

For those still in doubt, I will refer you to the 842 pounds of inedible, quite old Moon rocks returned by Apollo 11 and other Moon missions for sampling. Be sure to update your dental plan before doing so.

To the Moon, Baby

Moon myths flourish in modern times, depending on the year, month, or day—Supermoons, lunar eclipses, and Blood Moons may all be harbingers of the apocalypse, or perhaps they're just being marketed that way to move online merchandise. To clarify lunar myth perceptions, it seems like an article in the *Moon Sign Book* is the place to do it!

I realize that for some, the conspiracy theory of the Apollo Moon landings will remain an indelible Moon-related construct. But for me, lore and myths surrounding the Moon are less sinister, with a deeper connection to my childhood. Moon myths aside, what is childhood if not the expansion of memories to mythic proportion?

I will forever cherish memories of childish, drowsy wonderment as my mother read *Goodnight, Moon* nursery rhymes of cows jumping over the Moon, and later cherish my laughter and empathy at identifying with nearly every scene in *Moonstruck*.

Sometimes our memories feed into the myths, and vice versa.

Thirty years after that &#$@! test question, I'm a professor, administering graduate-level exams to my own students. I'd say Moon myths are just as prevalent today as three decades ago, and the internet will keep these and more like them thriving. Maybe I'll toss my students a trick question for old time's sake and test the current strength of Myth 1.

But most likely, I'll watch a DVD of one of my favorite films as the Full Moon rises, and sarcastically tell myself to snap out of it!

Resources

"Apollo 11 jokingly ordered to watch for Chang'e." 2013. Global Times. http://www.globaltimes.cn/content/829188.shtml.

Britt, Robert Roy. 2016. "It's Just a Phase: The Supermoon Won't Drive You Mad." Live Science. https://www.livescience.com/7899-moon-myths-truth-lunar-effects.html.

Mancini, Mark. 2019. "Why Do People Say the Moon Is Made of Cheese?" Mental Floss. http://mentalfloss.com/article/53107/why-do-people-say-Moon-made-cheese.

Myers, Robert and Robert Pearlman. 2011. "Apollo Moon Landing Hoax Theories that Won't Die." Space. https://www.space.com/12814-top-10-apollo-moon-landing-hoax-theories.html.

Plait, Phil. 2008. "Dark Side of the Moon." Bad Astronomy. http://www.badastronomy.com/bad/misc/dark_side.html.

Redd, Nola Taylor. 2014. "Bunnies on the Moon? 7 Lunar Myths Apollo 11 Debunked." Space. https://www.space.com/26640-moon-myths-debunked-apollo-11.html.

____. 2015. "Biggest Moon Myths for the 'Supermoon' Total Lunar Eclipse." Space. https://www.space.com/30632-Moon-myths-super Moon-lunar-eclipse-myths.html.

Essential Oils and the Moon

by Robin Ivy Payton

Like winds and waves, our vital life force shifts with the lunar cycle. We experience the rising energy of waxing Moon and the downward energy of waning Moon each month. When our bodies and minds are in harmony, we feel balanced and in rhythm with the universe. At those times, it's easier to flow or be resilient during the rise or decline of lunar energy, even on challenging days. For example, when the Moon engages in a square or opposition, our anxiety or stress level may temporarily increase with the conflict or uncertainty, and then naturally return to equilibrium. Sometimes though, we become overwhelmed, blocked, or uninspired, and experience strong emotions that persist. You may burn sage, clean the house, meditate, practice gentle yoga, or manage these fluctuations with other comforting rituals and routines. Essential oils for aromatherapy are another way to boost or release energy and increase feelings of clarity, well-being, and grounding. Families of oils associate with air, water, earth, and fire, and also with portions of the lunar cycle. With your Moon and Sun profile and olfactory preferences in mind, explore essential oils as another resource to support your intentions and rhythms as the Moon waxes and wanes, peaks and shines through each of the signs.

Organic oils are gifts of nature that we humans can use for self-care and mindful transitions. Coming from the plant, they hold the inherent wisdom of nature, so when we use them we are tapping right into the source. The oils found in the bark, roots, seeds, flowers, and peels of trees, fruits, and all sorts of plants have innate antifungal, antimicrobial properties. They protect plants from disease and threats, and they attract pollinators, perpetuating survival and reproduction. When diffused into the air, ingested by mouth or nose, or applied to the skin, many essential oils interact with the human body in beneficial ways. Because their molecules are small and lipid soluble, they cross the blood-brain barrier and create emotional and physical responses. The unique smell of an essential oil may create a positive feeling instantly, yet the influence can be even deeper and affect your body at a cellular level. Some types of oils, such as citrus, herbal, spice, floral, and camphor, sync well with the cycles of the Moon and the four elements of the zodiac. To bring oils into your life, begin by identifying four or five to use on a rotating basis, guided by the Moon's phase and sign. Note any shifts you feel as you breathe or absorb them, and create a set of supportive oils that flow with you daily and through the quarters of the Moon.

Monthly, or from one month to the next, the New and Full Moons grace particular signs, generally the polar opposites. Therefore, a New Moon in Leo leads to a Full Moon in Aquarius. When the cycle begins in Virgo, the Moon peaks in Pisces, and so on throughout the year. Your essential oils may also be based on polarities as you choose oils that align with or contrast your feelings and responses to the natural lunar rhythms. Considering the element the Moon lands in can also guide your choices.

New and waxing Moon times are for clearing the path, growing, warming, developing, progressing, and giving. These weeks correlate with air and fire elements. Citrus and spices nourish and invigorate our experiences during this half of the cycle. Yet, there are times when all of this activity feels overpowering and it makes sense to lean into herbal, floral, and tree-based oils for grounding. During the Full Moon, as we are finalizing, committing, celebrating, or healing, our emotions also reach their potential. Special oils assist in balancing hormones, moods, and how we respond to the intensity and peaks. As the Moon wanes, the energy of releasing, unwinding, adjusting, and disseminating is supported by floral, herbal, mint, and camphor. If you feel relieved or harmonious at this time, notice what oils you're most drawn to. Alternatively, if you feel down or unmotivated, the mints and florals offer gentle uplifting, as do citrus oils, such as bergamot. Finally, the balsamic Moon is for revising and resting, and oils that refresh and cool help prepare us for the upcoming cycle.

Here are some examples of essential oils to try as the Moon moves through each phase and zodiac sign. Also, take into consideration your own Sun, Moon, and rising sign, since your individual profile influences your preferences and tendencies. Let's start with the elements and some suggestions for how to use your oils creatively.

When the Moon visits a fire sign—Aries, Leo, or Sagittarius—add a bit of oil to a candle or warm some stones and drop oils on them to inspire your mind and activities. Anoint the chest, collarbones, shoulders, and hands, all of which relate to the heart chakra. During this time of action, creativity, and social energy, choose oils like wild orange, cinnamon, clove, and grapefruit to support your plans.

On earth sign days—when the Moon is in Taurus, Virgo or Capricorn—add a drop or two of oils while cooking, dilute in a carrier oil for hands or full body massage, or have some oil-infused Play-Doh made and stored in an airtight container. Knead the dough for stress release or to exercise tired/sore fingers or wrists. Anoint knees, mastoid bones, and other joints. Think building, prospering, productivity, and also grounding, as you incorporate rosemary, geranium, lavender, cedarwood, and other woodsy and herbal oils.

Diffuse and breathe the oils when the Moon sails through air signs Gemini, Libra, and Aquarius. Anoint your forehead, wrists, and ankles. If you're drawing or writing, scent your paper with one drop. Dip a toothpick in frankincense or peppermint or place a drop under your tongue to encourage clear speech. These Moon signs encourage collaboration, communication, inventiveness, and agreements. Citrus such as lemon aligns well with the clear focus needed for such activities, while cedarwood and geranium foster open minds and grounding for working together.

When the Moon is in water signs—Cancer, Scorpio, and Pisces—emotions are highlighted. Use oils that instill joy, such as tangerine, or those that support grief, like ylang-ylang or frankincense. Put one to a few drops of mint or lavender in tea or water, and drink your ingestible oils in tiny amounts. Bathe with a few drops of melaleuca (tea tree oil), jasmine, or eucalyptus with a proper dispersant, and allow your skin to absorb the oils through open pores. Anoint your abdomen, heart, and feet as you honor feelings and privacy, nurture others, and detoxify the body and mind.

Oils for Balsamic Moon

Balsamic Moon phase begins about three days before the New Moon when the Moon moves within 45 degrees of the Sun. Balsamic means restorative, and it's a time to replenish, clear energy, create space, and reflect. Essential oils in the mint and camphor families literally clear the air. Eucalyptus, a spa favorite, comes from the leaves of the eucalyptus tree. When diffused into the air, eucalyptus smells fresh and clean, opens the nasal passages, and may help boost the immune system. Though eucalyptus has a relaxing effect on many people, it actually stimulates blood flow to the brain and can help boost energy and alertness. If the dark phase of the Moon tends to pull your energy down a bit too far, diffuse, inhale, or massage diluted eucalyptus oil. Eucalyptus also has antimicrobial, antiseptic qualities that lend well to house cleaning as you prepare for New Moon.

Peppermint is also well suited to balsamic Moon phase. Mildly energizing, peppermint counteracts sluggishness or melancholy feelings characteristic of dark Moon days and cuts through murky energy in the body or the environment. Known to support res-piration and digestion, peppermint oil also aligns energetically with processing and digesting experiences before starting the next lunar cycle. Inhale organic, therapeutic-grade peppermint oil from your hands to open the throat chakra and open up commu-nication. Feel peppermint act powerfully to clear your head for decisions or conversations due with the oncoming New Moon.

Oils for New Moon

As New Moon arrives, enjoy the uplifting properties of citrus. New Moon favors initiating, regrouping, and diving into projects and plans. The citrus oils, often cold pressed from the rind, relate to motivation and fresh starts as the lunar cycle begins. They align well with our third chakra, the solar plexus, which is the home of self-esteem and sense of purpose.

Lemon and wild orange oils are energy boosters that increase our focus for tasks and decisions. Grapefruit, another citrus, supports dietary changes that begin with New Moon. If you use food-grade quality oils, brighten up your water with a few drops of lemon, orange, or grapefruit, and sip throughout the active hours of your day.

Bergamot oil is reputed to balance moods, so if anxiety comes with the uprising of New and waxing Moon, try this oil to reduce tension and feel grounded. High-quality bergamot is a wonderful addition to black tea. Like the other essential oils, it can be diffused or used in the shower as a steam.

Oils for Waxing Moon

As the Moon increases, warming oils like clove, ginger, and cinnamon can be added to your routine in similar ways. These spices add a fire element, which naturally aligns with the waxing Moon. Related to the heart chakra, our fourth energy center, they have inspirational and passionate qualities aligned with growth, creativity, and openness. Use them sparingly and dilute with carrier oils, like coconut, since they tend to be strong. Spices also blend with citrus and mint oils quite nicely. Awaken your senses and keep your mind alert with blends of clove, cinnamon, and

wild orange, or combine ginger and lemon for healthy digestion. Energetically, New and waxing Moon are an uprising, like the tide coming in. For some of us, this resonates and we embrace this time of progress with stronger and spicier blends. For others who tend to feel overpowered by lunar currents, milder choices like lemon or grapefruit soothe the nervous system without dimming or scattering our focus.

Oils for Full Moon

Full Moon is the high tide of the lunar cycle. Whatever you're feeling or involved in is likely to be magnified, and emotions tend to the extremes. Precious oils and specialized selections are appropriate to Full Moon circumstances and states of mind. Frankincense is lovely any time, and is a Full Moon go-to because it blends with or enhances almost any other oil. Historically, frankincense was used in spiritual practices and associates with emotional and physical healing. Good for the skin, the immune system, and cellular health, frankincense also has anti-anxiety and antidepressant qualities. As you seek comfort, peace, the guidance of higher power, or even right speech during Full Moon time, frankincense has much to offer. It can be inhaled, diffused, or taken by mouth as long as you have high-quality, food-grade oil.

Clary sage is well known for hormone balance, particularly for the female reproductive cycle. Closely aligned with lunar energy, clary sage can be rubbed on the abdomen or chest, or added to massage oil and bathwater. Women may use clary sage during their menstrual cycle, though this oil should not be used during pregnancy or if you are trying to conceive. Clary sage is also said to encourage restful sleep during this wakeful Moon time.

Copaiba, like frankincense, comes from the resin of a tree. It has a complex, spicy, and woodsy scent that is very unique. Interacting with many systems of the body, including immune, digestive, and respiratory, copaiba is a strong choice when physical issues or ailments are present. Since symptoms may increase during Full Moon, try copaiba for its reputed pain-relieving properties. This oil is also known to reduce feelings of anxiety that may peak at this time in our lunar cycle. Its earthy aroma contributes to a sense of stability and well-being.

Oils for Waning Moon

Trees and flowers offer essential oils aligned with the releasing and receptive natures of waning Moon time. Lavender, ylang-ylang, jasmine, and geranium are florals for relaxation, comfort, and sentimental feelings. The unwinding of waning Moon is similar to preparing for rest in the evening, and lavender on the feet promotes both calm and sleep. Jasmine is a richer, more exotic scent that uplights the Moon and is associated with love and romance. Ylang-ylang, also associated with love, has been used traditionally in wedding ceremonies. All of these floral oils are beautifying and often used in hair or skin care products. During waning Moon, add drops to your hair conditioner or a soothing bath.

Cedarwood and sandalwood, two of the tree oils, are sweet and woodsy. Breathe in during meditation to connect to the earth, while freeing your mind of extraneous thoughts once Full Moon has passed and it's time to let go. Either can be used to steam the face and detoxify the skin, as this phase of the Moon favors release.

Note: Before using any essential oils, read about their properties and safety warnings. Use carrier oils to safely dilute before applying any essential oil to the skin.

Put Your Heart Into It: The Moon's Role in Vocation

by Amy Herring

Many of us wonder what we are called to do, not just what we *can* do or what we have the skills for. We want to uncover our purpose, our mission; we want to know what we were made for.

The word *vocation* often means "a calling" and has long held an aura of divinity about it, probably because its earliest uses were aligned with the idea of being called by god. Even in modern, everyday usage, we still tend to think more reverently about vocation than we do when speaking about our career or our job. To speak of vocation gives us the sense that each person has gifts and talents that are innately suited for that singular, perfect calling that was meant for them. Many of us search for our vocation with the same intensity we may search for our soul mate—looking for "the one," our destiny. We long to fit like a key into a lock, where everything we've studied and all our past experience has prepared us for our right calling. We may imagine that when we get that call, we'll know that this is the first day of the rest of our lives, right?

But most of us don't get a letter in the mail telling us when and where to show up for the rest of that life! We follow our curiosity and develop our interests, looking for sparks that we can ignite into a flame. We have to draw from the clues we get along the way, and our vocational path is rarely a straight road with even terrain. We may sometimes feel that we are stalled if we don't know what we want or where we want to go, or that life is compelling us to stumble along without any sense of a meaningful direction. Whether we're just beginning to determine our path or we've been walking for a while and come to a crossroads or a dead end, feeling our way is sometimes the only option. When our map fails us or we're entering undiscovered territory, we do well to rely on our inner compass.

The idea of a calling can be inspirational and moving but also overwhelming and thwarting. It can cause us to discount quiet nudges from our inner compass because we are waiting for the trumpets to announce our cosmic job title. A profound sense of vocation may not always come in the ecstasy of prayer but in following the continuing nudges of things like our own curiosity, interest, and delight. After all, a compass doesn't tell you about your destination, it simply tells you in which direction you are moving.

The Moon's Role in Vocation

Finding and fulfilling our vocation is not something we can compartmentalize into one part of our life or one aspect of our personality. Centering on a sense of vocation involves many parts of us coming together and is therefore reflected through many symbols in our natal charts. The Sun can symbolize our overall sense of purpose; Mars represents our drive and style of pursuing it; and planets involved with the second, sixth, and tenth houses of money, work, and career all have their two cents to offer—and that's just the beginning! But when it comes to what you love and what makes you happy, you're speaking the Moon's language. The Moon symbolizes the inner compass that can help you orient on what you want or need.

The Moon's role in vocation can help you hone in on things like which pursuits, causes, or activities touch and move you deeply, or give you comfort and a sense of emotional rightness, peacefulness, or fulfillment. It can tell you what you instinctively want to shelter, nurture, protect, and encourage. It doesn't tell you what is reasonable, responsible, or practical, and it doesn't care what your resume looks like or what the current job market has to offer! "Follow your heart" is something we may hear in a pep talk or read in a greeting card but is easily dismissed advice in the so-called real world where we are trained to think that time is money and our professional pursuits mean entering "the rat race." Asking yourself what you want to be when you grow up seems like a childish practice, but sometimes that's precisely what you need to do, and especially without burying yourself in qualifiers ("you can't make money that way," "you're not qualified enough to be successful," "that's not a real job," and so on). Whether you're starting out or starting over, the Moon can take you to the heart of the question and its answer, if you dare to ask it seriously and make time to sit with the question long enough to hear the answers.

They may not be simple answers, especially since life finds a way of filling our time with its necessities and demands and entrenching us in routines we find it difficult to change. Maybe you need to go back to school for what you want to do. Maybe

you can follow a hobby into a career if you continue to build on it and branch out. Maybe you keep your day job but pursue your vocational interests in your free time. The Moon can whisper your desires to you but will leave you to put things into action in the real world.

Here are a few questions and ideas to get that conversation with yourself started. You can also look to your Moon's sign and house placement, as well as planetary aspects with your Moon for a more complete picture.

- What do I love to spend my time doing?

- What activities comfort me?

- What would I do, no matter how small, strange, or self-ish, if I didn't have to worry about making money, getting training, or scavenging for opportunities?

- What nourishes me and gives me life?

- How do I like to take care of others?

- In what circumstances do I feel the most rightness or peace within myself?

- What topics concern me or engage my empathy the most?

Fire Moon Signs (Aries, Leo, and Sagittarius)

You desire a level of passionate engagement with the world that continues to provide you with a sense that the world is a big place with lots of possibilities. You seek out motivation through inspiration, which requires autonomy to do your thing. You want to be uplifted and have a knack for uplifting and motivating others as well, depending on your preferred circumstances. While you need a level of independence, deadlines and friendly competition can push you to excellence. You need freedom to move. For some of you, travel may be an obvious way to get that sense of movement; others may need more of a figurative freedom to express their own creative style without being heavily monitored, controlled, or confined within someone else's vision. You have an entrepreneurial spirit, so working for yourself in contract or freelance work could be ideal, although the realities of that might be a challenge depending on your other, more practical needs beyond the heart.

Earth Moon Signs (Taurus, Virgo, and Capricorn)

You may take great pleasure in getting hands-on with something, sometimes literally. Making an actual object that one can see and touch at the end of the day can bring a level of satisfaction that sometimes the more cerebral pursuits don't provide, and can offer a way to measure their level of progress or productivity. Creativity and satisfaction can be expressed through craftsmanship in this way. While some may be more in a hurry than others, earth Moon signs have an innate understanding that things of quality take time and planning. Pursuits that involve planning or helping others plan in a practical way, from financial planning to launching

events, also involve a level of hands on-control and organization that help earth Moons stay grounded.

Air Moon Signs (Gemini, Libra, Aquarius)

You crave an exchange of ideas and information and feel happiest being able to express yourself in a way that will be heard and considered. You need to have a place where sharing your ideas and opinions is welcomed, whether that's inherent in the type of work you choose (such as research, journalism, marketing, and so on) or in the nature of your environment, with things like regular brainstorming sessions and open, cooperative environments. You may also enjoy a social aspect in your vocation as an outlet for these desires—after all, there's no air in a vacuum! You are a natural observer and sharing your observations is half of the pleasure. Taking in new ideas and pursuing your curiosity is emotionally stimulating and awakening for you.

Water Moon Signs (Cancer, Scorpio, Pisces)

You need to put an element of heart into your work, something that goes beyond enjoying what you do, but where the nature of the work involves a level of feeling, empathy, and imagination that adds a depth of meaning to what you spend your days doing. For some of you, expressing this by caring for others is most instinctual, and your vocational path may feel most aligned with healing arts, either of the body or the spirit (or both in unity!). Others of you may prefer a more solitary vocational path, where you have the time and space alone to draw from that deep well of creativity and imagination. You need a balance between a structure that allows you to feel secure and avoid getting too lost in your own private world, but deadlines or high-pressure may not be for you as it can short-circuit the heart. Built-in recharge time in the rhythm of work can also be important, as you may tend to invest deeply in your work, clients, or coworkers, which can lead to burnout.

The Moon and Metabolism

by Bruce Scofield

In astrology, the Moon is normally said to be an indicator of response and reaction. Consequently, it shows interests and tastes. Being ruler of the sign Cancer, it is also an indicator of nurturing, the most basic form of which is feeding. But at a deeper level, the Moon represents what it takes to put a process into action. It is a kick-starter that gets things going and keeps them moving along. It drives the rhythmic changes that are necessary to sustain and regulate a process, like the behavior of a crowd of people or the digestion of a meal. The Moon is the force behind some of the most basic characteristics of living things, made visible by our unconscious behaviors. We carry with us ancient memories of lunar response patterns and rhythms that keep us in balance with our environment. These memories may go back billions of years.

The first life on planet Earth appeared somewhere between 3.5 and 4 billion years ago, not that long after Earth and then the Moon were formed. We can only speculate on what first life was like, but "origins researchers," as these scientists call themselves, study how strings of molecules (polymers) that bond under natural conditions became more complex, eventually forming macromolecules such as RNA and enzymes that have the ability to start chemical reactions. Some researchers think that it was the spontaneous harnessing of natural chemical reactions in a closed cell that was the first life. The early oceans were devoid of oxygen but rich in iron and other elements that, when triggered by extreme temperature gradients, radiation from the Sun, or the immense tides pulled by the Moon (much closer to Earth than it is today), would begin to bounce electrons between themselves and generate energy. Some molecules capable of setting off chemical chain reactions, called enzymes, were also initiators of energy-producing reactions. Somehow these natural, energized, chemical reactions evolved into the first metabolic pathways and networks that all life today has in common.

Once metabolism got started, life could grow. It could thrive in environments where the materials for metabolic energy generation were readily available. Fast forward to about 600 million years ago, or maybe even earlier, when the first animals evolved in the ancient oceans. Sponges were likely the earliest animals and it is their primitive metabolism that is of interest. The way sponges feed is by pulling water into a special chamber where bacteria are trapped as the water is pushed back out into the sea. Individual cells then digest the bacteria. What is significant about this kind of feeding (called filter feeding) is that the sponge, which is attached to the ocean floor, is dependent on the movement of water. Of course, the movement of water is regulated by the Moon's ocean tides, which stir up the food and other nutrients from the sea bottom that the sponge needs. This may be the original link between the Moon and feeding. Life evolved in the seas and became entrained to a feeding schedule by the lunar tides.

In medical astrology, the Moon is said to rule the stomach and the breasts, each related to feeding. Both organs are—like the sponge chambers—containers, another concept associated with the Moon. Container formation is actually one of the first steps in the building of a body. When animal reproductive cells merge at fertilization, cell division begins and a ball of cells called a blastula is formed. The blastula soon becomes a ball with a hollow inside, now called a gastrula. This is the stage of embryo development when cells begin to differentiate and openings into the hollow container—what will become a mouth and anus—first form. Here we see the beginnings of the digestive tract, a container that later becomes a long tube within which metabolism occurs.

For humans, the activities of feeding and digestion come under the astrological rulership of the Moon, both of which are focused on internal containers, especially the stomach. Although most of us feed according to a meal plan, something that serves as a means of social coordination of groups from families to the national culture, left to our own devices we will most likely feed simply when we are hungry. But what makes us hungry? Hormones circulating in our blood make us feel like eating, or not eating. Some hormones are released by the stomach, intestines, and other organs like the pancreas, so their levels in the body are determined by how much food is being processed at the time. Therefore our feelings and sensations that tell us to eat or not to eat are driven by chemical messages sent from our food processing organs to our brain. It's all quite complicated, but it illustrates the idea of the regulation of rhythmic changes that sustain a process—exactly what the Moon does.

While the astrological Moon points mostly to the stomach and breasts, it also encompasses the entire metabolic system from

front to back. When the Moon in a person's birth chart is being transited by a slow-moving planet like Saturn, digestion can be slowed or even stopped. With a transit from Jupiter there may be problems with excesses; with Mars, stomach acid or muscle contraction problems; with Uranus, agitated digestion; with Neptune, weakness in the system; and with Pluto, problems with the microbiome that lives in our gut. All of these issues concern our metabolism, and the transiting planet that is making contact with the natal Moon is a key to understanding any metabolic problems that surface.

There are a few studies that have found connections between the Moon and metabolism. In one study, what nearly seven hundred people ate or drank over the course of the lunar cycle was tracked. An 8 percent increase in meal size and a 26 percent decrease in alcohol consumption at the Full Moon was found. The authors of the study suggest that this is evidence of a deep internal rhythm that exists within us. Another study investigated a possible connection between the Moon and hospital admissions for gastrointestinal bleeding. The authors looked at two years of records totaling 447 patients and found a higher incidence of hemorrhages in men at the Full Moon. It appears our bodies are responsive to the peak of the lunar cycle.

One of the most important areas of research today in regard to metabolism is the role that is played by the microbiome. Composed of a community of microorganisms, which includes bacteria, yeasts, protists, and even microscopic animals, microbiomes are found in many organisms. (Notice that plants are not in this list, so the term *gut flora* is wrong—a better word for the members of these communities is *microbiota*.) Termites digest wood only because of a dense microbiome in their hind gut that does the work for them. Cows digest grass the same way—they cannot live without the community of microorganisms living in their gastrointestinal tracts that break down cellulose.

Humans are likewise very dependent on a gut microbiome that has a greater cell count than the number of cells that make up our bodies. The microbiome is a consortium of microorganisms that, when all is well, keep pathogenic bacteria at bay and maintain a balance in our metabolic processes. It is the microbiome that breaks down the parts of our food that would be indigestible otherwise. Further, there are links between gut microbiota and our brains via the vagus nerve. This implies that we have vast numbers of symbionts living inside us that we desperately need, and that they can communicate with us by altering moods that will change our behaviors. It's now known that many digestion problems are due to a weakened microbiome and that depression may even be a symptom of something wrong with our symbionts.

The microbes in our bodies have their own circadian cycles, these being twenty-four-hour rhythms, and that this can have a big effect on the time of day we take medications. What we don't know is if there are lunar rhythms in the microbiome that are regulating our moods and health in general. One interesting finding was made by John Alden Knight, a fisherman who created the Solunar tables that plot the Sun and Moon and predict the best fishing times. He found that when the Moon (or Sun) was rising or setting that fish were caught more frequently. He thought that this was because the tidal pull of Moon and Sun, which is strongest when both are simultaneously rising or setting at Full and New Moon, stirs up the water and the microorganisms that other slightly larger organisms feed on. This feeding process moves up the food chain and soon big fish are seeking out meals. And then humans catch them. In other words, the response of the tiniest members of the ecosystem to the Moon results in the subsequent entrainment of other parts of it. If this is so, then it is reasonable to consider that our own microbiome may be responding to minute tidal forces and using these to keep the rhythms of metabolism going strong, not unlike life in the seas billions of years ago.

We now know that the microbiome is extremely important in understanding our health and well-being. As we age, our microbiome becomes less diverse and less adaptable to dietary insults we may happen to throw at it. We should respect our microbiome and not weaken it with too much of what can break it apart. Paying attention to our diet alone may not be enough—we probably need to consider when and what we eat in the context of the lunar cycle. Some people believe this is true—there may actually be something to the "werewolf diet," a fad diet that has fasting and eating scheduled according the phases of the Moon. Perhaps someday a study will show that eating by the cycle of the Moon is a good thing for our microbiome, and consequently for our physical and mental health.

Your Natal Moon: A Powerful Asset in Workplace Relationships

by Alice DeVille

Before I became an astrologer with various specialty areas in this appealing metaphysical science, I had a twenty-four-year career in the federal government and left early to pursue my career in consulting astrology and writing. Credentials for writing this article stem from my work as an executive coach and developer of training modules designed to elevate performance and improve the quality of the work environment. I offer material that builds team confidence and helps leaders understand the diversity of staff. Managers have often asked me to include the personality findings of the Myers-Briggs test in advance of specific training. One company head was visibly upset to learn that very few members of the staff had the same Myers-Briggs profile. "Won't we argue all the time if our types are so different?" the manager asked. I explained that if every employee had the same profile, the work would get stale, certain tasks would never be accomplished, and the passion and energy level would be low because everyone thought alike. Both managers and employees agreed that when talent wasn't used, the inclination was to look for a job that offers meaningful assignments.

One leader hired me to do teambuilding to look for ways to solve internal problems and requested that I collect birth information, so the natal charts of participants could be compared. All employees agreed and were excited to learn more about cohesiveness. They wanted to identify key work assets, find ways to get along better, and work harmoniously. What made staff members click or created tension with one another? The combination of planets tells the story of preferences for certain types of work, with the Moon playing a central role in defining the work personality. My private consulting work and monthly newsletter with a Readers' Q & A column are the inspiration for this article that highlights the importance of knowing your personality traits and developing quality work relationships.

Bonding with Your Workplace

What attracted you to your employment venue? Did you know that your Moon describes how well you navigate the workplace? Do you realize that your natal Moon is one of the most powerful career assets for displaying qualities, talents, and habits that enhance performance in your place of employment? While texts and e-mails dominate our business world, good business relationships reflect solid interface and quality communication. The work environment thrives when there is evidence that employees get along with one another, demonstrate honesty, take accountability, and deliver products and services on time. Today's highly effective organizations look for employees who adapt to rapidly changing markets and technology and are open to learning new skills. In any chart, the sixth house describes the work, the daily environment, and the individuals or teams who count on your expertise and cooperation.

Sampling the Signs

Let's give each Moon sign a little time in the spotlight. If you know your Moon sign, which of your personal assets do you recognize from these passages? Although it is impossible to cover every quality or career affiliated with each sign, here is an overview of what you can expect.

Aries Moons have strong personalities and a flair for individuality. They demonstrate enthusiasm for ever-evolving ideas and enjoy creating innovative concepts and plans—they leave implementation to more detail-oriented types. Aries Moons crave recognition to express their egos in leadership roles and are the perfect choice if you want to launch a new program or product and get the ball rolling quickly. Their bedside manners are not always polished—they can be combative and they rile colleagues by dismissing their ideas or showing impatience over the analysis and the decision process. Impulsiveness is often their downfall. They are quick to anger but just as quickly let it go and move on.

Aries Moons are action-oriented and want to be first to get the job done. Since Mars rules their Moon sign, many of them are well suited for military careers; emergency management; analytical work that includes handwriting analysis and clue detection; legal professions that involve interrogating individuals in lawsuits; mechanical expertise (auto, planes, and trucks); and careers involving weapons, such as butchering, artillery management, and police work. Aries Moons get along with those who have Gemini, Leo, Sagittarius, and Aquarius Moons and feel friction with cardinal sign Moons, Cancer, Libra, and Capricorn.

When you hire someone with a **Taurus Moon**, you usually have a pragmatic, reliable worker who enjoys physical material comforts yet watches expenditures, keeps the workplace orderly, and may show a flair for designing the work space. Put this person on the team you select to reorganize space. Taurus Moons keep their eye on the bottom line and often seek careers in financial management, investment, real estate, mortgage banking, setting pay scales, and maintaining the staff budget. Other career fields include music (composing, instructing, performing, writing); food connoisseurs (developing recipes, tasting, preparing, writing reviews, bakery work); positions in the flower growing industry; and careers associated with clothing design, makeup products, and home or office décor.

Self-development appeals to the Taurus Moon who looks for opportunities to move up the career ladder. They examine the cost and value of training that accelerates performance and eagerly apply for a new position. Stubbornness is their Achilles' heel and they think nothing of delaying a decision if they feel their ideas are not accepted. Taurus Moons generally work well with Capricorn, Pisces, Cancer, and Virgo Moons, yet frequently clash with fixed sign Moons—Leo, Scorpio, and Aquarius.

Gemini Moons bring the gift of gab to the work environment, along with diplomatic skills and wit. They use ice breakers in meetings to get conversation started. Known for their communication mastery, they tackle writing assignments or speaking engagements with passion. If you are looking for an in-house trainer, those with a Gemini Moon are natural educators—tailor-made for developing and presenting courses, facilitating meetings, and giving new employees a thorough orientation to the workplace. This Moon sign rocks the debate team, the advertisement field, assignments in research and development, running the library, or demonstrating professional driving skills.

They bring what they learn in life to the workplace; their fertile minds constantly look for solutions to problems and find them.

Other professions that attract Gemini Moons include acrobat, magician, mime, editor, journalist, linguist, news reporter, franchise owner, neurologist, speech pathologist, and weather forecaster. Their natural chattiness gets them in trouble at times—spilling the beans prematurely, fibbing, gossiping, and promising more than they can actually deliver. These outcomes occur because they are versatile and juggle so much data, taking in far more information than others can assimilate. Although they often work alone because their quick minds are busy fielding ideas, they get along well with individuals who have Leo, Libra, Aquarius, and Aries Moons. Relationships get rocky with those who have mutable sign Moons: Virgo, Sagittarius, and Pisces.

Those with a **Cancer Moon** reflect the psychological makeup of life experiences and often express their feelings through their work. Cancer Moons accommodate the needs of the organization, show loyalty, and focus on meeting deadlines while maintaining quality control. They have excellent memories and easily recall the institution's history and progress. They take a stand caring for children and their well-being, and in defending the underdog when it comes to social issues. Cancer Moons thrive on self-employment, all facets of food management and preparation (baking, catering, dairy farming, restaurant management), developing recipes with an eye on nutrition, analyzing and writing about relationships (personal and business), and the independence involved with real estate careers. Work as advisors, mentors, talent managers, and transpersonal psychologists appeals to them.

This cardinal Moon sign is very action-oriented and often earns income from two or more careers or moonlights and thrives on the never-ending supply of energy that passion for one's work brings. Other career fields with appeal: ancestry, genealogy, history, home improvement products, building and remodeling, landscaping and exterior design, produce growing, and professions related to the sea—fisher, cruise ship associate, navy officer, seafood harvester, and resort worker. The bane of the Cancer Moon is not getting enough sleep, being sensitive to criticism, or showing a crabby side when too many demands are made on their time without checking for availability. Cancer Moons get along well with those who have Taurus, Virgo, Scorpio, and Pisces Moons. Those with other Cardinal sign Moons—Aries, Libra, and Capricorn—clash over control issues.

If they're a **Leo Moon** sign, your employee wants recognition for accomplishments and often the starring role in the enterprise—director, leader, boss, manager, or star. They are dramatic and put passion into cherished enterprises, whether a stage production or their own business. Leo Moons take a gamble on the unknown and turn it into a creative enterprise. Their flair for spontaneity livens the environment of the workplace and builds camaraderie within the ranks. They will invite others home to dinner, throw inclusive parties, and make visitors feel welcome. This Moon seldom shies away from delegating authority. They believe in enjoying recreation, taking vacations, and encouraging others in their circle to take time to recharge batteries and return to work with renewed enthusiasm. Here's a Moon sign that exudes warmth, has a flair for entertainment, enjoys emceeing a show, and welcomes conversation and lively exchanges in any debate.

Many Leo Moons are teachers or coaches and connect well with their students. When employees seek solutions to problems, they take the same interest in reaching a resolution as they would with their children. Among the professions where you find Leo Moons: athletes, boxers, park rangers, manufacturers or salespeople of outdoor equipment, educators or school principals, theater workers, comedians, midwives or obstetricians, entrepreneurs, government workers, astrologers, and CEOs. This Moon sign resents anyone looking over their shoulder or checking to see when the work will be completed—they feel that anyone who knows them should recognize their integrity. Sometimes they take time off from work at inconvenient junctures, party too much, or have investment misses that take time to recover. Leo Moons get adventurous with those who have the Moon in Aries, Sagittarius, Gemini, and Libra; they clash with the Taurus, Scorpio, and Aquarius Moons over politics or management style.

Virgo Moons flaunt their superior attitude toward work and productivity while displaying organizational skills, and show a passion for meeting challenges. You'll find them in every type of service industry, including cleaning; fitness; holistic health care; government; pet care; medical and elder care environments; food preparation and nutrition; equipment sales and service; and clothing design, repair, and retail. They have sought-after analytical skills that include work in accounting, computer management, math, organizing, and writing fields.

They are at the center of workplace relationships with coworkers, colleagues, customers, or collaborators. A frequent role for a Moon in Virgo is disciplining employees or making such recommendations to management. A strong Moon in Virgo asset is the ability to develop work manuals, procedures, and policies, as well as implement or update electronic equipment and file management. If they have an interest in food benefits, they may write books or articles on proper nutrition, body cleanses, and lifestyle. Virgo Moons excel at conference or meeting planning and coordination of details. They make excellent bookkeepers, carpenters, druggists, inspectors, opticians, policemen, poll takers, and veterinarians. A Virgo Moon's downfall may deal with a tendency toward hypochondria, displaying nervous tension and a negative attitude toward dreaded facets of work, being too picky in critiquing others' work, or using sarcasm or passive aggressive behavior when something or somebody aggravates them. Virgo Moons get along best with those who have the Moon in Taurus, Capricorn, Cancer, or Scorpio, and may experience confusion from those with the Moon in Gemini, Sagittarius, or Pisces.

Libra Moons look for ways to compromise, find balance when it is out of bounds, reconcile ideology stalemates, create collaborative environments, restore harmony to turbulent conditions, and mediate differences. Partnership ventures and cooperation appeal to Libra Moons. Sometimes the partner is their spouse. These Moons are good at contract negotiation, excel in consulting environments, resolve personnel problems, encourage competition, keep abreast of legal issues, and would rather go to arbitration than go to court. Among other strong suits, they have impeccable manners, the gift of diplomacy, ability to recognize and reward excellent performance, and find it easy to acknowledge all players in the environment. As employees or bosses, these Moons advocate teamwork and often take an interest in the company baseball team, picnics, fundraisers, or holiday parties. This Moon resonates with artists, matchmakers, hair stylists, sparring partners, and sales representatives. Business psychologist, motivator, marriage counselor, and Equal Employment Opportunity specialist are careers in their wheelhouse.

While Libra Moon is known for sharing information and keeping everyone in the loop, sometimes they say too much by spilling the beans prematurely. You'll find this Moon looking for ways to be fair to others to avoid potential conflict; they are either the best listeners ever or so eager to share an experience or an "ah-ha" moment that they stop listening to a contact's message. Libra Moons get along well with Gemini, Aquarius, Leo, and Sagittarius Moons and frequently get rattled by those with Moon in Aries, Cancer, and Capricorn.

There is no lunar sign like a **Scorpio Moon** to get to the gist of a problem or keep you focused in a conversation. These Moons are deeply introspective and want to know more about the inner workings of contacts' minds and motives. They ask lots of questions yet don't always give up information—sharing does not come easily to them. Research is one of their strengths and they dig deeply until they find what they need. They are very good at eradicating what is no longer needed, such as debts, pests, people, garbage, addictions, and bad habits.

You'll find Scorpio Moons in businesses related to debt collection, insect control, mortgage lending and payoff, criminal undertakings, self-help psychology, sex therapy, waste management, and diverse careers in police work. Jobs in the medical industry fascinate Scorpio Moons—coroners, dentists, lab technicians, medical scientists, proctologists, and surgeons, for example. Wills and goods of the dead attract their interest as attorneys or legal specialists; so do careers as funeral directors, estate settlement attorneys, and insurance adjusters. This Moon sign can withhold information, be vindictive when things don't go their way, and be avid scorekeepers when they think someone else is getting more notice than they are. Scorpio Moons get along best with Moon in Cancer, Virgo, Capricorn, and Pisces and find the environment too competitive with Moon in Taurus, Leo, and Aquarius.

A **Moon in Sagittarius** capitalizes on a socializing nature by experimenting in careers that offer a breadth and depth of experience. They explore the map, choosing paths in journalism, medicine, law, philosophy, politics, religion, teaching, and the travel industry. Often they seek multiple educational degrees, studying languages and the culture of various countries. Residing in another country appeals to this Moon and they relish travel assignments to recharge their batteries whether at home or abroad.

This Moon frequently has two or more careers. They are abstract thinkers, founts of information, and impart knowledge as advertisers, broadcasters, clergy, editors, explorers, diplomats, animal trainers (especially horses), jurists, lecturers, legal analysts, international trade specialists, metaphysicians, and advocates of social change. Colleagues would refer to one as "perpetual student," "world traveler," "storyteller," and "vagabond." A Sagittarius Moon is not fond of keeping close records and often misses deadlines. They prefer to have a trusted assistant to make arrangements or polish off unappealing parts of the tasks. Although they are a lively and welcome part of the team, bosses complain that they lose track of time, talk too much or go off point in formal presentations or meetings. Valued connections include those with Moon in Leo, Aries, Libra, and Aquarius, while those with Moon in Gemini, Virgo, or Pisces seem too critical.

Capricorn Moon signs bring a serious note to the workplace, demonstrating high standards of performance while displaying ambition and a desire to lead. They want recognition for their achievements. Assign them to manage teams, lead initiatives, and develop mission objectives. Assign Capricorn Moons to your goal-setting and long-range planning initiatives. They are often CEOs in training and look forward to occupying the executive suite. Fame is often affiliated with this Moon sign and you'll find geniuses among them. You can count on Capricorn Moons to get a grip on problems in any situation. Employees consider them authorities, the boss, or sometimes father figures, and they are sought after as mentors. Capricorn Moons are found among presidents, commanders, company heads, governors, law enforcers, all facets of public service, royalty, statesmen, veterans, and business owners. Those who gravitate toward medicine often choose dentistry, hospital administration, geriatric care, and osteopathy. You'll find them in diverse facets of real estate—sales, construction (especially masonry), home inspection, land development, structural engineering, and appraisal. Other careers that may interest them include astronomer, economist, physicist, or soil scientist.

They let nothing slip by them and will hold your feet to the fire when expecting deliverables, as well as notice when you are late for work or meetings because they are very punctual. Although they never give up despite constraints in their plans, they can be very peevish or critical of others who do not perform as expected. Some in their circle find them too bossy, too cold, or too cheap in doling out compensation. Capricorn Moons work well with Taurus, Virgo, Scorpio, or Pisces Moons and get contentious with individuals who have Aries, Cancer, or Libra Moons.

Aquarius Moon signs relish the role of a change agent or internal consultant in various organizations. They take pride in their many affiliations and not only attend meetings and events but often run for office, head up task forces, or set up impartial panels to discuss emerging issues. This Moon fits in well with diverse groups and offers an array of skills that get the job done. Count them among the most analytical of Moon signs. Aquarius Moons are personable, blend in seamlessly, display versatility, and quickly get a sense of the work culture. They are joiners and thrive in settings that improve conditions for humanity, such as automation, charitable work, electronics technology, manage-

ment development, politics, and talent acquisition. Their impersonal manner allows them to analyze personal, organizational, and social problems without distressing the group members. They are champions of the underdog.

Aquarius Moons jump on the bandwagon to promote cybersecurity and make recommendations for culling out fraud, funds mismanagement, and information breaches. They excel in positions like advisor, advocate, airline personnel, astrologer, electrician, guide, inventor, legislator, political representative or senator, sociologist, trendsetter, and visionary. As crackerjack human capital professionals, their insight often uncovers the bias that prevents the best people from being hired. Critics of their style say they are too aloof, show indifference or boredom openly, are manipulative, unleash their rebellious streak, or make statements simply for shock value. Aquarius Moons create synergy with Gemini, Libra, Sagittarius, and Aries Moons, while interactions with Taurus, Leo, and Scorpio Moons can be testy.

Pisces Moons gravitate toward careers that call for behind-the-scenes activity, confinement, and privacy. Staff in hospitals, institutions, prisons, and drug or physical rehabilitation centers often have Pisces Moons. Telecommuting was made for them. Charities, fundraising firms, public service groups, welfare organizations, and educational venues attract their fair share of individuals with this Moon. Many Pisces Moons are holistic healers, have healing hands for practicing Reiki, and possess gifts of psychic insight and often mediumship. They encourage others to take five when stress builds up, to get back in balance, meditate, or practice yoga.

Pisces Moons make excellent teachers and clergy, including nuns, friars, priests, and those in cloistered religious orders. A number of Pisces Moons are really good with numbers and make excellent accountants or bookkeepers. Even in large companies, they like assignments that give them space and allow them to blitz through a pile of work behind the scenes. They are happy in freelance fields like writing, music, and acting. You'll find this Moon working in bars, breweries, oil refineries, and firms that manufacture perfumes and bath products. Throughout their lives, Pisces Moons benefit from taking inventory of their careers, goals, and relationships, releasing what is not working, and looking for the next meaningful step toward fulfillment. They are kind and considerate employees. Habits that rattle bosses include daydreaming, taking too long to complete assignments, lack of truthfulness about the status of work, misunderstanding circumstances (their Moon's ruler is Neptune and they sometimes get caught in its fog), and forgetfulness. Pisces Moons get along well with those who have Moon in Cancer, Scorpio, Capricorn, and Taurus, while managing to confuse individuals with Moon in Gemini, Virgo, and Sagittarius.

Heirloom Vegetable Gardening: Nourishing the Future by Preserving the Past

by Michelle Perrin, Astrology Detective

While globalization has brought some wonderful advantages, such as a worldwide sense of shared experience and multicultural understanding, the international marketplace has also caused the erasure of much local biodiversity.

Nowhere is this more evident than in the food supply. Worldwide, it is estimated that we have lost 75 percent of our edible plant varieties in the last hundred years, and that 60 percent of our plant-based calories come from just three crops—rice, maize, and wheat ("What Is Happening to Agrobiodiversity?"). Since much of our sustenance depends on so few crops, this places us at incredible risk of potential blights. Moreover, the modern, global-ized agricultural marketplace puts more emphasis on factors such as uniformity, sturdiness, and the ability to withstand long-distance shipping, as opposed to nutrition, culture, history, and tastiness.

Before World War II, most plants grown were heirlooms. By taking part in heirloom vegetable gardening, you can not only preserve the past, but ensure the future. To learn more about the increasingly popular heirloom gardening movement—what it is, why it is important, how to choose, and where to buy—read on!

What Is an Heirloom Plant?

The common definition of an heirloom plant is an open-polli-nated, non-GMO variety that is older than fifty years—preferably grown before WWII—and handed down from generation to generation. These plants can be old-timey commercial varieties or family treasures. Many of these plants were once extremely popular, but are no longer viable at an industrial level. It is hard to imagine the huge diversity of food available before 1950, much only at a local level.

Hybrids vs. GMOs vs. Open Pollinators

Things changed in the mid-twentieth century, when hybrid seeds were introduced on a mass commercial scale. Originally devel-oped in the twenties, hybrids are obtained by cross-pollinating two varieties, such as two tomatoes, to obtain desired character-istics like durability or large yield. These seeds do not form off-spring identical to the parent, so they cannot be saved and handed down; each planting season, new seeds must be bought. Hybrids represent the bulk of seeds on the market today, having been bred to conform to the profit-driven needs of big agriculture. These seeds produce vigorous plants that are uniform in size and color, ripen all at once, hold up well during mechanical picking and long-distance shipping, and can be pest and drought resistant. Taste, however, is sacrificed. Hybrid seeds are also widely used by home gardeners, due to their ease of use, predictable results, and dominance in garden centers and catalogues.

It is important to note that the term *hybrid* is not synonymous with *genetically modified organism* (GMO), which refers to seeds that are created in a laboratory by crossing the DNA of two different species. For example, corn could be crossed with bacteria to make it more resistant to pests. This type of crossing could never occur in nature or through traditional crossbreeding, and the seeds produced by the fully grown plant are sterile, so they cannot be saved or used. GMOs presently are for commercial use only.

Heirloom seeds, unlike hybrids or GMOs, are open-pollinated. These seeds will grow a plant that is identical to its parent. You can harvest, save, and share the seeds, as no one "owns" the rights to them, making them cost-efficient and sustainable. Open-pollination happens strictly through nature, via birds, bugs, wind, or other environmental occurrences, and does not need any intervention by man. Some heirlooms, such as potatoes, are grown, not by seed, but via vegetative propagation or cuttings that do not require pollination.

When seeking out seeds, remember that while all heirlooms are open-pollinators, not all open-pollinators are heirlooms, as many new varieties have been introduced in recent years. Heirloom seeds are carefully chosen and saved, passed down over several generations, because of their flavor, yield, hardiness, dependability, or adaptability to the local environment. They represent the gardener's fine eye for choosing and spotting the best plants and preserving them for posterity.

Hybrids have dominated the vegetable market since the 1950s, but starting in the 1970s, a growing interest in heirlooms has arisen.

Stories and History

Age is perhaps the most important factor taken into consideration when deciding if a plant is an heirloom. While some growers consider varieties that are at least fifty years old to be heirlooms, most place the cutoff date either at the end of WWII in 1945, or in 1951, which marked the dawn of industrialized agribusiness and widespread use of hybrid seeds. Others prefer cultivars that were around prior to the 1920s, when hybrid seeds were first invented. When you choose to plant heirloom vegetables, you are literally consuming history, by eating produce that can be traced back innumerable years, sometimes to prehistoric times.

There is a certain magic and awe in the realization that the little seeds you lovingly save from your heirloom plants have been passed down from generation to generation, farmer to farmer, friend to friend, since perhaps the dawn of time, and you are taking part in ensuring their survival into the distant future. Heirloom plants connect us not only to nature, but to history itself.

A wide variety of plants have fascinating stories to tell of their proliferation over time and space. George Washington would trade seeds with people from China, while Thomas Jefferson brought back seeds from his diplomatic missions abroad and planted them in his garden at Monticello, which can still be visited today.

Just like a priceless piece of antique furniture, the provenance of a seed is one of the key factors in its value as an heirloom. The stories and names attached to them are an intrinsic part of their charm, and as colorful as the plants themselves. There really was a Mrs. Hubbard who created the "Hubbard Squash" (Rupp 2015). Dr. John Wyche used elephant and tiger manure from his friend who owned a circus to fertilize his famous Dr. Wyche's Yellow Tomatoes (from the Seed Savers Exchange). One of the most famous heirloom stories is that of the Mortgage Lifter Tomato, developed during the Great Depression by a West Virginian named "Radiator Charlie." When his radiator business went belly up, Charlie took to gardening, and, after a few years of experimentation, developed this large, meaty tomato, whose popularity paid off his mortgage debt (from Slow Food USA).

The Amish, Mennonites, and Native Americans have made special efforts to preserve and save heirloom seeds, helping maintain their cultural heritage in the process. Native Americans domesticated many plants that are now common in gardens throughout the world—in fact, over 60 percent of what the world eats today was originated and developed by Native Americans. It is imperative to preserve the remaining lesser-known varieties of Native American fruits and vegetables, as many traditional dishes, medicines, and ceremonies rely on these rare, local breeds, which are on the verge of extinction, endangering not only the continuation of the plant variety, but key facets of entire cultures and traditions. These Native American plants—such as cattail broadleaf shoots, chokecherries, beaked hazelnuts, lambsquarters, plains pricklypear, prairie turnips, stinging nettles, and rose hips—are highly nutritious and deserve wider implementation into the standard modern American diet.

Family Legacy

While heirloom seeds often tell the sagas of the great sweep of history, they also are cherished for the loving personal tales they quietly tell of individual families. A family heirloom is a prized possession, whose value is often more sentimental than monetary, passed from one generation to the next. For the immigrants, natives, and pioneers of the American frontier, seeds often were an integral part of the family legacy, ensuring not only the survival of future generations, but a remembrance of past sacrifice and love.

Perhaps these seeds reminded first generation immigrant Americans of the old country and their faraway loved ones, while their successors remember, instead, great-grandpa or grandma's vegetable garden and the delicious home-cooked meals prepared by them. By preserving these seeds, they are also preserving their flavors, so the home cook really can make a dish that tastes and looks exactly like what grandma used to make.

Heirloom gardening can be a true multi-generational family affair. It is an excellent way to get your children involved in gardening, biology, history, nutrition, and cultural studies, as well as to create an activity they can enjoy with their grandparents, while learning the stories of their ancestors in the process.

The first, and arguably the most important, heirloom seed bank in the world, Iowa's Seed Savers Exchange, was created so that its co-founder, Diane Ott Whealy, could save for her children the seeds her great-grandparents brought from Bavaria in the 1800s (Iowa Agriculture Literacy Foundation 2018).

Taste and Nutrition

Even if your family did not pass down seeds themselves, many people get into heirloom gardening in order to enjoy food that has the same robust flavor enjoyed by their ancestors.

Things that are important now, such as a uniform appearance or sturdiness for shipping, were irrelevant in the past, when what mattered most was taste and freshness. Many Baby Boomers can look back with fondness to the savors of their childhood, and heirloom gardening gives a way for all generations to rediscover the amazing range and depth of flavors provided by heirloom plants. In fact, this is probably the most important factor in the resurgence of heirloom gardening; once people experience a vegetable bred for taste, it is hard to go back. It is not only the superior savor that tempts the curious, but the sheer variety of different tastes on offer—who knew that a tomato, bean, or potato could come in so many different flavors? It is also important to note that most homegrown heirlooms are much richer in nutrients than their hybrid, commercial cousins.

Visual Feasts and Flights of Fancy

Purple tomatoes, white eggplants, and watermelons with starry rind patterns that would put Van Gogh to shame—the sheer visual delight of heirloom vegetables draws many to the movement.

Imagine growing stalks of corn and for shucking each ear to be

like opening a present, never knowing exactly what combination of colors will adorn the kernels inside. The modern food business depends on mass distribution and standardization, but heirloom vegetables offer a huge variety of surprising shapes, sizes, colors, textures, and fragrances—even the names cause the imagination to soar. From Cherokee Trail of Tears beans to Howling Mob corn or Champion of England peas, the names evoke both hunger and curiosity.

Heirloom plants can also be used for dyeing fibers, home medicinal remedies, and decorative arts-and-crafts projects. They are of great inspiration to cooks and chefs, who increasingly use them for experimental dishes, or to make historically accurate recreations of the great meals of the past.

Bred for Local Conditions
One of the best advantages of heirloom seeds is that they are adapted for local conditions. By saving the seeds of the hardiest and tastiest varieties, season after season, the home gardener can develop the ultimate seed for their plot of land. Over time, open-pollinated seeds become adapted to that region's soil, climate, diseases, and

pests, making them more resistant, on a small, local level, than store-bought hybrids, which are bred to grow the same way under the largest number of conditions possible. Since heirloom seeds are often particularly suited to the local area, they can create higher yields than hybrids. Heirloom seeds are of particular interest in organic gardening because their hardiness in the local environment makes the use of chemical pesticides largely unnecessary.

Growing Peculiarities

For commercial reasons, hybrid seeds are engineered to produce an early harvest that ripens all at once. Heirloom plants, however, will continue to grow and produce over time. This means you will not experience the arrival of one huge glut of vegetables, but can enjoy your produce as it ripens and comes in gradually over the season. Heirloom plants are also less uniform; they form vegetables of varying sizes on the same plant—sometimes small and sometimes extremely large. One of the reasons heirlooms can grow so big is because their stalks keep shooting up even after setting fruit, creating a large, robust plant, unlike hybrids, whose stems stop growing and tend to be more compact. Heirlooms also have more foliage, which means more photosynthesis and, ultimately, a tastier final product.

Also, many modern seeds are bred for monoculture use, the industrialized practice of planting only one crop at a time. Heirloom seeds thrive in biodiverse environments, like those of our ancestors. Biodiverse systems tend to produce more output, as well as increase the diversity of other species, including beneficial insects and micro-organisms, helping to control pests and blight.

While heirloom seeds may be quirky to grow at first, due to their longer germination times and erratic ripening periods, they also offer the home gardener a fascinating experience of watching plants grow and adapt on their own time and in their own fashion, as true, unique, living parts of nature—drawing the grower back to the natural rhythms and wonders of life itself.

Biodiversity and Preservation

Plants make up over 80 percent of the human diet. Since their introduction in 1996, GMOs accounted for over half of all US cropland by 2013 (NutriFusion). Non-hybrid seeds sold by commercial seed companies fell from 5,000 in 1981 to less than 600 at the dawn of the 2000s (Vinje). It is estimated that there are currently between 60,000 and 100,000 plant species threatened with extinction, not based on natural selection, but due to man-made factors related to the commercial needs of a globalized food industry, which has drastically cut the genetic diversity of our overall food supply. These diverse genetic characteristics, however, allow a plant to adapt and mutate for survival.

Just five cereal grains account for over half of our caloric intake on a global level; this puts us at extreme risk in the event of crop failure, such as what happened during the famous Irish Potato Famine in the 1840s, when a new fungus wiped out potato crops. Due to their lack of genetic diversity, hybridized crops are especially at risk to new disease mutations.

It is imperative we maintain a store of open-pollinated seeds with a vast genetic makeup that can grow under a wide range of conditions and are resistant to a diverse number of diseases and pests, so that we can replenish our crops in case of massive crop failure. This makes sure that our food supply is protected. By taking part in heirloom gardening, each individual person can ensure the survival of threatened plants and their genes.

Food Self-Reliance

Roughly 30–40 percent of the global seed market is dominated by just one company, Monsanto. Our entire food supply has fallen into a small handful of companies, most of which are more concerned about commercial factors and money-making over nutrition. These companies are also at the forefront of the shift to GMO and hybrid seeds, and making it illegal to store or share patented seeds. Many farmers and gardeners prefer the freedom to plant what they want and how they want, as opposed to being ruled over by a large corporation.

By being dependent on so few companies, we also run the risk of what will happen in the event of a large-scale catastrophe. This is not just the paranoia of conspiracy theorists. When Iceland's Eyjafjallajökull volcano erupted in 2010, it caused European air traffic to grind to a halt, with a resultant temporary shortage in the food supply throughout the entire continent, as many products ran dangerously low or disappeared from the shelves completely. Having locally adapted seeds on hand ensures that individuals and farmers can keep on farming, in the case of such events.

Heirloom seeds are currently being preserved in three locations: governmental seed banks, such as the one run by the USDA; small seed companies and exchanges; and family-run farms. These are all at risk due to lack of funding, globalization, offshoring, small market share and other economic factors. If we turn our full output to GMO and hybrid seeds, we risk losing a seed reserve that can reproduce on its own, so we will become

completely dependent on manmade technology for our very survival, cutting us off totally from nature.

Food sovereignty, however, is more than just standing up to mega corporations, it is about embracing nature and maintaining ancient traditions that allow us to keep plugged into the cycle of life, death, and regeneration on planet Earth, and our role in its stewardship and survival.

Seed Saving

Seed saving and heirloom gardening is the way food was grown from prehistoric times up until roughly fifty to one hundred years ago. Many traditions, knowledge, and plant varieties have gone extinct in this period. While heirloom gardening requires a short initial learning curve and the purchase of starter seeds, in the future, you can save your own seeds from the plants you grow and never have to buy them again—saving money and resources, while ensuring biodiversity.

Things to Consider When Buying Your Starter Heirloom Seeds:

1. Buy seeds that are perfect for your region. While some heirlooms can flourish in a wide variety of climates, some will thrive in the more temperate areas of the South, while others are more suited to the cooler nights of the North. Also, your area may have modern local diseases and pests that these older plants are not resistant to. Talk to local farmers who can point you in the right direction, or even share their seeds with you. The websites of heirloom seed exchanges and companies are often family-run passion projects, containing a wealth of information; do not be hesitant to reach out with questions before you buy.

2. When starting out, it's okay to mix hybrids and heirlooms, so that you are guaranteed a fail-safe yield for your hard work. Don't feel heirloom gardening is an all or nothing game. It can take time and patience to get into the rhythm of planting like our forebears.

3. You do not have to save seeds to enjoy heirloom gardening. While many enjoy the experimentation and economy that comes with seed saving, it is a lot of hard work and success is not guaranteed. Also, you may prefer to buy and try new varieties each year.

4. Choose the right variety for your tastes and end use. Maybe you prefer a small, sweet tasting tomato, or a larger one that has been bred for longer storage. Your vegetable, your choice.

5. Experiment with varieties that reflect your ethnic identity or interests. Perhaps you would like to try plants that your ancestors ate in the old country. Or maybe you love Asian cooking and would like to try to grow authentic produce from these regions. How much more fun would it be to make pasta sauce with a true Italian tomato variety, just like the Italians would use?

6. Some of the easiest heirloom plants to grow are lettuce, beans, peas, radishes, turnips, sweet potatoes, winter squash, pumpkin, okra, chard, kale, spinach, beets, cucumber, tomatoes, eggplant, and peppers. The offspring of beans and tomatoes, especially, will remain true to the parent.

7. Try a variety of seeds from a variety of places; if you experiment planting a wide variety of heirlooms, a few are sure to make it to harvest.

8. Be aware of which seeds are self-pollinating and which ones cross-pollinate. Some vegetables easily cross with each other, making mongrel offspring. These include onions, squash, pumpkins, cabbage, cauliflower, broccoli, cucumbers, corn, beets, spinach, carrots, melon, radishes, chard, and others. If you wish to save the seeds from these plants, make sure to isolate them or stagger the period when you grow them, so they are not pollinating at the same time. Some plants will also pollinate with wild varieties, so be aware of what is growing in uncultivated nature nearby. Self-pollinating plants will not cross, and are true to the parent. These include: beans, peas, peanuts, lettuce, eggplant, peppers, and tomatoes. If this is your first time growing heirloom

plants, you may want to use only self-pollinators. For example, you could plant three varieties of tomatoes in one season, without fear of them cross-breeding.

9. Seeds can be harvested from annual and biennial plants, while perennials are saved through cuttings and division. It is easier to start off by saving the seeds from annuals—plants that grow to harvest the same season in which they are planted. Biennials require greater patience, skill, and commitment, as they don't complete their life cycle until the second season. Common biennials are: beets, Brussels sprouts, cabbage, carrots, cauliflower, celery, onion, parsley, parsnips, chard, and turnips. Annual plants include: beans, lettuce, peas, and tomatoes—these are also all self-pollinators that don't cross, making them the easiest plants to start with.

Tips for Saving Heirloom Seeds:

Locate the hardiest, healthiest, strongest, largest, most colorful, fastest-growing plants that have shown the most resistance to pests and diseases, and clearly mark those out for seed saving before harvest, so you don't eat them by accident. This way the following year's crop will be even more adapted and strong. Every season, your plants will adapt to local conditions, sometimes optimizing even after two or three growth cycles. Do not harvest too soon, as mature seeds are more likely produce. Always save double the seed you think you will need, so you can replant in case of unforeseen problems or low germination. Seeds are best matured in warm, dry conditions. Move the plants inside if the rainy season sets in.

Seeds should be dried before saving. Seeds will be damaged when exposed to temperatures above ninety-five degrees Fahrenheit, so be careful of placing them in direct sunlight. There are three primary methods of seed drying. Some seeds, such as beans, are best dried on the vine in the garden. Others, including tomatoes, need to be first soaked and fermented in water. Finally, the seeds of some plants, such as peppers, should be scraped out and dried. An excellent resource for learning the techniques specific to saving seeds from a wide variety of plants and how long the seeds can be stored is http://howtosaveseeds.com.

Keep seeds in airtight containers such as plastic bags or glass jars and store in a cool, dry location, away from sunlight. Peas and beans, however, need breathable bags. Do not open the containers until you are ready to plant, as moisture could collect on the seeds and ruin them. If you live in a humid area, put silica gel packs in the seed containers to help preserve them, or store them in the refrigerator, if you have room. Label each receptacle with the name of the variety, date collected, and any other relevant information. This is especially important if you are growing several varieties of one vegetable.

Where to Buy Heirloom Seeds

There are many small local seed saving exchanges throughout the United States and the world. Many are run by local farming groups, such as the Amish, Native Americans, and Mennonites, who have a vested interest in preserving their cultures and traditions. Some public libraries even offer seeds on loan. Ask around to local farmers or gardening associations in your area, or search online for heirloom exchanges near you. Many universities have ecology departments with a focus on preserving heirloom seeds.

Heirloom seeds can also be bought on a national and global level from seed companies and established seed exchanges. The oldest and most influential of these is Seed Savers Exchange, first established in 1975. It preserves a collection of over 20,000 open-pollinated, often rare, heirloom plants in its seed bank, and has passed on over one million seeds during its lifetime. They have a seed exchange for swapping that is open to everyone, with over 13,000 members, as well as a catalogue for online purchases. For more information, visit www.seedsavers.org/.

Among commercial seed companies, W. Atlee Burpee & Co., commonly known as Burpee, is the nation's largest vendor of heirloom seeds. Dating back to 1876, many varieties come from its own historic catalogue. Find them at https://www.burpee.com/.

Baker Creek offers an international blend of seeds from over seventy countries. They also bought out Comstock, Ferre & Co., which is the oldest continually operating seed catalogue in the United States, specializing in seeds particularly suitable to the Northeastern United States and New England, with many varieties tracing back to the pre–Civil War era. They can be visited at www.rareseeds.com.

References

"Half of Cropland Acres in the U.S. Were Devoted to GMO Crops in 2012." NutriFusion. https://nutrifusion.com/half-farm land-us-devoted-gmo-crops-2012/.

"How Do They Work? Seed Vaults." 2018. Iowa Agriculture Literacy Foundation. https://iowaagliteracy.wordpress .com/2018/10/16/how-do-they-work-seed-vaults/.

Rupp, Rebecca. 2015. "Blue and Warty, the Hubbard Squash Is Scary Good." National Geographic. https://www.national geographic.com/people-and-culture/food/the-plate/2015/11 /16/blue-and-warty-the-hubbard-squash-is-scary-good/.

Vinje, E. "The Charm (and Flavors) of Heirloom Vegetables." Planet Natural Research Center. https://www.planetnatural.com/ heirloom-vegetables/.

"What Is Happening to Agrobiodiversity?" Food and Agriculture Organization of the United Nations. http://www.fao.org /3/y5609e/y5609e02.htm.

About the Contributors

Mireille Blacke, MA, LADC, RD, CD-N, is a registered dietitian, certified dietitian-nutritionist, and addiction specialist residing in Connecticut. Mireille is the bariatric program coordinator for Trinity Health of New England at Saint Francis Hospital in Hartford, with years of experience as a bariatric dietitian, educator, and counselor. As an adjunct professor at the University of Saint Joseph in West Hartford, Mireille teaches graduate-level courses in nutrition and media. She has been published in Llewellyn's *Moon Sign Book*, *Herbal Almanac*, and *Magical Almanac*, *Today's Dietitian*, and *OKRA Magazine*. Mireille worked in rock radio for two decades before shifting her career focus to psychology, nutrition, and addiction counseling. She is obsessed with the city of New Orleans, the various works of Joss Whedon, and her beloved (if psychotic) Bengal cats.

Pam Ciampi was a professional astrologer from 1975 until her passing in 2019. She served as president of the San Diego Astrological Society and was President Emeritus of the San Diego Chapter of NCGR. Pam was the author of the Weekly Forecasts for Llewellyn's bestselling *Daily Planetary Guide* since 2007. Her latest contribution was an astrological gardening guide titled *Gardening by the Light of the Moon*. In its fourth printed edition, it is now available in a calendar format.

Sally Cragin is the author of *The Astrological Elements* and *Astrology on the Cusp* (both Llewellyn Publications). These books have been translated and sold in a number of countries overseas. She does readings (astrological and tarot). Visit "Sally Cragin Astrology" on Facebook, email sallycragin@verizon.net.

Alice DeVille is known internationally as an astrologer, consultant, and writer. She also has the pleasure of working as an executive coach, integrating spiritual insight while meeting the needs of clients in the corporate, government, and small business worlds. Alice specializes in relationships of all types that call for solid problem-solving advice to get to the core of issues and give clients options for meeting critical needs. Her clients seek solutions in business practices, career and change management, real estate, relationships, and training. She has developed and presented more than 160 workshops and seminars related to her fields of expertise. The Star IQ, Astral Hearts, Llewellyn, Meta Arts, Inner Self, ShareItLiveIt, Twitter, and numerous websites and publications feature her articles. Quotes from her work on relationships appear in books, publications, training materials, calendars, planners, audio tapes, and on World-Famous Quotes. Alice's Llewellyn material on relationships appeared in Sarah Ban Breathnach's *Something More*, Oprah's Website, and in *Through God's Eyes*, by Phil Bolsta. In 2018, Alice made a guest appearance on CUTV Blog Radio discussing soul mates and past lives. She is available for writing books and articles for publishers, newspapers, or magazines; conducting workshops; and doing radio or TV interviews. Contact Alice at DeVilleAA@aol.com.

Amy Herring is a graduate of Steven Forrest's Evolutionary Astrology program and has been a professional astrologer for over twenty years. She has written two books on astrology: *Astrology of the Moon* and *Essential Astrology*. She especially enjoys teaching and writing about astrology. Visit HeavenlyTruth.com for readings, classes, and educational videos.

Penny Kelly is a writer, teacher, author, publisher, consultant, and naturopathic physician. After purchasing Lily Hill Farm in southwest Michigan in 1987, she raised grapes for Welch Foods for a dozen years and established Lily Hill Learning Center, where she teaches courses in developing intuition and the gift of consciousness, getting well again naturally, and organic gardening. She is the mother of four children, has cowritten or edited twenty-three books with others, and has written seven books of her own. Penny lives, gardens, and writes in Lawton, Michigan.

Robin Ivy Payton is a yoga teacher and intuitive astrologer living in Portland, Maine. A lifelong student and practitioner of intuitive arts, Robin began writing and broadcasting her astrology forecast, Robin's Zodiac Zone, in 1999, and has been contributing to Llewellyn publications since 2003. She trains yoga teachers and tarot readers in southern Maine and offers weekly classes and workshops, including Vinyasa Flow, Yin, Restorative, Gentle Yoga, and Yoga Nidra. Find Robin's forecasts and schedule at www.robinszodiaczone.com.

Michelle Perrin, aka Astrology Detective, has built a reputation as one of the world's most trusted and sought-after astrologers for more than ten years. Her work has appeared in some of the most influential titles online and in print, making her one of the few astrologers who has garnered respect from both a mass audience and the astrological community. Her horoscopes have appeared on the websites for Canada's W Dish and Slice TV Networks, Tarot.com's Daily Horoscope site, and Dell Horoscope Magazine, among others. Her writings have also been featured in *The Mountain Astrologer*, the leading trade journal for the astrological community, and astrology.com.

Kris Brandt Riske is the executive director and a professional member of the American Federation of Astrologers (AFA), the oldest US astrological organization, founded in 1938; and a member of the National Council for Geocosmic Research (NCGR). She has a master's degree in journalism and a certificate of achievement in weather forecasting from Penn State. Kris is the author of several books, including *Llewellyn's Complete Book of Astrology: The Easy Way to Learn Astrology*, *Mapping Your Money*, and *Map-*

ping Your Future. She is also the coauthor of *Mapping Your Travels* and *Relocation and Astrometeorology: Planetary Powers in Weather Forecasting*. Her newest book is *Llewellyn's Complete Book of Predictive Astrology*. She writes for astrology publications and contributes to the annual weather forecast for *Llewellyn's Moon Sign Book*. In addition to astrometeorology, she specializes in predictive astrology. Kris is an avid NASCAR fan, although she'd rather be a driver than a spectator. In 2011, she fulfilled her dream when she drove a stock car for twelve fast laps. She posts a weather forecast for each of the thirty-six race weekends (qualifying and race day) for NASCAR drivers and fans. Visit her at astroweathervane .com. Kris also enjoys gardening, reading, jazz, and her three cats.

Bruce Scofield, PhD, is an author of numerous books and articles and teaches evolution at the University of Massachusetts and astronomy and astrology for Kepler College. He has an international practice as a consulting astrologer. His interest in Mesoamerican astrology, mythology, and astronomy has a web presence at www.onereed.com.

Christeen Skinner is a Director of Cityscopes London Ltd, a future-casting company. She holds a Diploma from the Faculty of Astrological Studies, where she has taught for some years, has been Chair of the Astrological Association, is presently Chair of the Advisory Board of the National Council for Geocosmic Research, and is a Director of the Alexandria I-base Project. Through www.financialuniverse.co.uk, her company offers services to investors and entrepreneurs who value the timing and trend services provided. She also writes regularly for www.horoscopes.co.uk and for www.star-horoscopes.com. Christeen is author of several books: *Exploring the Financial Universe* (2016), *The Beginner's Guide to the Financial Universe* (2017) and *Navigating the Financial Universe* (2019). She can be reached via office@cityscopes.com.

Charlie Rainbow Wolf is happiest when she is creating something, especially if it can be made from items that others have cast aside. Pottery, writing, knitting, astrology, and tarot are her deepest interests, but she happily confesses that she's easily distracted, because life offers so many wonderful things to explore. She is an advocate of organic gardening and cooking, and she lives in the Midwest with her husband and special-needs Great Danes. Follow her at www.charlierainbow.com.

Moon Sign Book Resources

Weekly Tips provided by Penny Kelly, Charlie Rainbow Wolf, and Mireille Blacke

"The Methods of the *Moon Sign Book*" by Penny Kelly

"Gardening by the Moon" by Pam Ciampi

GET MORE AT LLEWELLYN.COM

Visit us online to browse hundreds of our books and decks, plus sign up to receive our e-newsletters and exclusive online offers.

- **Free tarot readings • Spell-a-Day • Moon phases**
- **Recipes, spells, and tips • Blogs • Encyclopedia**
- **Author interviews, articles, and upcoming events**

GET SOCIAL WITH LLEWELLYN

Find us on 🐦 @LlewellynBooks

www.Facebook.com/LlewellynBooks

GET BOOKS AT LLEWELLYN

LLEWELLYN ORDERING INFORMATION

 Order online: Visit our website at www.llewellyn.com to select your books and place an order on our secure server.

Order by phone:
- Call toll free within the US at 1-877-NEW-WRLD (1-877-639-9753)
- We accept VISA, MasterCard, American Express, and Discover.
- Canadian customers must use credit cards.

Order by mail:
Send the full price of your order (MN residents add 6.875% sales tax) in US funds plus postage and handling to: Llewellyn Worldwide, 2143 Wooddale Drive, Woodbury, MN 55125-2989

POSTAGE AND HANDLING

STANDARD (US):
(Please allow 12 business days)
$30.00 and under, add $6.00.
$30.01 and over, FREE SHIPPING.

INTERNATIONAL ORDERS, INCLUDING CANADA:
$16.00 for one book, plus $3.00 for each additional book.

Visit us online for more shipping options. Prices subject to change.

Notes